Guides to Wines & Top Vineyards

Barolo and Barbaresco

2024 edition

Benjamin Lewin MW

Preface

This Guide is devoted to Barolo and Barbaresco. The first part discusses the region, and explains the character and range of the wines. The second part profiles the producers. There are detailed profiles of the leading producers, showing how each winemaker interprets the local character, and mini-profiles of other important estates.

In the first part, I address the nature of the wines made today and ask how this has changed, how it's driven by tradition or competition, and how styles may evolve in the future. I show how the wines are related to the terroir and to the types of grape varieties that are grown, and I explain the classification system. For each region, I suggest reference wines that illustrate the character and variety of the area.

In the second part, there's no single definition for what constitutes a top producer. Leading producers range from those who are so prominent as to represent the common public face of an appellation to those who demonstrate an unexpected potential on a tiny scale. The producers profiled in the guide represent the best of both tradition and innovation in wine in the region. In each profile, I have tried to give a sense of the producer's aims for his wines, of the personality and philosophy behind them—to meet the person who makes the wine, as it were, as much as to review the wines themselves.

Each profile gives contact information and details of production, followed by a description of the producer and the range of wines. For major producers (rated from 1 to 4 stars), I suggest reference wines that are a good starting point for understanding the style. Most of the producers welcome visits, although some require appointments: details are in the profiles. Profiles are organized geographically, and each group of profiles is preceded by maps showing the locations of producers to help plan itineraries.

I owe an enormous debt to the many producers who cooperated in this venture by engaging in discussion and opening innumerable bottles for tasting. This guide would not have been possible without them.

Benjamin Lewin

Contents

Tables

Appellation Maps

Producer Maps

The Langhe: Powerhouse of Piedmont

"Finally winemaking in Italy is becoming unchained, today producers are making wine completely differently from the past. There is no other region like Langhe, with such consistent high quality. I think Piedmont is like it is because we had the confrontation between modernism and tradition, so we moved to cleanness, producers have a proper style, and now there is a new way of pushing the boundaries, to be more natural. Modernism helped the traditionalists even more than the modernists. In the last ten years we've focused more on the vineyard, less on the oak," says Gaia Gaja, whose father, Angelo Gaja, was as instrumental as anyone in bringing Piedmont to the forefront of quality wine production in Italy.

In the northwest corner of Italy, Piedmont means "foot of the mountain," and the Alps are a pervasive influence. With 12 DOCGs and 44 DOCs, Piedmont has more appellations than any other part of Italy (ahead of Tuscany's total of 43). DOC(G) production is around 90% of the total, which is largely devoted to indigenous grapes. Asti Spumante is its well known sparkling wine. Gavi is probably the best-known white.

The Langhe is the catch-all DOC at the base of the appellation hierarchy in the province of Cuneo. It was created in 1994 to allow a more detailed description for wines that previously had been only Vino di Tavola. The Langhe DOC extends from north of Alba to south of Barolo and is not as large as the general name suggests, only about 1,600 ha of vineyards.

Langhe Rosso or Bianco can contain any proportions of a wide variety of authorized grapes, including both indigenous and international varieties, but varietal-labeled wines are more important. Indigenous varieties are most important in reds, dominated by Nebbiolo, Barbera, and Dolcetto. Arneis is the most important indigenous white, but international varieties are important here, dominated by Chardonnay, Sauvignon Blanc, and Riesling. Varietal Langhe must contain at least 85% of any named variety.

The most important DOCs within the Langhe are in the center. To the north of the river Tanaro, not far from Alba, is Roero, where the predominant grape is the indigenous white variety, Arneis. Immediately south of the river, Barolo is to the west, and Barbaresco is to the east, both devoted exclusively to Nebbiolo. Wines made from other grape varieties grown in Barolo or Barbaresco are usually labeled as varietal Langhe.

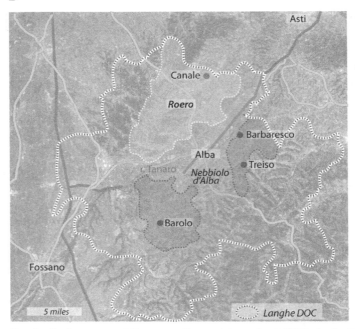

Barolo, Barbaresco, and Roero are the most important DOCs in the Langhe.

Some Langhe Rossos are blends of the indigenous varieties Nebbiolo and Barbera with some combination of Merlot, Cabernet Sauvignon, and Syrah, but international black varieties have not had a great impact here, unlike Tuscany, where they are the basis for most super-Tuscans. "The super Tuscan concept does not apply in Piedmont—there is a super-Piedmont and it is called Nebbiolo," says Angelo Gaja.

The general view is that Nebbiolo stands alone. "The wines from Tuscany made from Cabernet Sauvignon or other international varieties can be great wines, but are not Italian. Nebbiolo is the greatest wine in Piedmont, and by itself has great complexity, and does not need anything else," says Giorgio Rivetti at La Spinetta.

Nebbiolo

It's generally thought that Nebbiolo originated in Piedmont and that its name refers to the nebbia, the local fog that forms in the Piedmont hills in the autumn. Several references from the thirteenth century probably identify this variety growing in Piedmont. There is a continuous stream of subsequent references to the importance of the grape, and it is viewed as the highest quality grape of the region in a famous treatise of 1606.

Nebbiolo is a difficult grape to grow. It buds very early and it ripens very late. The proximity of the Alps keeps the average growing season temperature a little cooler than you would expect from the latitude, and producers regard the climate as traditionally on the cool side for Nebbiolo. The need for a very long growing season makes it susceptible to problems at both ends of the season. Frost is the problem in the Spring. The summers can be dry, but the big climatic problem has been whether the grapes can be harvested before the autumn rains in October. Earlier harvests resulting from global warming have reduced the problem.

Nebbiolo is fussy about its location. It used to be planted exclusively on south-facing slopes, but in today's warmer conditions is also planted on eastern and western exposures. "It's only in the past 20 years that the hillsides have been completely planted with vines," says Alan Manley at Luciano Sandrone. "Nebbiolo does not like to be grown too low down. Nebbiolo hates wind—that's why we plant Barbera on the tops of hills where it's windy. At the bottom of the hill, where cold collects, many people plant Dolcetto or Chardonnay."

This is changing with global warming. "We can now plant vineyards at higher elevations. The limit for Nebbiolo was 400m, now it is 500m," says Pietro Ratti. "It's difficult to plant new vineyards but we can convert Dolcetto vineyards to Nebbiolo. I call the increase in planting Nebbiolo the nebbiolization of the land."

Nebbiolo is not a grape with obviously fruity qualities. Fruit aromas can be transitory, sometimes in the same spectrum as Pinot Noir, but tending more towards cherries. Roses and violets are often mentioned in describing the aromas. Nebbiolo can be a deceptively light garnet color, and rapidly develops an orange appearance. The light color can lead to a mistaken impression that the wine has aged prematurely.

Tannins are just in the DNA of Nebbiolo. It's possible to make wines that are soft and approachable by tricks of vinification, but this takes away the whole point and character of the variety. Nebbiolo really does fit the old view that if the wine isn't a little tough when it's young, it won't achieve greatness when it's older.

The basic issue with Nebbiolo is how to handle the tannins and get them into balance with the fruit. "Nebbiolo has nearly 3.5 g/l of tannins—it can be more than Bordeaux—but with only half the color. So the main task is to allow color and tannin to blend together," says Flavio Fenocchio

Fermentation in Barolo

The big issue in fermenting Nebbiolo has always been how to tame the high tannins. Historically, Nebbiolo had so much tannic structure that years were required for the tannins to integrate. Some alternatives to conventional fermentation were developed to help soften the tannins.

Conventional Fermentation

Destemmed grapes or whole bunches are put into a fermentation vat, which is effectively a vertical cylinder of stainless steel, a concrete vat, or a wood vat. The skins rise to the surface during fermentation and form a cap that must be periodically immersed in the juice, either by punch down (mechanically pushing the cap down from the top into the juice) or pump-over (pumping the juice up from the bottom of the tank to spray it over the cap).

Submerged Cap Fermentation

The submerged cap is a technique that is popular in Barolo because it allows very gentle extraction from the skins. A steel grid about halfway up the fermentation tank stops the skins from rising to the surface. Because the skins do not move, extraction is less than with pump-over or punch-down.

Rotary Fermenters

A rotary fermenter is a fermentation tank turned on its side, so that it is horizontal instead of vertical. Inside there are large paddles that turn slowly to mix the skins with the juice. This makes for gentle extraction and a soft wine. This was popular at one time for Barolo, but is less used now because the wines can be so soft as to lose typicity.

at Marchesi di Barolo. Differences of opinion on how best to accomplish this were at the heart of the clash that dominated the seventies between traditionalists, who believe in aging in large casks, and modernists, who switched to barriques.

Nebbiolo always has high alcohol. "You cannot make a great Barolo at 12.5%, we need that extra kick that gives more sugar in the grapes. That's why Nebbiolo is planted facing south," says Aldo Vacco at the Produttori del Barbaresco. So alcohol levels are usually high, typically about 14%, but the alcohol is naturally integrated into the palate and is rarely at all obtrusive. (Nebbiolo's advantage over other varieties is reinforced by the fact that it occupies most of the vineyard sites that face full south.)

Today Nebbiolo is almost always vinified as a single variety, but before the regulations of the DOCs came into effect, it was customary to soften the wine and darken the color by including small amounts of other varieties, typically Barbera. But today, in the modern style, fruits are more obvious, color is deeper, and the tannins are less aggressive anyway. (In fact, just as Barbera was used to soften Nebbiolo, so in the other direction a little Nebbiolo was used to give more power to Barbera.)

Nebbiolo tends to be productive, calling for stern pruning to keep to low yields. Officially three recognized subvarieties are permitted in Barolo: Lampia, Michet, and Rosé. Lampia is more productive than Michet (where yields are reduced because the subvariety is virused); Rosé has pretty much disappeared because it has very little color (and it now turns out that may be a progeny of Nebbiolo rather than a variant).

In reality there is much wider variation than the three names would suggest. Like Pinot Noir, Nebbiolo is highly subject to mutation, and throws off clonal variations frequently. Whereas producers were often planting clones twenty years ago, today they tend to regard them as too productive, and selection massale from their own vineyards has become more common.

Barolo and Barbaresco are the great names, but Nebbiolo is grown all over Piedmont. There are two generic DOCs for Nebbiolo. Nebbiolo d'Alba is a broader appellation in the immediate vicinity of the great appellations; in effect it is a DOC for 100% Nebbiolo that does not come from Barolo or Barbaresco. (If it is labeled Superiore it must spend at least 12 months aging in oak.)

Langhe Nebbiolo can come from anywhere in the Langhe (and like other varietals in the Langhe can include up to 15% of other varieties.) It can be used to declassify Barolo or Barbaresco, and there's a wide range of styles from those that age in oak and mimic the great appellations to those that are produced directly as simple entry-level wines in stainless steel. Cesare Benvenuto at Pio Cesare explains that, "We decided we needed to have the possibility to declassify Barolo in vintages that weren't good enough. But the first wines were very good and now we find them in top vintages because Nebbiolo has started to become an everyday wine for the region."

Elsewhere in Piedmont, the best appellation is Gattinara (near Lake Maggiore), where Nebbiolo must be at least 90% (usually it is blended with a little Bonarda), and the wines tend to be a little lighter and less alcoholic, reflecting the more northern location.

Barbera and Dolcetto

Nebbiolo is without question the greatest variety in the area, but Barbera is the most widely planted variety in the Langhe. "Barbera is planted where Nebbiolo can't grow, which is why it is—let us say—very variable," says Elena Currado at Vietti, where producing Barbera from top vineyard sites is an unusual priority.

6

Barbera has very high acidity but very little tannin, so the problem is typically to tame the acidity and give it some structure. "There are oceans of Barbera where there's only acidity wrapped around a thin veneer of fruit," says Alan Manley at Luciano Sandrone. "This is where global warming really has made a difference. Barbera loves heat. In the cold vintages of the fifties and sixties, Barbera was often thin and really acid. Barbera is a grape that's characterized by its acid, it should have that incredible liveliness on the tongue that's typical of Barbera."

For me the authentic note of Barbera is a faintly savory note, briary, leathery, and animal; it can turn medicinal. Today, however, a Barbera is more often smooth and juicy, although often at the expense of dimension. "Barbera is a good wine to introduce people to Piedmont because it is rounder and more approachable, it's a good introduction for people who are used to New World wines," says Elena Currado. Acidity varies from quite tart in entry-level wines to nicely balanced in the best wines. But "Barbera has to have acidity. If you lose acidity, you lose the soul of the wine," Stefano Chiarlo says

The Barberas you are most likely to encounter are from the Langhe (that is, anywhere in the region and Barbera d'Asti (more masculine and rustic) or Barbera d'Alba (finer and more feminine). They can include up to 15% of other varieties. Superiore means that the wine has spent a year aging, including several months in oak. Within Barbera d'Asti, the best area is the *sottozone* (sub-zone) of Nizza, which was promoted to a DOC in its own right in 2014. This must be 100% Barbera, with minimum aging of 30 months, including at least 6 months in barrel.

"The old idea of Barbera was the family wine on the table, it's difficult to change people's opinion," says Paolo Monti, who is one of the producers making Barbera as a 'serious,' ageworthy wine. The best Barberas d'Alba are likely to come from vineyards that are actually within the Barolo DOCG. Good examples are from Vietti, Elio Grasso, Giuseppe Mascarello, Giovanni Viberti, and Giacomo Conterno. The move to highlighting the best vineyards in individual cuvées has spread to Barbera, and these can be serious wines, with some aging potential. The wines can be quite dark in color and purple in hue, quite a contrast with Nebbiolo. One problem in making 'serious' Barbera is that alcohol can rise up to 15%. (A trend to make Barberas where the style has been influenced by Barolo is called baroleggia locally.) If the label says 'Vigna,' the wine comes from a single vineyard.

Reference Wines for Barbera d'Alba from Single Vineyards		
Producer	Vineyard	Location
Burlotto	Aves	Verduno
Ca'Viola	Bric du Luv	Montelupo Albese
Giacomo Conterno	Francia	Serralunga d'Alba
Elio Grasso	Vigna Martina	Monforte d'Alba
Marchesi Di Barolo	Peiragal	
Giuseppe Mascarello	Scuditto	Monforte d'Alba
Cordero Di Montezemolo	Funtani	La Morra
Paolo Monti	San Martino & Merenda	Monforte d'Alba
Pio Cesare	Vigna Mosconi	Monforte d'Alba
Prunotto	Pian Romualdo	Monforte D'Alba
La Spinetta	Gallina	Neive
Giovanni Viberti	Bricco Arioli	Vergne (Barolo)
Vietti	Scarrone Vigna Vecchia	Castiglione Falletto
Roberto Voerzio	Pozzo dell'Annunziata	La Morra

The attitude towards handling varieties in new oak is the reverse from Burgundy or Bordeaux, where the most powerful wines get the most new oak. Barbera tend to get new oak to provide the structure that it intrinsically lacks. "It has very little tannin, that's why we put it into the most new oak," says Alan Manley. And often enough Lange Nebbiolo gets more new oak than Barolo, again because intrinsically it has less structure.

Dolcetto is almost the opposite of Barbera: it has very low acidity, quite high tannins, and is deeply colored. (The name, which means "little sweet," may relate to the low acidity.) Usually given only a short period of skin maceration and fermentation, and matured only in stainless steel, giving a soft, round, and fruity flavor spectrum, it is somewhat Piedmont's equivalent to Beaujolais, intended for drinking in the two or three years after release. Some of the best Dolcettos come from Diano d'Alba, one of the communes of the Barolo, but a DOC specifically for Dolcetto in its own right. (Sorì on the label means the wine has reached 12.5% alcohol instead of the minimum 12% for Diano d'Alba.)

White Wines

There's been something of a move towards white wines in recent years, as much to round out the range as anything else, but it's difficult to find a white grape variety that gives distinguished results. Arneis is the white variety of the Langhe, and is the predominant variety in Roero (to the north of Barolo), giving wines that are lightly aromatic and pleasant, but it's revealing that at La Spinetta, Giorgio Rivetti, who is committed to indigenous varieties, produces white wine from Chardonnay and Sauvignon Blanc. "We wanted to make high quality white, but couldn't find local varieties to do it." Farther to the northeast, crisper wines are made from the Cortese grape in Gavi.

Many Barolo producers who want to offer a white choose Chardonnay, with Sauvignon Blanc a second choice, and Riesling in a rather distant third place. Chardonnay tends a bit to go to either of two extremes: over-oaked so it's hard to see the underlying fruits and typicity; or soft and even a touch exotic, showing more the amorphous character of Italian whites than a recognizable trait of Chardonnay.

Given the (relatively) warm climate, it is surprising that Riesling is sometimes more successful than Chardonnay in the Langhe. The best Rieslings have crispness and sometimes minerality.

White wine is something of a work in progress. "When the region started to make whites, they followed the French style, and the wines were a bit heavy, but now we are making white wines with out own identity," says Pietro Ratti. It's fair to say that the tendency to make overoaked international style whites has dissipated, but even so, it's hard to pinpoint any variety or style as typifying the region yet.

In terms of a getting a bead on whites of the area, Ceretto's Arneis from the Langhe is the largest selling wine, with a fresh, light style. Styles of Chardonnay are the most variable, lightly aromatic from Elio Grasso or Ratti, quite soft from Massolino or Cordero Di Montezemolo, or distinctly oaky from Gaja. Sauvignon Blanc tends to be creamy or fruity rather than herbal or herbaceous: good examples come from Ratti (aged in stainless steel) and Parusso (aged in oak). Vajra was the first to introduce Riesling, and this remains a benchmark for minerality, joined by Oddero.

Some producers have turned to reviving old indigenous varieties. "All the local varieties are aromatic," says Sara Bertola at Elvio Cogno, where an effort was made to resurrect Nascetta, was popular in the 19th century

Reference Wines for Indigenous White Grape Varieties in Piedmont

Region	Grape	Producer
Roero	Arneis	Bruno Giacosa
Langhe	Arneis	Ceretto
Langhe	Rossese	Manzone Giovanni
Derthona	Timorasso	Borgogno
Derthona	Timorasso	Massa
Langhe	Nascetta	Elvio Cogno

but abandoned after World War II. By 1994 there were only a few vines left. Elvio bought all the production, decide he liked it, and planted his own vineyards. It's now grown by 13 producers in Novello, for which there is a special DOC (Langhe Nascetta Communale Novello. There is also a general Langhe label for use for other sources. Rossese is another Piedmont variety that was all but extinct when Giovanni Manzone revived it. The best-known revival is Timorasso, revived in the area of Colli Tortonesi, largely by Walter Massa, and given the DOC of Derthona, about 50 miles northeast of Barolo.

Tar and Roses

The classic description of Barolo as "tar and roses" is wonderfully evocative of the crucial contrast between the delicacy of the fruits and the stern backbone of the Nebbiolo grape. (Actually, "tar" is not found so much these days and may have partly reflected faults of old-fashioned wine making, but it's not quite as much of a contrast with roses as it sounds. Perfumed aromatics resembling roses can become more phenolic, melding into impressions moving in the direction of tar.) Nebbiolo is undoubtedly a great variety, but it has been successful only in Piedmont, where it prospers in the climate protected by the nearby mountains. It is at its peak in Barolo and the smaller neighboring area of Barbaresco.

Together Barolo and Barbaresco occupy only about 2,000 hectares (little larger than the Margaux appellation in Bordeaux). Nebbiolo is the only grape that can be grown for either DOCG. Sites are restricted to hillsides between 170m and 540m elevation. (Other varieties are also grown in the appellations, mostly on plots that aren't suitable for Nebbiolo, and carry lesser labels, such as Barbera d'Alba.)

Looking north (from Serralunga d'Alba), on a clear day, the Alps can be seen in the far distance beyond the steep vineyards of Barolo.

The Barolo DOCG rules require aging for at least 36 months, including 18 months in wood (a compromise between the original two years and a proposal to shorten the period to one year). Riserva wines must have 5 years of aging, but do not require any extra time in wood, so it's purely a matter of whether the producer wants to hang on to the wine longer in bottle before releasing it.

Until the 1980s, producers tended to use Riserva as a description for wines they had been unable to sell previously, making the label more a marketing than production decision. Since the move towards quality in the 1990s, there has been an increasing tendency to make Riservas only in top vintages for the best wines, and often they are matured for a year longer in wood, but there is no legal requirement to do so. "The emphasis on Riserva has really diminished. Most producers focus on single vineyard wines now," says Jeffrey Chilcot at Marchesi di Grésy. Of course, sometimes the single vineyard wines are also Riservas.

Politics deprived Barbaresco of some of its best wines in the nineties. When the Consorzio defined the regulations for Barbaresco, Angelo Gaja believed they should allow the wine to contain 5% of another indigenous variety; this accorded with historical precedent and the belief that it made better wine. When the Consorzio decreed that Barbaresco had to be 100% Nebbiolo, he simply labeled his top wines as Langhe, as they continued to have 5% Barbera. This was a major loss for the appellation, as Sorí Tilden and Sorí San Lorenzo are two of the best, and best-known, wines of Barbaresco. (Sorí means a south-facing site at the top of a hill.)

It's a sign of the change brought by global warming that Gaia Gaja decided in 2016 that Nebbiolo no longer has so much need of Barbera, and

The nebbia descends on the vineyards of Barolo.

the wines would return to Barbaresco as of the 2013 vintage. "We decided to go back to Nebbiolo at 100% because we would like to express things the way they are today in the Langhe," Gaia says. "Nebbiolo is more juicy today, it has sweeter and softer tannins, it's a purer expression, the wine will be more vertical."

Historically, there have usually been only one or two great vintages every decade, but since 1995 there has been a succession of exceptional vintages, broken only by the disastrously wet season in 2002 and (perhaps) the heatwave of 2003. "Climate change has been positive for viticulture," says Chiara Boschis. "I remember that up to the seventies, in a decade we would have three extraordinary, two good, and five average vintages. Now there are still three extraordinary vintages, but all the others are great." Aldo Vacco at the Produttori Del Barbaresco emphasizes the difference this has made. "In vintages when we don't make Riservas from the single vineyards, in the seventies we would have made them, those vintages would have been regarded as great."

Barolo was one of the very first DOC regions in 1966, and became a DOCG in 1980 as soon as the new level was introduced. Total production is tiny; it's been rising steadily to its present level of about 13 million bottles per year, roughly one percent of the production of Bordeaux. The vineyards are highly fragmented, with the 1,800 hectares of Barolo divided among 1,300 growers, so the average holding is less than 2 ha.

You would think all quality vineyards must be long established, given the history of the area, but in fact the planted area increased 50% after the start of the twenty-first century. Some growers mutter that the new vineyards are on land that will lower the overall quality of Barolo. The demand for Nebbiolo is so great that "many people are planting Nebbiolo in north-facing vineyards where Dolcetto used to be grown," says Alan Manley.

Communes of Barolo and Barbaresco

Barolo is organized into eight communes, but most (about 80%) of the wine comes from five core villages. In spite of small size of the appellation, there are significant stylistic differences between the west and the east. The road from Alba to Barolo is the dividing line. The soils are older and have more clay to the east; the soils to the west are younger and have more sand (increasing as you go north into Roero). "There are differences in the wines moving across from La Morra to Monforte, but they are narrowing as producers concentrate on eliminating astringent tannins," says Roberto Bordignon at Elio Grasso.

The wines of La Morra are the finest and most supple. This is the largest commune and the farthest west. Soils are calcareous, with the best vineyards in an amphitheater around the town facing south and southeast. In most wine-growing areas you might turn your nose up at

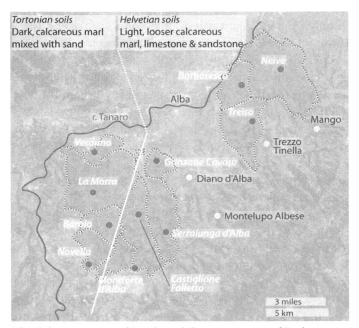

The eight communes of Barolo and three communes of Barbaresco are the glory of the Langhe.

Communes and Top Crus of Barolo

Commune	Top Crus	Reference wine
La Morra has soils of marl and gives the finest, most aromatic, wines, sometimes described as feminine.	Arborina Brunate Cerequio Rocche dell'Annunziata	Elio Altare Michele Chiarlo Voerzio Renato Ratti
Barolo is broader, more open than La Morra, elegant but moving towards a plush character.	Cannubi Cannubi Boschis	Scavino Sandrone
Monforte d'Alba has the most structure and greatest aging potential.	Bussia Romirasco (in Bussia) Colonnello (in Bussia) Ginestra	} } A. Conterno Prunotto Elio Grasso
Serralunga d'Alba has soils of white (calcareous) marl and sandstone, bringing a unique combination of power and elegance.	Falletto Francia (Monfortino) Vigna Rionda Ornato	Giacosa G. Conterno Oddero Pio Cesare
Castiglione Falletto is balanced between the elegance of La Morra and the power of Serralunga or Monforte.	Rocche di Castiglione Bricco Rocche Villero Monprivato	Vietti Ceretto Vietti G. Mascarello
Verduno is the small most northern commune; the wines can be on the tough side.	Monvigliero	Burlotto
Novello at the southwest corner lacks the refinement of the other crus.	Ravera	Cogno
Grinzane Cavour has young vineyards; relatively unknown, it is a work in progress.	Garretti	La Spinetta

There are also some classified areas in the communes of Cherasco, Roddi, and Diano d'Alba.

sandy soils, but here it gives the most elegant wines of the DOC. "Nebbiolo that's grown in sand becomes incredibly fragrant, light bodied, like a grand cru Burgundy. Clay gives structure to Nebbiolo, longevity and power," says Alan Manley at Luciano Sandrone. Rocche dell'Annunziata may be the finest zone of all, but there are several top zones in La Morra, including Brunate and Cerequoia.

Barolo (meaning the commune) shows elegance and finesse, but on the other side of the divide, the wines are stronger. The top vineyards are below the town. on the east side of the main road, with Cannubi and

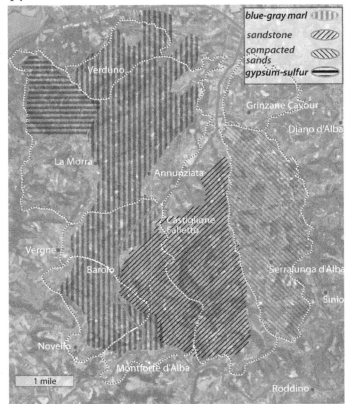

blue-gray marl

sandstone

compacted sands

gypsum-sulfur

Verduno

Grinzane Cavour

Diano d'Alba

La Morra

Annunziata

Castiglione Falletto

Vergne

Barolo

Serralunga d'Alba

Sinio

Novello

Montforte d'Alba

1 mile

Roddino

The most important soil types are divided by the Alba-Barolo road, but do not exactly follow communal boundaries.

Cannubi Boschis standing out. This is where the soils from the west and east parts of the appellation meet.

Monforte d'Alba gives the most structured Barolos, very long lived. This is the southernmost commune, with vineyards up to 500m altitude. Bussia is the best known cru, but it is very large, and it is really only the best zones within it that are superlative.

Castiglione Falletto gives powerful wines, the most full bodied of the appellation. People who make comparisons with Burgundy say that Serralunga is the Vosne Romanée of Barolo: "The Serralunga tannins are special. Serralunga gives an impression that the fruit is rounder, but it isn't—it's just that the tannins are different," says winemaker Oscar Arrivabene at Domenico Clerico. "If you love Barolo you have to love Serralunga."

From Castiglione Falletto in the foreground you can see across the deep valley to Serralunga in the background.

Serralunga can be more austere than the other crus. The wines have great finesse, due to a high concentration of limestone in the soils known locally as white marl. Traditionally the tannins required significant time to soften.

"For a long time, the idea was to take grapes from the western side for finesse and elegance, and from the eastern side for tannins and structure, and to blend to get a well balanced wine," says Emmanuele Baldi at Prunotto. "Bussia (a very large cru in Monforte d'Alba) is right in the middle and can express the two sides of Barolo, feminine and powerful," he adds.

There are three communes in the Barbaresco appellation. With soils based on limestone and clay, Barbaresco itself has the greatest concentration of what would be grand or premier crus if there were a full classification. The best three, Asili, Rabajà, and Martinenga, which would be the grand crus, are south of the town on a ridge facing south-southeast. "Asili is probably the most feminine expression of Barbaresco," says Stefano Chiarlo. "There's a calcareous marl that gives florality and an elegant precise expression of fruit." Nearby, Pajè and Rio Sordo might be considered as premier crus, together with Montestefano farther north, where higher elevation is proving an advantage during climate warming.

Neive falls into two parts. West of the town, where the soils are like Barbaresco, the tend to be more powerful and structured; Santo Stefano

The hilltop village of Serralunga dominates the surrounding vineyards.

would be the grand cru, and Gallina would be a premier cru. East of the town, soils are sandier, and the wines are lighter; Serraboella would be a premier cru. Treiso has the coolest microclimate, giving the lightest wines. Pajorè would be its grand cru. A fourth area is the least well-known, where around the village of San Rocco Seno d'Elvio, the vineyards are nominally attached to Alba.

The terroirs of Barolo and Barbaresco are infinitely complex. Although there is something of a move towards putting communal labels on wines today, the problem with any simple description is that soil types very quite a bit within each commune, and sometimes the most famous Crus are not on the terroir that's most typical of the commune. Even aside from differences in soil types, constant twists and turns in the land change the exposure of every plot. Adjacent plots can be quite distinct. This extensive variation is brought into greater relief today by the focus on single vineyard wines.

It's a fine palate that can reliably discern a difference between Barolo and Barbaresco. In fact, in the nineteenth century grapes from Barbaresco were often sold to make Barolo. Barbaresco became independent when proposals to incorporate it as a village in a wider Barolo area were rejected. "Barbaresco is more elegant and approachable than Barolo, which is more powerful. Barbaresco is about flowers, Barolo about fruit. Barbaresco tannins are softer," says Giorgio Rivetti at La Spinetta. And although there are definitely differences in terroir, it is also true that Barbaresco is not required to age as long in wood as Barolo; Barbaresco

Communes and Top Crus of Barbaresco

Commune	Cru	Reference wine
Barbaresco gives the most complete and balanced wines.	Asili	Bruno Giacosa
	Rabajà	Bruno Rocca
	Martinenga	Marchesi di Grésy
	Montestefano	Produttori Barbaresco
Neive shows the most variation in style, typified by more power in the northwest to the lighter southeast.	Santo Stefano	Bruno Giacosa
	Gallina	La Spinetta
	Serraboella	Cigliuti
Treiso is the coolest commune, with more vineyards at higher elevations, and gives the lightest wines.	Pajorè	Sottimano
	Rombone	Nada Fiorenzo

must age 2 years including at least 9 months in wood, while Barolo must age three years with at least 18 months in wood.

But the differences are narrowing. "The main difference is in the tannins, but this has changed with the use of barriques; differences are now smaller than in the past," says Giorgio Lavagne, winemaker at Bruno Giacosa until 2011. I would be inclined to say that Barbaresco can show a more obvious sense of tension, even a touch of austerity, which is hidden by more of an opulent sheen to the palate in Barolo.

Some of the difference between Barolo and Barbaresco has been due to slower ripening in Barbaresco, but the warming trend of recent years has brought convergence. "Global warming has been incredibly helpful for Barbaresco," says Angelo Gaja. "It used to be considered a lower quality appellation than Barolo. This was partially true in the sixties through eighties. Until the mid nineties, several of the villages in Barbaresco regularly failed to reach the minimum 12% alcohol level for the appellation, where Barolo was usually 13%. Since 1995 every year has been in the range 13.5-14.5% in Barbaresco, and Barolo has reached up to 15% or higher. So now it is perfect for Barbaresco. I am certain Barbaresco's reputation will become higher than Barolo's."

Modernists versus Traditionalists

Wine has been sold under the name of Barolo since the early nineteenth century and the wine has undergone several transitions in style. In the nineteenth century, it was made in both a sweet version with residual sugar and a fully dry version. By the twentieth century, dry wine became the norm, with high acid and tannins. Barolo used to be famous for its dense tannins, and was undrinkable when young. (It used to be the cus-

Traditional winemaking used to involve very old wood vats in dank cellars.

tom to warm the wine a little so as to minimize the effects of the tannins.) In the past twenty years, modernization of vinification has led to more approachable wines.

Traditionally Barolo was fermented and matured in large oak vats of Slovenian oak (called botti). After a long period of maceration, the wine was aged for several years. A traditional top Barolo would take years to soften, but when mature evolves vegetal, gamey characteristics, with predominantly mineral and animal aromas. (It has to be admitted that many "traditional" Barolos were oxidized with high volatile acidity and very harsh tannins. As recently as 1983, one authoritative opinion was that "Barolo appears most often to be bitter-astringent when young and also when old... We do not know whether [Nebbiolo] is grown elsewhere, but apparently not (and justifiably so.)" Indeed, it was this sort of opinion that led to the modernist movement.

The clash between traditionalists and modernists played out more forcefully in Barolo than most places. The methods of the modernists were introduced by a group of (then young) producers who were known as the "Barolo boys;" today they are the elder statesmen. When they introduced green harvest to reduce yields, it was regarded as wasting the grapes. "Do you know what your daughter is doing?" other producers asked Chiara Boschis's father, even though she did green harvest at night in order to avoid being noticed. When the modernists introduced barriques of new wood in order to improve hygiene, it was regarded as scandalous. Elio Altare's father did not speak to him for ten years after he took a chain saw to remove the rotten old botti.

The final straw was when some modernists introduced rotary fermenters in order to get softer tannins. "The problem with Barolo is the aggressive and bitter nature of the tannins—not the quantity but the quality," says Enrica Scavino at Paolo Scavino. "The long paddle rotates very slowly and extracts more tannins but, but only from the skins, as the seeds drop down and out of the tank."

The clearest dividing line was replacing botti with barriques. By giving greater exposure to oxygen, the barriques soften the tannins and make the wine more approachable. Modernists believed that the barriques make more elegant wine, traditionalists that the barriques introduce flavors of vanillin obscuring Nebbiolo's delicate flavor.

The modernist movement is often represented as part of the general movement towards globalization of wine style. But this is to misunderstand the situation in Barolo in the 1960s and 1970s. Wine production was scarcely economic, and often was being abandoned; Elio Altare recollects that making wine in Barolo became regarded as something you did only if you were not capable of doing anything better. Asking himself, "Why don't consumers like my wine?" and why wine production was economically successful in Burgundy but not in Barolo, he decided to adopt Burgundian methods. "The foudres used in Barolo were filthy, everyone recognized Barolo because of its barnyard smell; the typicity of Barolo was of flawed wine," he says. So he introduced modern hygiene into handling wood, and switched to barriques.

Elio credits Angelo Gaja with being the first to realize that better wine is made by using modern techniques. Gaja says that, "Respect for tradition can be a hindrance. It is simply ridiculous to believe that introducing barriques instead of using large casks is a problem." He too views the barrique as simply another example of equipment used in the winery. "After all, no one is using iron anymore, everyone is using stainless steel, this is not controversial, it is a benefit." Altare and Gaja, and most other producers, now regard the whole question of modernist versus traditionalist as an irrelevant distraction from the real issue: making good wine.

In retrospect, what was seen at the time as an abrupt clash of cultures has now melded into an acceptance of modern practices. "The green harvest was when they most changed the style of Piedmont wine," says Stefano Chiarlo. "People talk about tradition and modernists, but really

Rotary fermenters are large horizontal tanks, with paddles that rotate slowly to extract soft tannins.

the important thing was the introduction of green harvest from 1984 to 1987. The problem in Piedmont was the high yields."

Indeed, there is now general agreement that the issue between modernists and traditionalists is largely resolved. Some merging of the two has occurred since the modernists have reduced the extent of oak, and it's now a fairly common regime in the region to use one year aging in barriques (including some but not all new oak) followed by a second year in the large botti. A measure of the convergence is that whether you visit an arch-modernist or a traditionalist, the cellars look much the same; there will be stainless steel tanks for fermentation, and very likely both botti and barriques for aging. The proportions used of each may vary, and whether there is any new oak, but now it's more a matter of degree than an absolute divide. A lot of this has to do with the change in generations as the Barolo Boys and their contemporaries hand over to the next generation. "It's funny, but a lot of the sons are more traditional than their fathers," says Paolo Grasso.

I don't think the issue is so much the size of the container as whether and how much new oak is used. I side with traditionalists to the extent of believing that overt expression of oak clashes with the aromatics of Nebbiolo. This is now relatively rare, however. A modern Barolo favors sweet, ripe, finely grained tannins over harsh and astringent ones, and purity of aroma and flavor over "animal" extraction. Wines vary from delicate to forceful at both modernist and traditionalists, and many producers are now hard to pigeonhole in one category or the other. It's a great sign of

Wine maturing in the traditional botti at Giacomo Conterno.

the change that when I visited a producer still using 100% new oak, the intensely oaky taste of the wiens seemed distinctly old-fashioned!

Modernism has a rather different meaning in Barolo from what you might expect casually elsewhere in the world of wine. It is not at all synonymous with the concept of "international" wines, that is, powerful wines with dark colors and lots of extraction. In fact, modernists use shorter periods of maceration than traditionalists. Full force Nebbiolo can mean delicacy rather than power.

The main change in Barolo and Barbaresco over the past twenty years is almost universal. As Isabelle Oddero, from one of the most traditional producers, says, "The most important difference in style is that even when young, the wine is in balance. It used to be that young Barolo was too tight and needed ten years." Of course, some vintages are ready sooner than others, but the striking feature now is that even the most recent vintages tend to be relatively approachable. Personally, I think it's a rare vintage that should be drunk within, say, five years, as it will reveal much more as the tannins begin to resolve, but it is certainly true that young wines no longer have that brutal tannic character.

There's no doubt that the quality of Barolo has never been higher than it is today. Aging wine for five years or more in large casks required a great level of expertise to avoid oxidation and volatile acidity, and required very high levels of sulfur dioxide. Today the few producers who still do this are highly skilled, such as Giacomo Conterno, who makes wonderful wine; but the life of the modernist is somewhat easier. Change is inevitable, and as Angelo Gaja says, "The profile of wine has completely changed, it is stupid for a producer to say that he makes the same wine as his great grandfather. Forget it." There is common ground with all good producers believing that the best wines are made from lower yields, good equipment (whether or not this includes barriques), and of course Nebbiolo. As Davide Voerzio of Roberto Voerzio points out, much of what is described as modernism is simply catching up with what has been done in France for a long time in both the vineyard and cellar. Barolo and Barbaresco have now reached a similar situation to France where everyone claims to be perpetuating the tradition and no one admits to being a modernist.

Defining Crus: Missed Opportunities

The tradition in Barolo was for a producer to make a single wine by blending lots from various plots to make a wine with the maximum complexity. The concept of making Crus from named vineyards dates from the suggestion of Veronelli (an influential Italian wine critic) in the 1960s. The first single vineyard wines came from unquestionably great vineyards. In Barolo, Prunotto's Bussia and Vietti's Rocche di Castiglione appeared in 1961. In Barbaresco, there were Giacosa's Santo Stefano in 1964 and Gaja's Sorí San Lorenzo in 1967. Others followed in a steady stream. Recognizing the trend, in 1992 the regulations in Barolo were changed to allow single vineyard names to be identified on labels.

Most producers now have a hierarchy of wines, starting with a generic Nebbiolo. There is some divergence of opinion about style. Some producers, in fact probably most producers, make it in fresh, fruity style, very much designed for easy-drinking at entry-level. "We want to showcase the pure character of the grape," they tend to say. These can be perfectly decent wines in their own right, but in my opinion they do not give much insight into the style of the producer or the character of Nebbiolo.

Generic Nebbiolo come from either of two sources. Sometimes it is in effect a second wine declassified from plots within the Barolo DOCG, usually those have younger vines or aren't in the best locations. Sometimes it comes from vineyards in the Langhe outside the Barolo DOC (in which case it is more likely to be called Nebbiolo d'Alba.) "Nebbiolo from Roero area is more approachable, and less structured, with more fresh-

Producer	Name	Source
Elio Altare	Giàrborina	La Morra
Pio Cesare		10 vineyards in Barolo
Aldo Conterno	Il Favot	Bussia (Monforte d'Alba)
Oddero		La Morra + Castiglione Falleto + Villero
Luigi Pira		Serralunga d'Alba
Paolo Monti		Monforte d'Alba
Giuseppe Rinaldi		Barolo
Sottimano		Basarin (Barbaresco)
La Spinetta		Stardieri (Barbaresco)
Giovanni Viberti		Vergne
Vietti	Perbacco	Barolo + Barbaresco
Roberto Voerzio	San Francesco	La Morra

Reference Wines for Langhe Nebbiolo from Barolo or Barbaresco

ness: it's an expression of Nebbiolo that's different from Barolo and Barbaresco," says Francesco Vierzo at Bruno Giacosa. Actually, with the warming trend of climate change, some producers are now considering expanding their vineyards in the Langhe, thinking they may be able to make really good Nebbiolo from vineyards at higher elevations.

The big distinction about the nature of generic Nebbiolo is not so much the source of the grapes as the style of winemaking. Producers who want to distinguish the Nebbiolo from Barolo tend to vinify it in stainless steel instead of wood. Other producers make a 'baby Barolo,' by aging the wine in the same way as Barolo, but with shorter maceration (so there is less extraction from the skins) and shorter aging in in botti or barriques. This can offer the chance of seeing the producer's style in a more approachable way at a lower price point.

Perhaps the most significant change in Barolo is that now the best plots are almost always used to make single vineyard wines, so a Barolo *tout court,* the traditional blend from different vineyards, has less interest because it's deprived of the best lots. It is a step up from the Langhe Nebbiolo, but less interesting than the wines from the Crus. Most producers still produce a blend, and they often describe it casually as their Barolo Classico (although classico is not allowed on the label).

The Crus is the casual description that producers give their single vineyards. The system was informal until the Consorzio finally made a geographical classification of regions within Barolo and Barbaresco. The formal name for each defined area is the MGA (Menzione Geografica Ag-

Carta del Barolo

Renato Ratti

Antiche Cantine della Abbazia dell'Annunziata

Renato Ratti's map identified two levels of Crus (dark [red in the original]) is the top level, shaded [orange in the original] is the second level). Courtesy Renato Ratti Winery.

giuntive or Additional Geographic Mentions). However, it represents an unfortunate compromise to make sure that every single piece of land is entitled to a single vineyard name, thus to a large extent undermining the whole purpose of the exercise.

Although producers often refer to the MGAs as 'Crus,' these are absolutely not Crus in the sense in which the French use the term, where premier or grand crus are considered to produce better wines. The MGA is nothing more or less than a place name, the equivalent of the French *lieu-dit* or *climat*, meaning a circumscribed area: there is wide variation in size (and therefore the homogeneity of each MGA), and there is no implication that any one is better than any other. "Our intention has never been to classify, rather, to register and administratively delimit areas that are more restricted than the main denominations," according to Giovanni Minetti, former President of the Consorzio di Tutela Barolo.

In fact, there is a complete range from those that would be classified as village level (if this concept existed in Piedmont) to those that would be premier or grand cru. Its not really a classification system at all: just a more refined description of origin. It would be ever so much more useful if each MGA were assigned a level: village, premier cru, or grand cru... but that would involve a lot of politics...

With 170 MGAs in Barolo and 66 in Barbaresco, only the top names are likely to have any impact. Nor is there any assurance that a name on the label will correspond to a single vineyard, as it's still possible to trademark fantasy names. The classification is not consistent, as each commune set its own rules. The MGAs vary widely in size, and there's no guarantee that a name represents a homogeneous terroir. Bussia, in Monforte, for example, is so large that it actually contains several famous historical sites, each with its own character. Further, when an MGA is named on the label, it's permitted to include up to 15% of another MGA. In terms of conveying information about the character of a wine, the name of the commune (which has been allowed on the label since the MGA system was introduced in 2010) is probably generally a more useful guide to subregional differences.

While there is now a tendency for producers to indicate the commune for a Barolo that is blended from grapes all coming from one commune, this is not quite equivalent to the use of a village in, say, Burgundy; a communal wine is not necessarily superior to a Barolo Classico, blended from more than one commune, but means that the wine is likely to have the character of a specific commune.

The basic problem is that instead of defining a hierarchy—Barolo to Commune to Cru (premier or grand)—the official system left out the communal level and went straight from Barolo to the flat level of more than 100 MGAs. In many cases, perhaps most, the MGAs are really not very interesting by themselves, they can be somewhat one-note, and would actually make better wine as part of a blend with other MGAs. There might be some point in such situations to a blend with other MGAs in the same commune, in order to showcase communal character. Indeed, the Consorzio is trying to develop the concept of village wines to represent each commune, but it's difficult to retrofit the communes into the classification.

Is there in any case a consensus on the best Crus? Ratti remains a good guide, but of course there have been changes as Barolo has developed since then. Critics don't agree entirely, but the best sites certainly would include: Brunate, Cerequio, and Rocche dell'Annunziata in La Morra; Cannubi in Barolo; Bricco Rocche, Rocche di Castiglione, Monprivato, and Villero in Castiglione Falletto; Vigna Rionda, Francia, and Falletto in Serralunga. In Barbaresco, the best two Crus are Asili and Rabajà. One side effect of the introduction of MGAs is that is perhaps less tendency to make Riservas.

The Fame of Barolo

Until the 1960s, the production of Barolo was dominated by a handful of negociant firms who purchased grapes from many growers and blended to produce a Barolo (quality being determined by the negociant). Now grower bottling is the norm, but production is still on a fairly small scale. The average plot size is only 1.5 ha.

For the major players, Barolo and Barbaresco are only a small part of their total production; a typical producer might also have some Nebbiolo in the more general Langhe classification, vineyards of Barbera and Dolcetto, and perhaps some Arneis across the border in Roero. Barolo and Barbaresco are often only a third to a half of the total production for an average producer.

Most of the top producers concentrate on estate production, but the estate often includes rented vineyards. However, the success of Barolo has caused a sharp increase in land prices that is making rentals more difficult. "Rentals used to be done with a handshake, now you have to go to a notary and have everything certified," says Silvia Altare.

Rental agreements have become shorter—"the longest rental we have now is seven years," says Silvia—and sometimes the owner decides to sell rather than renew. "Farmers may want to sell, but wineries won't be able to afford to buy," says Elena Currado at Vietti. Prices have risen to €2-3 million for a hectare of vineyards in a good cru. "You can only buy vineyards if you buy for the next generation; it's a 50-year project to break even," says Emmanuele Baldi at Prunotto.

Will this lead to a transition like Bordeaux where owners are no longer local, but are rich investors, either personal or companies, with some looking to establish lifestyle wineries? The proportion of foreign owners is growing, and some old producers have changed hands. It was a shock when Vietti, known as an artisan producer, was sold in 2016 to a chain store magnate from Iowa.

The concern is that Barolo will now follow Bordeaux and Burgundy in transitioning to conglomerate ownership, because the high land prices make it difficult to expand as a small producer, and hard to resist the feeling that you can't afford not to sell. As yet this has not reached a point at which you feel any change when visiting the region, although the level of investment is indicated by some stylish wineries in post-modern architecture appearing on the landscape.

Aging Barolo

Barolo has a historic reputation for requiring very long aging before it can be drunk. This is no longer true. Like wines everywhere, better tannin management means that the aggression that used to be evident in young wines is a thing of the past: you are not forced to wait a decade before the wine becomes approachable. But there is a great difference between saying that a wine can be drunk now and being ready to drink. The success of Barolo has the unfortunate consequence of causing it to be drunk too young. "This is Nebbiolo. They're not made like they used to be, you don't *have* to wait to drink them, but you should be patient," says Roberto Bordignon at Elio Grasso.

"The characteristic of Barolo is that it ages. Otherwise it's not Barolo, you should change the name on the label. But our Barolos are different every year so you can always find a vintage that is ready to drink young or one that needs time," says Davide Voerzio. Since the run of good vintages that started in the mid nineties, there have been few poor vintages, but there are certainly vintages that need aging and vintages that can be drunk quite young. The latter may never reach the level of the complexity of the former, but they can be excellent restaurant wines. "We are pleased to have vintages like 2011 and 2012 that are more approachable as opposed to 2006 that still need 20 years," says Elena Currado at Vietti.

And it depends what style of wine you prefer. "All the hot vintages in the past were thought to be the best. Today we can't continue with this mindset. I feel that the cool vintages today are when we get the best balanced wines," says Gaia Gaja. "When it's too hot we say Barolo is not classical," says Elena Mascarello. The top recent vintages—2016, 2010,

2007, 2004—produced forceful wines, but sometimes you can see the delicate typicity of Nebbiolo much earlier in the lesser vintages, such as 2005 or 2012. The greater approachability of even the top vintages raises a question. "Thirty years ago you could drink Barolo and Barbaresco only after a long time. The great vintages now—2004 or 2007—are not like the typical great vintages of the past. We have to wait to see whether today's vintages will age as well as the ones in the past, but I think ours will age a long time," said Bruna Giacosa.

Vintages

Barolo and Barbaresco usually run more or less parallel, but there are vintages where one is significantly more successful than the other due to localized conditions. "2010 was excellent in Barolo but only good in Barbaresco. We had three rainy days in September that made the soil a bit moist, and the berries were a little too big. In Barolo they were able to wait another 10 days, the later picking gave shrinking of the berries." It was the other way in 2014: "2014 is the opposite of 2010, it was much better in Barbaresco. Barolo had two heavy rain days that we missed," says Aldo Vacco at the Produttori del Barbaresco.

Global warming has affected Barolo and Barbaresco like everywhere else. "Hot years are becoming more common, but since 2003 we have learned so much about how to manage them, now you don't see the problems of a hot year in the wine," says Isabelle Oddero. So while 2017 was the hottest vintage since 2003, the results are much better.

2021	**	The season started with some frost and rain, which meant lower yields at the end. Summer was long and warm with good diurnal variation. It's likely to be a classic vintage.
2020	**	Producers began to call this a great vintage immediately after the harvest, but the truth may be more heterogeneous. The growing season was on the warmer side, but there was always enough water due to frequent, but brief rains—to the point at which humidity sometimes became a problem. Heavy rains on October 2 meant results were problematic for grapes not harvested by then; otherwise the wines have midweight balance.
2019	**	Not entirely an easy year because of the alternation of rain and heatwaves. Producers describe this as a classic vintage. "It reminds me most of the classic vintages of the 1990s," Gaia Gaja says. Harvest in second half of October. Wines are more generous than 2018.

2018		Everyone starts descriptions of 2018 with one word: rain. There were 24 days of rain between May 1 and June 15, and the vintage never really recovered. Several producers did not make their single-vineyard wines, but put the grapes into blends. Wines are on the light side for Barolo, and many can be enjoyed immediately.
2017		A very dry, hot season with drought conditions led to the earliest harvest in ten years. Not well regarded.
2016	***	Shaping up to be a classic as good season was followed by perfect harvest conditions; richness may equal 2015 but tannic structure should be riper and acidity higher.
2015	*	A good water supply resulted from rain and snow over the previous winter, it was very hot from June to August, but then cooler than average for September and October. Results are mixed.
2014		"2014 was a difficult year. It started raining in March and did not stop until November," says Alan Manley at Luciano Sandrone.
2013	*	Wet at first, then hot, leading to late harvest. Wines now give somewhat of a cool climate impression, a little thin and tannic.
2012	*	The 2012 vintage was much derided by the international press, but there are many wines showing the essential character of Nebbiolo, fragrant and sometimes even delicate. The problem is that flavor variety can be a bit one dimensional, but in another four or five years, the best wines should show an elegance that should last for another four or five years. Better in Barolo than Barbaresco.
2011	**	A hot vintage gave very ripe grapes and forceful wines, but not absolutely top notch as some have too much alcohol. Good for Barbera.
2010	***	A classically cool growing season but with consistent good weather. Widely regarded as a great year in Barolo, perhaps even legendary, although not as good in Barbaresco.
2009	*	Warm year; heat caused vines to shut down, causing erratic ripening. Everything depends on individual harvest conditions.
2008	**	Cool growing season followed by Indian summer gave quite powerful wines on the austere side.
2007	***	Warm, dry year gave low yields and well-structured wines.
2006	**	Cool weather made tannins the big issue this year. Many wines require significant aging for the tannins to calm down. Most are not ready yet.
2005	*	"2005 was a very variable vintage. There were five days of solid rain. Every producer harvested some before the rain and some after. Results depended on what you did afterwards with the lots," says Giacomo at Aldo Conterno.

2004	***	A classic vintage, one of the top three of the decade.
2003		It was too hot for Nebbiolo to make classic wines, but very good for Barbera.
2002		The one really poor year of the decade due to too much rain.
2001	***	Classic vintage with wines maturing to elegance.
2000	**	Over-rated by some critics, this is a very good but not great, year.
1999	**	Perhaps a touch better than 1998, certainly very good.
1998	**	A very good year, but overshadowed by 1997.
1997	***	A great year, wines are universally harmonious, the best are at their peak now.
1996	***	A top year with strongly structured wines that often required a decade or so to come to their peaks.

Visiting the Region

The region is tiny. It is barely 5 miles from one end of the Barolo DOC to the other. Barbaresco is even smaller. The two regions are about 15 miles apart, less than half an hour. However, within each area it can take much longer than you might expect to go from one producer to another. Serralunga d'Alba and Castiglione Falletto are less than a mile apart as the crow flies, but to drive between them, you have to go all the way to one end of a deep valley, and then all the way back along the other side. Short cuts are best avoided as they can be extremely narrow and precipitous. The village in which a producer is nominally located may not be the best indication of how to reach the estate, as postal codes do not necessarily conform to access routes; sometimes the easiest route is in fact from the next village over.

It is perfectly reasonable to visit several producers in a day, but it helps

La Morra is the largest of the hilltop villages in Barolo DOCG, with a historic center, and restaurants and hotels for tourists.

The church in the medieval hilltop village of Barbaresco can be seen for miles around. Gaja is just on the right in the main street, and the Produttori cooperative is in the main square just to the right of the church.

enormously to organize a schedule in which successive visits are in the same or adjacent communes. Always allow at least half an hour between visits as finding a producer isn't always straightforward. The maps showing the locations of producers should be helpful for this.

The medieval hilltop villages are one of the sights of the region, especially La Morra and Monforte d'Alba (in Barolo) and Barbaresco and Neive (if you drive along the main road where most of the wineries are located, you may miss Neive village, which just off to the north). They can, of course, be rather busy in the season.

When producers basically made one Barolo blend plus perhaps a Riserva, tastings used to be relatively short, one or two other varieties, one or two Barolos. The emphasis in recent years in Crus means that many producers have quite an extensive range, typically a Nebbiolo Langhe, a Barolo, up to six or so Crus, and perhaps some. Even so, it is unusual for a visit to last much longer than an hour.

Neive is a typical walled medieval village of the region perched on a mountaintop.

While many producers have tasting rooms that are generally open, it's necessary to make appointments at the top producers. It is a good idea to book well ahead, especially in the peak season (which is the Autumn here) when some producers may fill up their appointments two or three months ahead.

As oenotourism has picked up, more producers have opened dedicated tasting rooms, but at smaller producers tasting may be in the cellar. The etiquette of tasting assumes you will spit. A producer will be surprised if you drink the wine. Usually a tasting room or cellar is equipped with spittoons, but ask if you do not see one. Of course, some tourists do enjoy drinking the wines, but producers will take you more seriously if you spit.

Maps

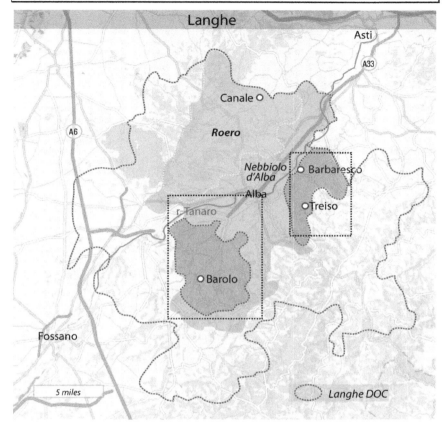

34

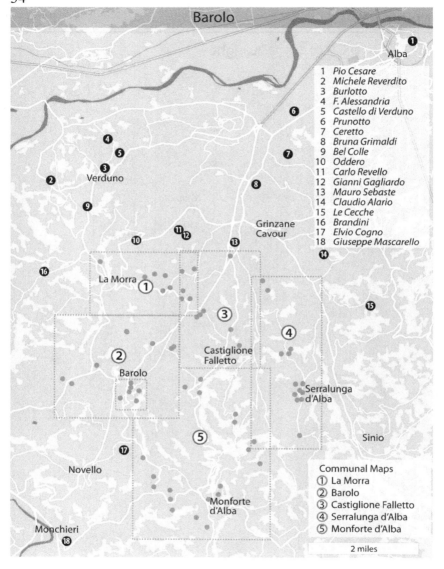

Barolo

Alba

1 Pio Cesare
2 Michele Reverdito
3 Burlotto
4 F. Alessandria
5 Castello di Verduno
6 Prunotto
7 Ceretto
8 Bruna Grimaldi
9 Bel Colle
10 Oddero
11 Carlo Revello
12 Gianni Gagliardo
13 Mauro Sebaste
14 Claudio Alario
15 Le Cecche
16 Brandini
17 Elvio Cogno
18 Giuseppe Mascarello

Verduno

Grinzane
Cavour

La Morra

Castiglione
Falletto

Barolo

Serralunga
d'Alba

Sinio

Novello

Monforte
d'Alba

Monchieri

Communal Maps
① La Morra
② Barolo
③ Castiglione Falletto
④ Serralunga d'Alba
⑤ Monforte d'Alba

2 miles

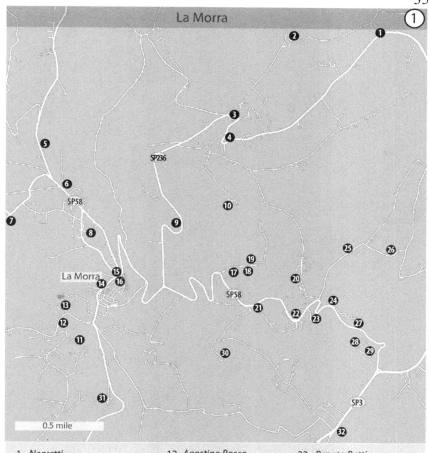

La Morra

0.5 mile

1 Negretti	12 Agostino Bosco	23 Renato Ratti
2 Luigi Oddero	13 Boglietti	24 Fratelli Revello
3 Burzi	14 Mario Marengo	25 Cordero Di Montezemolo
4 Oddero	15 Rocche Costamagna	26 Batasiolo
5 Andréa Oberto	16 Marcarini	27 Molino
6 Voerzio Martini	17 Renato Corino	28 Monastero
7 Alberto Voerzio	18 Mauro Veglio	29 Silvio Grasso
8 Roberto Voerzio	19 Elio Altare	30 Trediberri
9 Ciabot Berton	20 Aurelio Settimo	31 Giulia Negri
10 Crissante Alessandria	21 Bovio	32 Damilano
11 Serradenari	22 Corino Giovanni	

36

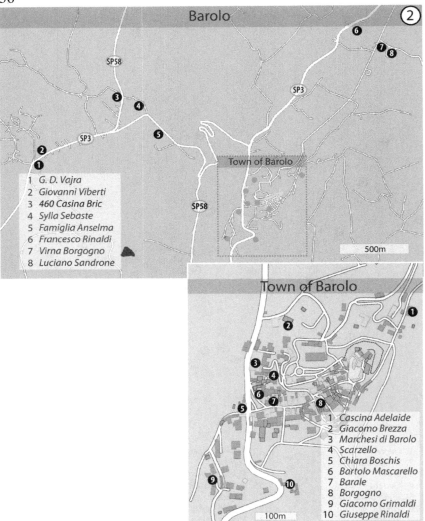

Barolo ②

SP58

SP3

SP3

SP58

Town of Barolo

500m

1 G. D. Vajra
2 Giovanni Viberti
3 460 Casina Bric
4 Sylla Sebaste
5 Famiglia Anselma
6 Francesco Rinaldi
7 Virna Borgogno
8 Luciano Sandrone

Town of Barolo

1 Cascina Adelaide
2 Giacomo Brezza
3 Marchesi di Barolo
4 Scarzello
5 Chiara Boschis
6 Bartolo Mascarello
7 Barale
8 Borgogno
9 Giacomo Grimaldi
10 Giuseppe Rinaldi

100m

37

Castiglione Falletto ③

1 Terre Del Barolo
2 Bongiovanni
3 Giovanni Sordo
4 Brovia
5 Luigi Scavino
6 Paolo Scavino
7 Boroli
8 Francesco Sobrero
9 Cavallotto
10 Vietti
11 Monchiero
12 Cascina Fontana

SP3 SP9

Castiglione Falletto

0.5 mile

Perno

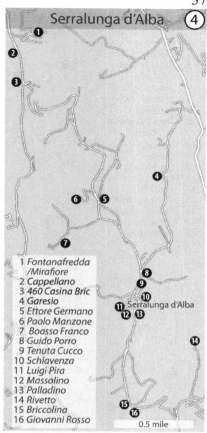

Serralunga d'Alba ④

1 Fontanafredda /Mirafiore
2 Cappellano
3 460 Casina Bric
4 Garesio
5 Ettore Germano
6 Paolo Manzone
7 Boasso Franco
8 Guido Porro
9 Tenuta Cucco
10 Schiavenza
11 Luigi Pira
12 Massolino
13 Palladino
14 Rivetto
15 Briccolina
16 Giovanni Rosso

Serralunga d'Alba

0.5 mile

38

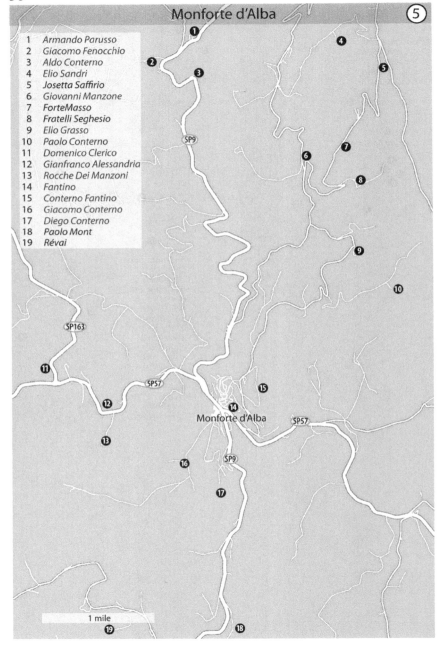

1   Armando Parusso
2   Giacomo Fenocchio
3   Aldo Conterno
4   Elio Sandri
5   Josetta Saffirio
6   Giovanni Manzone
7   ForteMasso
8   Fratelli Seghesio
9   Elio Grasso
10 Paolo Conterno
11 Domenico Clerico
12 Gianfranco Alessandria
13 Rocche Dei Manzoni
14 Fantino
15 Conterno Fantino
16 Giacomo Conterno
17 Diego Conterno
18 Paolo Mont
19 Révai

SP9

SP163

SP57

Monforte d'Alba

SP57

SP9

1 mile

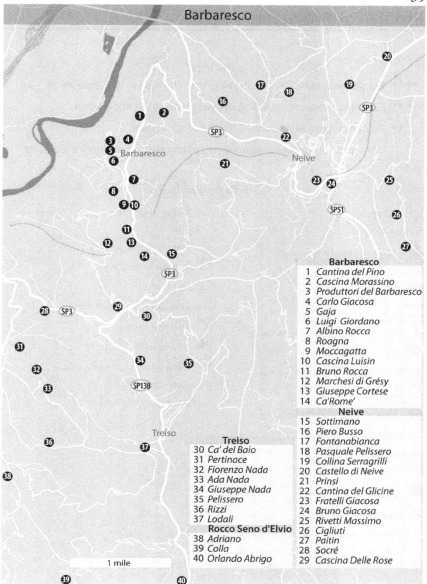

Barbaresco

Barbaresco
1 Cantina del Pino
2 Cascina Morassino
3 Produttori del Barbaresco
4 Carlo Giacosa
5 Gaja
6 Luigi Giordano
7 Albino Rocca
8 Roagna
9 Moccagatta
10 Cascina Luisin
11 Bruno Rocca
12 Marchesi di Grésy
13 Giuseppe Cortese
14 Ca'Rome'
Neive
15 Sottimano
16 Piero Busso
17 Fontanabianca
18 Pasquale Pelissero
19 Collina Serragrilli
20 Castello di Neive
21 Prinsi
22 Cantina del Glicine
23 Fratelli Giacosa
24 Bruno Giacosa
25 Rivetti Massimo
26 Cigliuti
27 Paitin
28 Socré
29 Cascina Delle Rose

Treiso
30 Ca' del Baio
31 Pertinace
32 Fiorenzo Nada
33 Ada Nada
34 Giuseppe Nada
35 Pelissero
36 Rizzi
37 Lodali
Rocco Seno d'Elvio
38 Adriano
39 Colla
40 Orlando Abrigo

1 mile

40

Profiles of Producers

Ratings

★★★★	Sui generis, standing out above everything else in the appellation
★★★	Excellent producers defining the very best of the appellation
★★	Top producers whose wines typify the appellation
★	Very good producers making wines of character that rarely disappoint

Symbols for Producers

Address

Phone

Owner/winemaker/contact

Email

Website

DOC

Red White Reference wines

Grower-producer

Negociant (or purchases grapes)

Cooperative

Conventional viticulture

Sustainable viticulture

Organic

Biodynamic

Natural Wine

Wine with No Sulfur

Vegan Wine

Tasting room with especially warm welcome

Tastings/visits possible

By appointment only

No visits

Sales directly at producer

No direct sales

Winery with restaurant

Winery with accommodation

ha=estate vineyards

bottles=annual production

Profiles of Leading Estates

Elio Altare ★★

Fraz. Annunziata, Cascina Nuova, 51, 12064 La Morra (CN)	📞 +39 0173 50835
@ *elioaltare@elioaltare.com*	👤 *Silvia Altare*
🌐 *www.elioaltare.com*	⊙ *Barolo [map p. 35]*
📅 ⚏ 🍇 ℃ *11 ha; 70,000 btl*	🍷 *Barolo*

"Our passion today is the same as when my father started; it's Burgundy," says Silvia Altare, explaining the focus on individual terroirs. She has now formally taken over from Elio, who remains involved, but is also busy trying other things; he's bought a small farm in the mountains of Liguria, and is making cheese and honey and some white wine there. "He loves to experiment," Silvia says.

Elio Altare was one of the "Barolo Boys" who revolutionized Barolo in the seventies. "I asked myself, why don't consumers like my wine," he recollects; after visiting Burgundy, he decided to use new methods. Yet he says, "I am a son of the soil, I am a vigneron, not an entrepreneur." He developed the vinification technique that the house still uses: short maceration of about only four days on the skins with rotary fermenters. "The results show better fixation of anthocyanins for color than in wines with the conventional 20 day maceration; the oenologists say it's impossible, but that's their problem."

Altare remains a small producer, with half its vineyards owned, and half rented. In a courtyard surrounded by other houses, the winery looks like a residence, but underneath is the cellar, stuffed with barriques; there are no botti here. The focus is on Nebbiolo, although there are also Dolcetto, Barbera (labeled Vigna Larigi without varietal identification because Elio thought it would be criticized for being too dark if it was labeled as Barbera), and a Barbera-Nebbiolo blend (La Villa). There are also two Nebbiolos, one labeled simply Langhe Nebbiolo, the other Vigna Giàborina. L'Insieme is blended from indigenous and international varieties.

The heart is in six Barolos. The Barolo *tout court* is a blend from four vineyards in La Morra. The four single-vineyard cuvées are Arborina and Brunate in La Morra, Cannubi in Barolo, and Cerretta in Serralunga. Finally there is Unoperuno, which comes from Arborina, but where berries are cut off the stems individually. "When you compare this with the others, it tastes completely different," says Silvia, but she adds ruefully, "of course, we can't make a profit on it."

The common factor to the house style is a silky smoothness, increasing from the Langhe, to the sophistication of the Barolo, showing the typical elegance of La Morra, to the greater density of Cerretta. Fruits are cut by a savory edge, the tannins get finer and silkier going up the range, and the fragrancy of the variety comes out more clearly. The wines have good tannic structure and usually need time for full flavor variety to show itself.

Azelia Di Luigi Scavino ★★

Via Alba Barolo 143, 12060 Castiglione Falletto (CN)	📞 +39 0173 62859
@ *l.scavino@azelia.it*	👤 *Luigi & Lorenzo Scavino*
⊕ *www.azelia.it*	🔴 *Barolo [map p. 37]*
📅 ⛰ 🍇 🍷 *16 ha; 80,000 btl*	🍾 *Barolo, Bricco Fiasco*

"We are one of the most historical wineries in the region, founded in 1920. We started bottling wine in the 1930s, which was unusual for the time. I am the fifth generation. I am the only child—there is no pressure! My father (Luigi) is still the big boss. We are very family run; there is a family member in charge of each process. We don't want to grow more because we would lose that," says Lorenzo Scavino.

The approach here is determinedly traditional. "We've always had the three local varieties. We have many plots of land where we could plant other varieties, especially whites, which customers ask for, but we are true to our roots. My father only wants to work with old vines, he does not want to work with young vines. The oldest vines are in a plot that's used for the Riserva, the oldest is 120 years, including some on own roots. We replace vines only individually as they die, using selection massale from the oldest vines."

The Dolcetto comes from a single vineyard of 55-year-old vines at 600m altitude at Monteluse, about 20 km from Barolo. The vineyard faces full south. "Dolcetto would never be planted in such a good position in Barolo," Lorenzo Scavino says. "If you have Dolcetto facing south on the top of a hill, it can be an incredible wine." Barbera d'Alba comes from Castiglione Falletto.

70% of plantings are Nebbiolo, with a focus on old vines. "My father only wants to work with old vines." The oldest are in a plot that's used for the Riserva, going as far back as 120 years, including some on own roots. Vines are replaced individually as they die, with selection massale from the oldest vines.

The Langhe Nebbiolo is declassified from vineyards in Castiglione Falletto and Serralunga d'Alba. "These are the young vines–20 years is too young for my father." Aging is 1 year in stainless steel. "For us, Langhe Nebbiolo is not a baby Barolo, it is a different wine. That's why we don't age it in wood, it should be refreshing, drink younger, so you can really see the grape."

The Barolos get 50 days maceration with a submerged cap, and then age in 30 hl Tini (botti with untoasted oak). The Barolo is a blend from 7 vineyards in Castiglione Falletto(with sandy soils) and Serralunga d'Alba (with more clay). "You get Castiglione on the nose and Serralunga in the mouth," Lorenzo says. There is a serious jump in intensity and also approachability going from Classic Barolo to Bricco Fiasco, from the original vineyard where the estate started in Castiglione Falletto, planted in 1938. This is always the most floral and aromatic cuvee of the house. Its first vintage as a separate release was 1978. Sweet, round, ripe, it is more approachable than the classic Barolo because fruit intensity balances the tannins better.

With the transition from Castiglione Falletto to Serralunga, there is more evident power, Margheria from Serralunga is the most obviously structured of the cuvées. Based on dark clay, San Rocco was the first vineyard (2 ha) that Luigi bought in Serralunga.. It is more powerful and richer than Margheria but the power is hidden by the finer texture.

Cerretta is only 200m from San Rocco, and is the top of the line with that typical Rolls Royce impression of Serralunga, round at the front but with silky power behind. Luigi replanted most of the vines in the 2.5 ha plot by hand 30 years ago because he was not satisfied with the condition of the vineyard when he bought it. For the first 10 years after planting it was declassified to Langhe, then it was part of the Barolo blend until the 2016 vintage was released as a single vineyard. A thread of minerality runs through all the wines.

The Riserva comes from Bricco Volghera, under 1 ha of 95-year-old vines, aged for 5 years in botti. More intense than the individual crus, it retains the overall elegant house style with an impression of minerality, and a firmness that makes the individual crus seem softer. "We never decide during harvest, we wait three years to decide whether to make a Riserva." It is made in about half the vintages.

Enzo Boglietti

Via Fontane 18/a, 12064 La Morra (CN)	📞 *+39 0173 50330*
@ *info@enzoboglietti.com*	👤 *Enzo & Linda Boglietti*
⊕ *www.enzoboglietti.com*	🌐 *Barolo [map p. 35]*
📷 🏭 🍇 🍷 *23 ha; 100,000 btl*	🍷 *Barolo, Fossati*

The family has been here for many generations and had a self-sustaining farm engaged in polyculture before switching to viticulture. Grapes were previously sold off. Enzo makes the wine and his brother Gianni manages the vineyards. They built a new winery in 2006, a modern but practical building built into the hillside just outside the village of La Morra. The striking labels with backwards lettering (this can be confusing on signposts when you are looking for the winery) were designed in 1991 by a cousin who was an architect. Most of the vineyards are inherited, but sources are sometimes supplemented by purchasing grapes.

The vineyards are in La Morra except for Fossati (in Barolo) and Arione (in Serralunga). There is some Dolcetto in Monforte. There are three cuvées of Barbera d'Alba, all from La Morra. The Langhe Nebbiolo comes from vineyards in the Barolo area (but not classified for Barolo because they are north-facing) and Roddino. Plantings are

60% Nebbiolo, 25% Barbera, and 15% Dolcetto. The Langhe Nebbiolo is an entry-level wine; the communal La Morra is smooth and elegant, less obvious than the Langhe Nebbiolo, but a little on the light side, in fact light enough to start on release. The Commune La Morra is the base of the Barolos, and then there are 5 crus. The little-known cru of Boiolo is the most northern and usually the freshest of the cuvées. The silkiness is true to La Morra, but it's rather tight when young. Fossati is more muscular, but greater fruit concentration makes it more approachable, although it still needs a couple of years after release. Case Nere has greater structure but the structure is less obvious because the fruits are deeper. Brunate is sleeker, rounder, and the most complex of the crus. Going up the hierarchy, there is more structure and also greater roundness and intensity, so the wines seem more approachable, with structure better hidden. Moving out of La Morra, Arione shows the restrained power of Serralunga in a clear demonstration of the difference between the areas. The wines now age mostly in 40 hl Tini (botti of untoasted oak).

It is like night and day when you taste older vintages compared with recent vintages. "Around 2014 I started to move to bigger casks and older barrels to be more respectful of Nebbiolo," Enzo says in a rather understated way. Wines from 2010 or 2009, for example, are still powerful and massive today. Before 2014 the wines are almost aggressively modern; today they are more subtle.

Giacomo Borgogno & Figli *

Via Gioberti 1, 12060 Barolo (CN)

@ info@borgogno.com

⊕ www.borgogno.com

30 ha; 250,000 btl

📞 +39 0173 56108

👤 Andrea Farinetti

Barolo [map p. 36]

Barolo

This is one of the oldest producers in the region, established in 1761. The modern era started in 1920 with Cesare Borgogno, who ran the estate until 1968. His children and grandchildren, the Boschis family, continued until 2008 when they sold to Oscar Farinetti, a local entrepreneur who had started Eataly; shortly after he also bought Fontanafredda (see profile) in Serralunga. Cesare and Giorgio Boschis stayed with the company for three years. (Giorgio later joined his sister Chiara at E. Pira; see profile). Today Andrea Farinetti is the winemaker.

Located in the heart of the pedestrianized part of the village of Barolo, the cellars are a major feature of the town. You wonder how grapes and equipment can get in and out. The domain encourages oenotourism and has a wide range of tastings and tours available. The tasting room is always busy (there is a charge for visiting the cellars). Underneath, the cellars are vastly more expansive than you would ever guess from their location. "The cellars are bigger than Barolo," Andrea says.

"We have not changed philosophy, we have changed nothing. I studied oenology in Alba for 6 years and I started to make the wine here in 2010," Andrea says. Wines ferment in concrete and age in botti of Slavonian oak (except for some French oak for the Barbera). The house used to be known for sourcing grapes from many small growers, but today relies only on estate grapes.

Although the focus remained on blending for a long time, Borgogno's most historic vineyard, Liste, has always been made as separate release. Cannubi and Fossati were added as single vineyards in 2008. The Crus were all in the commune of Barolo until Andrea bought 2 ha in in 2019 in Annunziata (in La Morra) from an old family friend.

The wines from the Langhe are not labeled with varietal names in the usual manner; Andrea believest this undercuts the value of the Langhe and uses his own names: Ancum is the Dolcetto, Bompé is the Barbera, and Bartomé is the Nebbiolo. (The back label states the varieties.) The Nebbiolo is not intended to be a baby Barolo: "it's stupid to try to make a baby Barolo. Nebbiolo d'Alba should be soft and drinkable. Barolo is Barolo."

The Barolo is the largest cuvée. A blend from all five vineyards, and from 2019 from six vineyards as it includes a small amount of Annunziata, it gives a good insight into the style, fine and elegant, and ready to start a couple of years after release (5-6 years after the vintage). From 60 cm of sandy soil on top of blue clay, Fossati is elegant and silky, and quite approachable on release.. Cannubi comes from two plots at the top of the hill and has the finest structure and greatest elegance of all the cuvées. Coming from sandy soil, Liste has similar finesse, but with a stronger, sturdier impression of tannic structure and a greater impression of minerality. It needs more time than the others to open out. The Riserva is the most structured of all (it usually contains 70% Liste), but greater fruit density hides the tannins so the structure is not too evident. All the same, it needs more time.

The house is famous for its holdings of old wines (currently about 120,000 bottles of vintages from 1961 to 1990), following a policy established in the 1920s to hold back about 20% of production to provide library wines from top vintages. In addition to the range of Barolos and the Langhe, there are communal Derthona and a single-vineyard release from the Timorasso grape. Andrea has expanded out of Piedmont by buying 7 ha on Etna, where he produces both red and white wine.

G. B. Burlotto   *

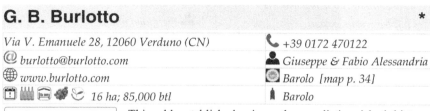

Via V. Emanuele 28, 12060 Verduno (CN)

@ burlotto@burlotto.com

🌐 www.burlotto.com

📅 🏭 🖼 🐛 ☙ 16 ha; 85,000 btl

📞 +39 0172 470122

👤 Giuseppe & Fabio Alessandria

📍 Barolo [map p. 34]

🍷 Barolo

This old established winery has a distinguished history. Founded by Giovan Battista Burlotto, known as 'Il Commendatore,' in 1850, it sold wines bottled under the estate's name (very rare in that era) to a clientele including the royal court of Savoy. G. B. Burlotto continued to make the wines until 1927, after which the estate somewhat faded. The estate remains in family hands, run today by Fabio Alessandria, Burlotto's great-great grandson, an oenologist who has revived and expanded the estate. Located in the original house of the Belle Epoque era, it has expanded into the adjacent property, with cellars on either side of a gracious courtyard, now connected by a new underground cellar.

"We look for elegance, freshness, and lifted aromatics, not so powerful or structured or muscular," Fabio says. "Elegance is the character of wines made in this area (Verduno)." That description applies to Barbera as well as to Nebbiolo. It's emphasized by traditional winemaking, with grapes trodden by foot, fermentation in large open-topped oak vats, and aging in botti.

Vineyards are mostly (12 ha) in Verduno, with the rest split between Roddi and Cannubi, and a plot added in Monforte in 2018. The Langhe Nebbiolo is declassified from younger wines in Barolo—"the age depends on the cru and the vintage, it's different each year." Aged for 10 months in botti, it is fragrant with lifted aromatics. All the Barolos age for 33 months in botti. The communal Barolo includes grapes from all the vineyards except Cannubi and Monvigliero; very fine and silky, it shows more subtle aromatics than Langhe Nebbiolo. Activi is a blend from the best plots in three vineyards in Verduno, but their proportions change each year. "This is the old philosophy of Riserva, but we don't want to use the classification." It's rounder with more sense of tannic grip and structure, but follows the elegant house style. The flagship wine is the Monvigliero Cru in Verduno, south-facing and known for its soil of white marl, which was the source for Burlotto's original Nebbiolo. This has a more herbal character, but although it is firmer than Activi, structure is less obvious because of the greater fruit density.

There are two cuvées of Barbera d'Alba, the regular bottling (aged in steel) and the more intense Aves (aged for one year in tonneau). Pelaverga is an unusual red wine, light and fresh, from an ancient variety that the estate has grown since its inception, and for which there are 17 ha left in Verduno.

Piero Busso *

Via Albesani 8, 12052 Neive (CN)	+39 0173 67156
info@pierobusso.com	Pierguido Busso
wwwpierobusso.com	Barbaresco [map p. 39]
10 ha; 45,000 btl	Barbaresco, Albesum (Vigna Borge)

"The idea of the winery started when my grandfather bought the Albesani vineyard in the 1940s. But he died very young, when my father was only 5; so my grandmother sold the grapes just to be able to keep the property. My father decided to start wine production at the end of the 1970s, bought another hectare, and his first vintage was 1982. Piero Busso is named for my father not my grandfather. My father slowly built the winery and increased production," says Emanuela, who has now taken over with her brother Pierguido.

Piero Busso

BARBARESCO
ALBESANI
VIGNA BORGESE
2014

The winery is a small property just outside the village of Neive. All the vineyards are around the winery, except for ha at Treiso. Winemaking is traditional. "My father never used any small barrels. He felt big barrels respect the integrity of the grape better." The range starts with Langhe Nebbiolo, which comes from grapes around the winery. "In the past we aged the Langhe Nebbiolo for 12 months in Slavonian botti, but it was always a little bitter and too tannic. So now we do 8 months in botti and 4 months in stainless steel. It's more drinkable." It has a classic, slightly briary, flavor spectrum.

The range moves straight to the single-vineyard Barbarescos, which are the major part of production. They age in large casks of Slavonian oak for 24 months. Albesani is faintly smoky and mineral, smooth and silky, and quite approachable. Gallina is more fragrant, more polished, more feminine. There are no Riservas, but there are Viti Vecchia cuvées from very old (more than 80-year) vines. Albesani has been made since 2010—"from vines planted by my grandfather"—and Gallina was added in 2015. They are made only in top years and age for 4 years in oak. The intensity of old vines shows through, with greater concentration on the palate; as with the regular cuvées Gallina is more refined than Albesani, but the difference with the regular cuvée is more marked for Albesani than for Gallina.

In other cuvées, the Barbera d'Alba Majano comes from Neive and ages in steel, while the Stan Stefanetto cuvée comes from Treiso and ages in oak. There's a Dolcetto d'Alba, and a modern touch in the form of the equal blend of Sauvignon Blanc and Chardonnay in the Langhe Bianco.

Ca'del Baio   *

Via Ferrere 33, Loc. Tre Stelle, 12050 Treiso (CN)	📞 +39 0173 638219
@ cadelbaio@cadelbaio.com	👤 Giulio Grasso
🌐 www.cadelbaio.com	Barbaresco [map p. 39]
📅 ⛪ 🍇 ⏱ 25 ha; 140,000 btl	🍷 Barbaresco, Vallegrade

BARBARESCO
VALLEGRANDE
CA' DEL BAIO

"Great grandfather bought the property in 1887. The family came from Monferrato but bought here because the price of land was lower. It was forest at the time of purchase, and had been a hunting preserve. Basically it was a self-contained farm with polyculture. My grandfather started to make Dolcetto for every day drinking in the fifties. My father wanted to do something different, to make Barbaresco, because my mother came from Barbaresco," Paolo Grasso says. Together with her sisters Valentina and Federica, she took over in 2020 when their father, Giulio, 'retired' in 2020, although he remains involved. Paola is mostly concerned with winemaking, and is the driving

48

force for experimentation in the winery; Valentina and Federica are more concerned with the commercial side. "We've experimented with yeast, temperature, tanks," Paola says. "We age in botti of 25-70 hl (mostly Slavonian oak, with some Austrian oak) which we found was the best size."

The range starts with the Red Label Langhe Nebbiolo, with grapes from various sources, a pleasant entry-level wine vinified in stainless steel. BriccdelBaio is s higher level, mostly declassified from the Crus; aged for 10 months in Slavonian oak, it is more of a preview of Barbaresco. Vineyards include five crus in the communes of Barbaresco and Treiso. Marcarini and Ferrere have blended into the Autinbej cuvée since 2014 as the holdings are really too small to vinify separately. The vineyards are at high altitude in Treiso, and the wine gives an impression of coming from a cooler climate than the other Barbaresco cuvées. There is a step up in interest from Autinbej to Vallegrande (the plot next to the winery) and again to Asili. All Barbarescos spend 26 months in botti. Asili was the only Riserva until Vallegrande was added with the 2018 vintage. They spend 36 months in old tonneaux, and Asili then spends a further 6-8 months in amphorae, which adds freshness. There are also Chardonnay and Riesling cuvées under the Langhe label.

The wines are superficially in the new approachable style of Barbaresco, seeming silky and approachable on opening, but this can be deceptive, as the tannic structure becomes more obvious ion the glass and flattens the fruit profile. In fact, they have the classic character of needing time to resolve tannins and develop flavor variety, but that style should be most elegant as they develop. Give Autinbej a year, Vallegrande a couple of years, Asili 3-4 years, and the Riserva at least 5 years.

Cascina Delle Rose   *

Strada Rio Sordo 58, Barbaresco 12050 | +39 0173 238292
cascinadellerose@cascinadellerose.it | Riccardo Sobrino or Giovanna Rizzolio
www.cascinadellerose.it | Barbaresco [map p. 39]
| Barolo, La Serra
5 ha; 30,000 btl | Barbaresco, Tre Stelle

"My grandfather purchased the property in 1948, my mother took over in 1974," says Riccardo, who has run the estate with his brother Davide since their parents 'retired.' "We have Dolcetto, Barbera, and Nebbiolo, but it might make sense for us just to have Nebbiolo," Riccardo says, a touch ruefully. "We consider ourselves a classic producer, so we like to represent the range (of varieties)." Vineyards are all close to the winery in the Tre Stelle area of Barbaresco. The estate has been bottling its own wines since 1992, starting with the old cellars under the house, until a new cellar was built in 1994, and then extended in 2017.

Except for the Langhe Nebbiolo, Aging is in 10-20 hl foudres, all Slavonian oak except for the latest two, which are Swiss oak. There is no influence of new oak.

"We don't want to taste the wood, the label says Tre Stelle, Barbaresco, it doesn't say 'forest'," Riccardo says. Barbera d'Alba is a blend between east-facing plots in Tre Stelle and south-facing plots in Marcarini, and ages for 12-15 months in botti. The Barbera d'Alba Superiore comes only from a single vineyard in Tre Stelle, and spends a bit longer in wood, 18-20 months. Both show purity of brambly black fruits, with greater intensity for the Superiore.

The Langhe Nebbiolo comes from young vines in Tre Stelle. "From 2004 we have used only stainless steel and concrete, so you are getting the pure taste of what Nebbiolo tastes like on our soils." There is no general blend of Barbaresco: there are cuvées from Tre Stelle, Marcarini, and Rio Sordo (the plot right around the cellars). "We make them every year, we like the idea you can taste the vintage in each Cru. We do not produce Riserva—it's just a marketing tool. Sometimes we do a late release. Alcohol is moderate—we've never had more than 14%."

The mark of the house style is purity of fruits, shining through the Barbera as well as the Barbaresco. Maceration uses pump-over, except for Tre Stelle and Rio Sordo, which use the traditional submerged cap. Tre Stelle is bright and approachable, with such fine texture and such clear fruits, it can be enjoyed soon after release. Rio Sordo is deeper and more structured, and benefits from a little time. You might say that Tre Stelle is more feminine and Rio Sordo is more muscular.

Cavallotto   *

Via Alba Monforte Bricco Boschis, 12060 Castiglione Falletto (CN)   📞 +39 0173 62814

@ info@cavallotto.com   👤 Alfio Cavallotto

🌐 www.cavallotto.com   Barolo [map p. 37]

📋 🏭 🍇 🍂 25 ha; 110,000 btl   🍾 Barolo, Bricco Boschis

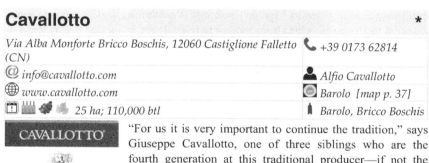

"For us it is very important to continue the tradition," says Giuseppe Cavallotto, one of three siblings who are the fourth generation at this traditional producer—if not the most traditional, certainly one of the most traditional in Barolo. The domain has been bottling all its production since 1944. Just off the road through Castiglione Falletto, the winery is a series of buildings around a courtyard. The old cellars were extended into new cellars in 2002, using red brick construction to control the humidity naturally. The first impression is that production must be on a large scale because there are such large casks, with botti from 20 hl to 100 hl, mostly 50-60 years old. But because of long aging, there are usually 5-6 vintages in the cellar at any time.

Located on the slopes of the Bricco Boschis cru, the vineyards are unusually in a single plot, the major part around the winery planted with Nebbiolo, and other parts planted with Barbera, Dolcetto, and some other varieties. The range goes straight from Langhe Nebbiolo to Bricco Boschis and Vignolo Crus. "Our philosophy is different, it is important for us to maintain the same quality in Nebbiolo and Barolo.

The quality selection is the same. We change the maturation, but the decision is made only at a later stage," Giuseppe says. "We always put the Cru on the label. It's been allowed for the past few years to put the village on the label, but we have the two crus. If you blend the areas it's impossible to recognize; it's important for us to recognize the terroir. Bricco Boschis is completely different from Vignolo, it's important for us to maintain the difference." Langhe Nebbiolo spends two years in botti, the Crus spend 3 years, and Riserva spends 5 years. (Everything ages in botti: Dolcetto for 6-7 month, Barbera for two years.)

For a traditional producer, Cavallotti is highly cognizant of technology. This extends to using rotofermenters. "People say, you are a traditional producer, why are you using rotary fermenters which are technological, but for us this has been completely different, it does not crush the seeds, so we don't get green tannins, and we get more color. Unlike using pump-over we don't get a big sediment, the wine is clear. This machine has completely changed our wine, it's removed the risk of green tannins," Giuseppe explains.

The style is consistent across the range, giving impressions of fruit purity supported by fresh acidity. Traditional vinification gives the impression here of really bringing out the fruit, the whole fruit, and nothing but the fruit. Unlike some producers, the Langhe Nebbiolo is not in a different style, but is in a continuum with the Barolos. just less intense, less tannic, and more approachable. Certainly there is jump in intensity and firmness to Vignolo (from limestone terroir), and an increase in refinement to Bricco Boschis (from sandier terroir). There is another big increase in refinement going to the Giuseppe Riserva, which comes from the central part of Bricco Boschis, and has been a separate cuvée since 1970. The Langhe Nebbiolo is immediately approachable on release, but the others need time, a couple of years for the Crus, perhaps four or five for the Riservas. Barbera similarly reflects a traditional style, with briary fruits supported by good acidity.

Ceretto   *

Loc. San Cassiano 34, 12051 Alba (CN)	☎ *+39 0173 282582*
@ *ceretto@ceretto.com*	👤 *Roberta Ceretto*
⊕ *www.ceretto.com*	🍷 *Barolo [map p. 34]*
📅 🏭 🍇 🍷 *170 ha; 900,000 btl*	🍾 *Barolo, Brunate*

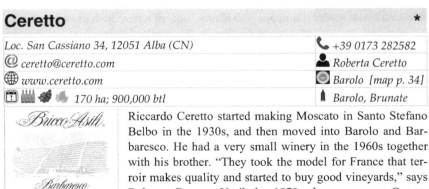

Riccardo Ceretto started making Moscato in Santo Stefano Belbo in the 1930s, and then moved into Barolo and Barbaresco. He had a very small winery in the 1960s together with his brother. "They took the model for France that terroir makes quality and started to buy good vineyards," says Roberta Ceretto. Until the 1970s there was one Ceretto winery in Alba; this became the vast emporium of today, which contains a major production facility and rather splendid tasting room, with a space bubble poised over the vineyards. It's a test for visitors to find the tasting room, as you have to follow a route through the winery that is a bit obscure. The Arneis from Roero is made here; representing a significant proportion of the appellation, it is claimed to be the largest selling white wine in Italy.

Only the classic Barbaresco and Barolo blends are produced at the winery, as they preceded the establishment of the DOC and the rule that wine must be produced in the DOC. The blends were originally called Zonchera for Barolo, and Asij for Barbaresco, but lost their names from 2011, and are just labeled as Barolo and Barbaresco today. Separate wineries were built in 1971 and 1973 at Bricco Roche in Barolo and Asili in Barbaresco. "We are going more deeply into the single vineyards. This is something we learned from Burgundy," Roberta says.

Through the nineties, the wines aged in barriques, with half new oak. "Slavonian oak has somewhat lost its quality since the 1980s," Roberta says, explaining the move to French oak in the nineties. The philosophy changed again after 2000. "We want to show the terroir, we don't want the oak to add flavors, so use of new oak is very small. Barriques are still used but for a shorter period, just six months to smooth things out." Then the wine ages for another 12 months in botti of Austrian oak, and is kept in bottle for a year before release. (The barriques you see in the cellar are mostly for Monsordo, a wine in international style, originally made from an equal blend of Cabernet Sauvignon and Merlot, today half Cabernet and a quarter each of Merlot and Syrah.)

The style is lighter than it used to be, but since this is Barolo, of course there is always tannic structure. It's more finely textured than before, but most of the wines still need time. Roberta describes the range in Barbaresco and Barolo as a crescendo building from the finest to the most powerful. "It is really shocking to have Brunate and Prapò one after the other because they are so different. Brunate is so elegant and Prapò is so rich and smooth," she says. These are the two extremes of the range in Barolo, which now includes three single-vineyard cuvées from Barbaresco and six from Barolo.

There's a classic view of lightness in Barbaresco compared to more weight in Barolo. "The Barbaresco has beautiful smells of berries, compared to Barolo where they disappear," Roberta says. "It's already ready. For a blend it's easier to find a compromise with the tannins." The Barbaresco blend is elegant rather than powerful, fragrant rather than pungent, and can be ready to enjoy on release. In the single vineyards, Gallina is soft and elegant with stronger impressions of red berries; Bernadot is fuller with more obvious fruits and a glycerinic sheen; Asili is the most forceful cuvée from Barbaresco, holding back when it's young.

The Barolo blend is more muscular than the Barbaresco, moving towards a chocolate coating. Brunate is supremely fine and elegant, and can even be more approachable than the Barolo at first. From a small plot in the heart of the large MGA, Bussia has more overt fruit sensations, backed by a firmer tannic structure. Rocche di Castiglione is firmer with a more obvious sense of structure. Bricco Rocche is back to elegance, although more forceful on the palate than Brunate, with something of the sheen of Bussia. Prapò (from Serralunga) is the most muscular of

52

the cuvées, chocolaty and potentially full-flavored. Cannubi is a bit different from all the others, because it ages longer and is released only after 10 years.

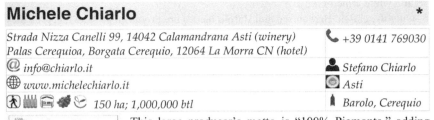

Michele Chiarlo   *

Strada Nizza Canelli 99, 14042 Calamandrana Asti (winery)   📞 +39 0141 769030
Palas Cerequioa, Borgata Cerequio, 12064 La Morra CN (hotel)
@ *info@chiarlo.it*   👤 *Stefano Chiarlo*
🌐 *www.michelechiarlo.it*   📧 *Asti*
🧍 🏭 🏠 🍴 🍷 *150 ha; 1,000,000 btl*   🍷 *Barolo, Cerequio*

This large producer's motto is "100% Piemonte," adding "no international varieties, no blends." There are seven estates all over Piedmont, with wineries in Monferrato, Gavi, and Langhe. The range includes Gavi, Moscato d'Asti, Barbera, and Nebbiolos, which consist of Langhe Nebbiolo, two Barbarescos, and five Barolos. The estate is considered to be a benchmark in Asti. It owns 10 ha in the Barolo appellation (more than half at Cerequio), and produces 100,000 bottles in Barolo and Barbaresco.

The estate was founded in 1956 by Michele and Giuseppina Chiarlo. Their son Stefano is now the winemaker. "For four generations we have owned a vineyard in Monferrato," he says, "but my father's idea was to make quality wine and try to export. It was a crazy idea at the time." Its most important vineyards in Barolo are Cerequio (planted in 1972) and Cannubi, where Michele purchased land in 1988 that had been considered too steep to cultivate, but he terraced the land and planted a vineyard. Other important holdings are the La Court vineyard in the old Aluffi estate in Castelnuovo Calcea, in the heart of the Barbera d'Asti zone, and the Fornace di Tassarolo vineyard in Gavi. The estate owns just under half of its vineyards; the rest are rented. The principal winery is located in Monferrato, but Chiarlo has also opened a boutique hotel in the heart of the vineyards in La Morra, where the wines can be tasted.

The supple house style favors a silky sheen to the palate. The Langhe Nebbiolo comes from hills in the Langhe. Barbaresco Reyna is a blend from several vineyards, and the single vineyard wine is Asili; it makes a very fine perfumed impression, which Stefano describes as feminine. Tortoniano is a classic Barolo (named for the Tortonian geology in the west part of Barolo). It includes grapes from all the vineyards in Barolo, but more than half come from Cerequio, as not all are used for the Cru. It makes a firmer impression with a more obvious sense of structure. Cerequio has the refinement of Asili, but with the firmer character of Barolo. There are also Riservas from the single vineyards. All the wines are matured in large (55 hl) casks. The Crus take about a decade to begin to develop.

Aside from Nebbiolo, Chiarlo is proud of the single vineyard Barbera, La Court, now labeled with the new Nizza DOC. It ages half in new barriques and half in large vats, and showcases smooth, silky, black fruits. The top white is a Gavi di Gavi from the Rovereto vineyard.

Domenico Clerico ★★

Località Manzoni 22a, 12065 Monforte d'Alba (CN) 📞 *+39 0173 78171*
@ *info@domenicoclerico.com* 👤 *Giorgia Zucco*
🌐 *www.domenicoclerico.com* 🖼 *Barolo [map p. 38]*
📅 ⚜ 🍇 🕰 *21 ha; 120,000 btl* 🍷 *Barolo, Ciabot Mentin*

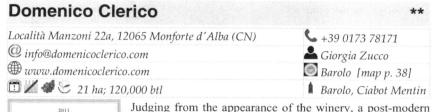

Judging from the appearance of the winery, a post-modern building with something of the appearance of a flying saucer, dominating the intersection of roads leading to Monforte, Domenico Clerico should be an arch modernist. The wine has been made here since 2011. There's a spacious tasting room, and the cellar extends three storeys underground.

One of the Barolo Boys, Domenico had various work experiences, including a period with olive oil, before he decided to join his father, who was a grower selling grapes to the coop. "The first revolution was in the vineyard when he introduced green harvest, while his father was away on holiday, and his father was not so happy when he counted his grapes. The second revolution was introducing new barriques in the cellar. After a few vintages, his father felt the wines were better and handed over the operation," is how they now tell the story at the winery. Domenico extended the domain by buying and renting more vineyards. He died in 2017.

Today there are ten wines: Dolcetto, Barbera, Langhe Nebbiolo (from a single vineyard), a Nebbiolo-Barbera blend, and six Barolos, which include one blend and five single vineyard wines. The Barolo *tout court* is a blend, and is aged in a mixture of French barriques and Slavonian botti. It is based on selection. "We taste from barrel. Everything that is ready to drink goes into the blended Barolo. Anything that is too oaky is discarded. The rest go into the single vineyard wines," says winemaker Oscar Arrivabene.

From different parts of Monforte, Ciabot Mentin and Pajana come from Ginestra, Bricotto comes from Bussia, and Percristina comes from Mosconi. Aeroplanservaj comes from a rented vineyard in Serralunga. The single vineyard wines are aged for 24-30 months in barriques, with around 80% new, except for Percristina which then has an extra 24 months in Slavonian botti. Two Langhe wines, Capsime-e and Arte are effectively declassified from Barolo, although Arte also includes a small proportion of Barbera.

The style here is strong (you would expect no less from Monforte). This is most evident with the Ciabot Mentin, then the Aeroplanservaj. There's a definite masculine impression reflecting the area. The wines are a very fine example of a modernist who has stayed true to modernism.

Elvio Cogno   *

Via Ravera 2, 12060 Novello (CN)	📞 *+39 0173 744006*
@ *elviocogno@elviocogno.com*	👤 *Valter Fissore*
🌐 *www.elviocogno.com*	🔵 *Barolo [map p. 34]*
🗓️ 🏭 🍇 ☙	🍶 *Barolo, Cascina Nuova*
15 ha; 100,000 btl	*Langhe Nascetta*

Elvio Cogno started as a restaurateur in La Morra, made wine with Marcarini starting in 1961, and then founded his own winery in 1990, buying an old farmstead in Ravera (he was 60). He renovated the farmhouse, converted from polyculture to viticulture, extended the winery, and expanded the vineyards. The family lives in the house over the winery. A new tasting room was added in 2021. In 1996 his daughter Nadia and son-in-law Valter Fissore (now the winemaker) took over.

Most of the vineyards (11 ha) are in the Ravera cru, which was unknown when Elvio started. (Elvio Cogno is now the largest holder of the cru). Originally there was only one label of Barolo. Then they decided that even though it is a single Cru, there are plots with different properties. Plantings are mostly Nebbiolo with a little Barbera and Dolcetto. The other 5 ha are in Novello, some in the Barolo DOCG, some out of the DOCG.

The range of Nebbiolo started with the Langhe. "When we started to produce the Langhe Nebbiolo we wanted to show a different expression of Nebbiolo, not a baby Barolo. First we use grapes that come from a hill on the other side of the Novello hill, outside the DOCG. It would not be possible to produce a wine like this with grapes from Barolo. Maceration is only 5 days and there is 25% carbonic maceration to preserve super-fresh character. It ages only in stainless steel for 6 months. For sure you see that the strength of this wine is not the complexity but the drinkability," says marketing manager Sara Bertola.

The soil in Ravera is basically compact clay and limestone, and the differences between plots are due to variations in the microclimate. There are now cuvées from 4 separate plots. Cascina Nuova comes from the youngest vineyards, a plot immediately below the winery planted 20 years ago. It does not carry the name of the cru although it is in Ravera. This is the basic Barolo. It is quite approachable for Ravera, quite fragrant and elegant. "When the vines get older we will have to do something different to make this style of wine," Sara says.

The only difference between Cascina Nuova and Ravera is that Ravera comes from two plots of the oldest vines, 80 year old. The exposition is the same. "This is our flagship because of our history and because it is representative of Ravera." Vinification is identical, except that Valter started to use some whole bunches in 2017, 15% for Cascina Nuova and 50% for Ravera. Ravera is deeper, richer, and rounder, almost to the point of better hiding the structure, but it does need more time.

There are two cuvées labeled for single vineyards. Bricco Pernice (the hill of the partridge) comes from the south-southwest-facing hill opposite the winery. Protected as it is less exposed to wind, it is a warmer spot, and the first to harvest. Usually it has more tannins and is more classic. Vigna Elena is a 2 ha plot planted with the rosé subcultivar of Nebbiolo in 1991 a cooler microclimate. The original intention was to blend with the other plots, but Elvio liked it so much that he decided to make it separately. It is produced as a Riserva and shows a classic character, firm and reserved, and needing time. All the Barolos age in 23-30 hl botti. There has been a cuvée from the Bordini cru of Barbaresco since 2006. It is planted with 30 year old vines of the Lampia cultivar at an altitude of 250m.

In terms of overall style, I would go from Cascina Nuova (relatively approachable) to Bricco Pernice (more structured), as both will become silky: and from Ravera (deeper and richer) to Vigna Elena (the most powerful), as both will become velvety. The style across the range is quite tight and reserved; you can see the tradition of Barolo with all the cuvées needing time to develop.

"We intend to produce traditional Barbera in a fresh style," Sara says, "but this is not so easy with climate change because Barbera is very susceptible to the heat." It's actually quite full and fruity. A second Barbera comes from an 0.25 plot of pre-phylloxera vines in the Berri cru of La Morra. Elvio had made Barbera from pre-phylloxera vines at Marcarini, and searched for a plot for his estate. The Pre-Phylloxera cuvee is smoother and more refined, with an extra layer of aromatic complexity, quite velvety at the end.

The least traditional cuvée (or possibly the most, depending on your view) is the white Nascetta, which Elvio resurrected from an almost extinct condition in 1994. The style is quite fresh when young, and a little nutty; it becomes flinty with time.

Aldo Conterno ★★

Loc. Bussia 48, 12065 Monforte d'Alba (CN)	📞 *+39 0173 78150*
@ *info@poderialdoconterno.it*	👤 *Giacomo Conterno*
⊕ *www.poderialdoconterno.com*	🔲 *Barolo [map p. 38]*
📅 🏭 🌿 🍇 *25 ha; 80,000 btl*	🍷 *Barolo, Cicala*

Conterno is an emblematic name in Barolo. The Conterno family started making wine in 1770, continuing as one family until 1961, when Giacoma Conterno retired. His sons Giovanni and Aldo had a difference of philosophy, which has been simplified as traditionalist versus modernist. The family had interests in Serralunga and Bussia, so the brothers divided the territories. Vineyards were mostly rented at the time, but Aldo purchased the estate in Bussia, which has remained the sole source of grapes. It consists of a rather splendid complex of buildings on a commanding height as you drive from Monforte to Castiglione Falletto. Today, Aldo's three sons, Franco, Stefano, and Giacomo, run the estate.

In addition to Nebbiolos, there's a Barbera d'Alba, and two wines under the Langhe DOC, a red blend based on international varieties, and a Chardonnay. The Langhe Nebbiolo is declassified from Barolo: "Vines older than 3 years can be used to make Barolo but we believe they should be 15 years. So the Langhe Nebbiolo here is from young vines, all in the Barolo DOC. It's a classic second wine, with the same vineyards but younger wines," says Giacomo.

The estate is within the very large and varied Bussia cru, so the various hills of the estate represent a microcosm of the terroirs in Barolo DOC. The three single vineyard Barolos represent three different hills, historically recognized as different vineyards. Colonnello's sandy soils give a feminine wine along the lines of La Morra. Only 50m away, Cicala has very poor soil with more clay and lots of fossils. It's a bit warmer, and the smooth coating gives an elegant sheen. Romirasco is full force grand cru, much in the style of Serralunga. The wines have the same vinification, with 30 days skin contact, and 28-30 months in botti of Slavonian oak.

The Gran Bussia Riserva is a blend made by selecting lots from all three areas, 70% from Romirasco and 15% from each of the other two. It's made only in top vintages, and the decision on whether to make it is made at time of harvest. Plots on all three hills are harvested on the same day, the grapes are cofermented in wood, and there is two months skin contact, "so it's a very old fashioned approach," says Giacomo. The 3,300 bottles all come from one (large) barrel.

So is Aldo Conterno modern or traditional? Although the details of vinification might lead you to expect traditional wine, for me the style is more towards modern, as I often see oak influence on young vintages. The Barbera is relatively well structured, the Langhe resembles a Barolo, and the single vineyards are quite expressive of their terroirs, but will be more so as the wine ages. However, the more savage impression of the Gran Bussia Riserva is definitely traditional. Giacomo doesn't care how he is described: "The discussion between Taliban and modernists is just a rhetoric for journalists, it has no real meaning today. To me it's more important whether the owner is the winemaker."

Giacomo Conterno   ***

Loc. Ornati 2, 12065 Monforte d'Alba (CN)	☎ *+39 0173 78221*
@ *conterno@conterno.it*	👤 *Roberto Conterno*
⊕ *www.conterno.it*	◉ *Barolo [map p. 38]*
📅 🖊 🍇 ☕ *23 ha; 80,000 btl*	🍶 *Barolo, Cascina Francia*

This is one of the most famous (and traditional) estates in Barolo. Conterno was founded in 1908 when Giacomo Conterno started a wine bar. There was a single Conterno estate until 1961, when it was split between two brothers: Giovanno was a traditionalist and retained the name Giacoma

Conterno and continued production from Serralunga, while Aldo established a new estate with modernist principles in the Bussia locale of Monforte.

The cellars are in Monforte, at the southern tip of the appellation. For one of the most traditional producers, the winery looks surprisingly modern, although in fact it was built in 1985. All the vineyards are in Serralunga. Conterno had started conventionally by purchasing grapes from growers, but Giovanno bought the Cascina Francia vineyard in 1974; a 14 ha monopole, with 9 ha Nebbiolo and 5 ha of Barbera, it's now the heart of the estate. Another vineyard, farther north in Cerretta, was added in 2008. The Arione vineyard, adjacent to Cascina Francia, was purchased in 2015. It has 3.6 ha in Barolo and another 2.4 ha outside the DOCG, used to produce Nebbiolo d'Alba. "The big difference between Arione and Francia is the exposure," Roberto says. Cascina Francia faces southwest but Arione faces full south. "Arione harvests 7-10 days earlier."

Third generation Roberto Conterno has been running the estate since 2003, and is not particularly concerned how he is described. "The distinction between modernists and traditionalists is a different vision, I've never considered that so important, every winemaker has his own beliefs, we have our opinions and ways, but others can be different." Roberto says there has been virtually no change in winemaking from the methods of his father and grandfather.

The two historic Barolos from the estate are Cascina Francia and Monfortino. One of the most famous, perhaps the most famous, Barolos, from 1978-2014, Monfortino was a selection of the best parcels in Cascina Francia, "but it is not the same parcels every year," says Roberto. Since the acquisition of Arione, some lots from there have been included in Monfortino. Monfortino (a Riserva) is made only in top years. (Indeed, in much older vintages it may not even have come from Cascina Francia; when it was first produced, in 1920, it was made from grapes purchased from different parcels in Serralunga.) The Cascina Francia bottling represents the rest of the vineyard. Winemaking is traditional, maceration lasts for 25-35 days, and Cascina Francia sees 4 years in botti before bottling, while Monfortino sees 7 years. Since 2010, Cerretta has been the third Barolo, and since 2015 there has also been Arione. The Barberas are aged for two years in botti. There are old botti, some up to fifty years, but many were bought in the past decade. Just before 2000, the source switched from Slavonian to Austrian oak, "but there was no change in the wine, because the oak is neutral," Roberto says.

The house style is dense but elegant. The Francia Barbera d'Alba is considered to be one of the top Barberas of the region; indeed, its intensity and depth would give you a completely different view of the variety. Cerretta is the lightest, and perhaps the most elegant, of the Barolos, with a surprising sense of delicacy for Serralunga. "We always get more red fruit expression at Cerretta," Roberto says. Arione shows its southern exposure with a firmer palate, and a more chocolaty impression on the finish.

The new cuvées certainly broaden the range, but neither has the sheer presence of Cascina Francia, which shows as a mid weight Barolo, traditional in style with a tendency towards the herbal and savory. It's more aromatic than Arione and gives a

58

more structured impression. Monfortino is darker in every sense than Cascina Francia; restrained when young, it shows the classic character of tar and roses as it matures, with well defined tension between smoky notes of gunflint and perfume of roses. It is simply classic.

In 2018, Roberto was offered the opportunity to buy Nervi, the oldest producer in Gattinara, and now also makes wine there under the name of Nervi-Conterno. The range includes a blend and two single-vineyard cuvées from Nebbiolo, and a rosé from 90% Nebbiolo plus 10% Uva Rara.

Corino Giovanni

Fraz. Annunziata 25/b, 12064 La Morra (CN)	📞 *+39 0173 509452+393347803895*
@ *info@corino.it*	👤 *Giuliano Corino*
🌐 *www.corino.it*	📷 *Barolo [map p. 35]*
🔲 🏭 🍇 🍷	*10 ha; 52,000 btl*

"The family arrived in La Morra starting at Santa Maria in the 19th century and were sharecroppers. They moved to Annunziata in 1952. When the price of fruit fell and the price of grapes increased, they moved to viticulture," says Stefania Corino. "My husband (Giuliano) and his brother (Renato) started to produce wine in 1985. They worked together until 2005 when they divided the estate as each of them wanted to work with his children." Renato founded a new domain (see profile), and Giuliano kept the name of Corino Giovanni. The original winery now seems small and cramped, and a striking new winery, constructed next door in 2023 with cellars underground and a residence above, now dominates the road through Annunziata.

All the vineyards are in La Morra. Winemaking was modernist with short maceration using rotary fermenters, and aging in barriques, and that remains the style. "The Dolcetto and Barbera d'Alba are both simple wines for drinking soon," Stefania says. They have a similar style showing clean, pure lines. The Barbera Ciabot Dù Re comes from a single vineyard in La Morra facing west-southwest, with very poor soil, which reduces the productivity of Barbera. It spends 18 months in barriques with 50% new oak. It is smoother and finer, altogether more serious. The Langhe Rosso, L'Insieme, was a blend of 40% Nebbiolo, 30% Barbera, and 15% each of Cabernet and Merlot, which were originally planted as an experiment. The blend changed to equal Barbera and Nebbiolo in 2019 when they were taken out and replaced with Barbera.

The Langhe Nebbiolo comes from younger vines "We wait at least 10 years to produce Barolo. It's not a baby Barolo, it ages only in stainless steel. We would like to produce something totally different from Barolo and we want to show the freshness and red fruits of Barolo." It has a clean, pure impression of red fruits with just some bare hints of structure.

The Commune di La Morra cuvée is a blend from two vineyards, one in Ciabot dù Re (next to the Barbera), the other in Giachini. In fact, there are two plots in Giachini, one facing west, used for the blend, the other facing south, which is used for the Cru. Both plots are rented from the Church. Maceration is relatively brief, then the wine ages for 24 months in used barriques followed by 6 months in stainless steel. It is quite fragrant, but the sense of oak and accompanying spiciness is prominent enough to require a year after release to subside.

Coming from white calcareous soil, just down the hill from the winery, the Giachini cru is weightier than the communal La Morra, with a finer texture, also quite approachable, but oak is more noticeable, requiring longer to integrate. Arborina comes from sandy soil facing southeast and has a fresher style than Giachini, showing more forward fruits, but also more structure. With Giachini you see the fruits and tannins together, with Arborina, the fruits come first and then the tannins kick in later. Bricco Manescoto is at the border with Serralunga, and the wine has a bigger structure, weightier and sterner, with more grip on the palate. The Riserva usually comes from a plot of 70-year-old vines in Giachini. It is dense, deep, and rich, very much a modern take, although greater intensity of fruits pushes the oak more into the background. Overall the style is decidedly modern, from the light oak on the Commune di Morra Barolo to the increasing sense of oak as you go up the hierarchy of Crus.

Podere Luigi Einaudi   *

Borg. Gombe 31/32, 12063 Dogliani (CN)	📞 +39 0173 70191
@ einaudi@poderieinaudi.com	👤 Matteo Sardagna
🌐 www.poderieinaudi.com	💿 Dogliani
🗓 🏭 🍇 🚜 60 ha; 350,000 btl	🍾 Barolo, Terlo

The winery was founded in 1897 by Luigi Einaudi, who went on to become President of Italy in 1948. It's a leading estate in Dogliano, where Dolcetto is the most important grape. The estate is famous for its Dolcetto, in particular Dogliani Superiore Vigna Tecc, which is regarded as a benchmark, but also has holdings in Barolo. Current production of Barolo is just over ten per cent of total, coming from two vineyards, Cannubi and Terlo (both in the commune of Barolo). However, this will be doubled by the purchase in summer 2016 of 9 ha in the Dardi subzone of Bussia in Monforte, which contains 4 ha of Nebbiolo and 1 ha of Barbera, as well as a truffle forest and other unplanted land.

The estate is managed by Giorgio Ruffo, who is married to Luigi's granddaughter, Paola, together with their son Matteo Sardagna. In addition to three Dolcettos from Dogliani, there are Barbera and Nebbiolo Langhe, red and white Langhe, and the international cuvée Luigi Einaudi (a red Langhe) which is a blend of Cabernet Sauvignon, Nebbiolo, Merlot, and Barbera.

There are presently four wines from Barolo. The Barolo *tout court* is a blend from vineyards in the commune of Barolo, Terlo comes from the named Cru while Costa Grimaldi comes from a specific vineyard within it, and Cannubi of course comes from the famous Cru. The wines are fermented in stainless steel and matured for one year in a mixture of half large casks and half barriques, with a third new; then the wine is moved into large casks for a second year.

I have always found the Einaudi Barolos to be on the lighter side, but the investments of recent years have led to improvements, and the purchase of land in Monforte should certainly extend the range and broaden the style.

Fontanafredda   *

Via Alba 15, 12050 Serralunga d'Alba (CN)	📞 *+39 0173 626117*
@ *info@fontanafredda.it*	👤 *Alice*
🌐 *www.fontanafredda.it*	📷 *Barolo [map p. 37]*
🗓 ⚒ ✕ 🏠 🍇 🛢 🍶 ● *122 ha; 7,000,000 btl*	🍴 *Barolo, Serralunga*

Fontanafredda has unusual origins. It was created when Vittorio Emmanuele II, the first King of Italy, became infatuated with Rosa Vercellana, and gave the land to her, making her Countess of Mirafiore and Fontanafredda. (Mirafiore and Fontanafredda are effectively two adjacent estates.) Twenty years later in 1878, their son began to run the estates as a commercial business. Subsequently the family lost interest, and in 1932 the estate became the property of the Monte dei Paschi di Siena bank, which sold it in 2008 to local entrepreneur Oscar Farinetti (founder of the supermarket chain Eataly and also owner of producer Borgogno). Reflecting its origins, the estate has a Royal Villa, gardens, and woods, as well as vineyards. It is well into oenotourism, with a hotel and multiple restaurants.

The largest single contiguous estate in Barolo, the 100 ha in Serralunga are the heart of the holdings, but Fontanafredda also owns vineyards in Barolo commune and Diano d'Alba. Single vineyard wines come from La Rosa (Serralunga), Lazzarito (Serralunga), and Paiagallo, formerly called La Villa (Barolo). In traditional blends from various areas, there are Barolo, Barbaresco, and Barolo Riserva (produced only in top vintages from the vineyards in Serralunga). The domain also buys grapes from around 400 growers. It's the largest single producer of Barolo, which amounts to more than 400,00 bottles annually. The adjacent estate of Casa E. di Mirafiore (see profile) is smaller. The boutique has wines from all the estates, including Fontanafredda, Casa Mirafiore Brandini (based in La Morra), and Borgogno.

The local varieties from Langhe and Alba are divided into regular and prestige ranges. Due Vini is a traditional Langhe blend of Nebbiolo and Barbera. There are also Gavi, Moscato d'Asti, are sparkling wines from Alta Langhe, and some grappas.

In short, this is a very large winery operation in which Barolo is only a part. When you ask how many cuvées there are altogether, the answer is a shrug.

The approach to winemaking is traditional, with the old cellars (dating from the late nineteenth century) stuffed with botti, mostly of Slavonian oak, but some with French oak, and only a small number of barriques. Danilo Drocco was the winemaker from 1999 until 2018, when Giorgio Lavagna took over, and his mandate is to introduce more precision into the wines. The Barolo is a blend from all 11 villages in the appellation; at communal level there is also a Barbaresco (from purchased grapes). The domain considers the Serralunga cuvée to be its most traditional wine—"this is our iconic cuvée"—and it's quite light and elegant: it is traditional, but without the rustic tannins of tradition. The wine from the vineyards surrounding the winery is called the Proprietà in Fontanafredda (the entire MGA is a monopole), and this is denser, moving from elegance towards the usual power of Serralunga. The top Barolo is the La Rosa single vineyard wine, which shows the most concentration. The wines are good, but I can't help feeling that with all Fontanafredda's resources, they could be finer. The attitude towards tastings for visitors is a little commercial.

Gaja   ****

Via Torini 5, 12050 Barbaresco (CN)	📞 +39 0173 635158
@ info@gaja.com	👤 Gaia Gaja
🌐 www.gaja.com	🔘 Barbaresco [map p. 39]
🚫 🔲 🚜 🚛	🍷 Barbaresco
100 ha; 350,000 btl	Langhe, Gaja & Rey, Chardonnay

Gaja is sui generis, not to be pigeonholed as modernist or traditionalist or any sort of -ist, but simply standing alone. Angelo Gaja is a force of nature—and not one to do things by halves. Famous for his Barbaresco (and Barolo), where his single vineyard wines are at the top of the hierarchy, he expanded into Montalcino by acquiring the Pieve Santa Restituta vineyards in 1994. Having decided he wanted also to make wine in Bolgheri, he conducted a long and patient search until he was able to purchase an estate in 1996. The scale of production is limited: each winery should stay at a size appropriate to remain an artisan winemaker, Angelo says. This is not the end of the process: the latest projects are wineries at high altitudes, in Sicily and Alta Langhe, where the focus will be on white wines.

Gaja's original premises are discretely located in the main street in Barbaresco. Inside is a large courtyard, with the cellars around and underneath. Angelo bought the castle across the street in 1994. It took ten years to restore, and it now provides an elegant venue for tastings and visits. The winery has been extended into Wines are now effective made in a modern winery built into the hillside, operating by gravity feed. All the Piedmont wines are made here. Angelo says proudly that Gaja's history is different from other producers, in starting as an estate from the beginning, rather than as a negociant.

Gaja started in 1859 with a restaurant that later expanded into selling wine. The market for the wines expanded so much that in 1904 they closed the restaurant to concentrate on wines. The direction to quality came from Clothilde Rey (Angelo's grandmother).

The more recent expansion came under Angelo who bought the Sorì San Lorenzo estate from the Church in Alba in 1964, and in 1967 bought Costi Russi and Sorì Tildin from local nobility; neither estate was making wine commercially at the time. Sperss in Barolo was bought in 1996, also Conteisa (which comes from La Morra).

It's no exaggeration to say that Gaja's innovations reshaped Barolo and Barbaresco. He led the drive to single vineyard bottlings from Barbaresco, with Sorì San Lorenzo in 1967, followed by Sorì Tildin (1970) and Costa Russi (1978). Sperss is a single vineyard bottling from Serralunga in Barolo. Not only are these now some of the most famous wines of the region, but when Gaja created the wines, he did not do so by buying existing vineyards of any reputation; he planted vineyards on land that had been used for sharecropping. His eye for land that can be converted to vineyards has not deserted him; the Ca'Marcanda property in Bolgheri was a farm until Gaja decided it was perfect for vineyards.

The blend for Barbaresco, has come from the same 14 vineyards (in the commune of Barbaresco) for many years. "It's important to maintain the history by continuing to produce a single blended Barbaresco," Angelo says. However, there was a famous disagreement about the single vineyard wines. When the Consorzio defined the rules, they decided that Barbaresco should be 100% Nebbiolo, but the three single vineyard wines had always contained a small proportion of Barbera. (And who can argue with the results?) So the three single vineyards were labeled as Langhe; the Barbaresco blend remained the only wine under the DOC. "This is paying our debt to the community of Barbaresco producers." The single-vineyard wines use names reflecting the history of the plots. "Angelo started to vinify each plot separately before the MGA existed. So we decided to continue with our existing single vineyard names," Gaia says.

The big news of 2016 was that the single vineyard wines would return to the Barbaresco DOC with effect from the 2013 vintage. "The news about our return to the Barbaresco DOC was read as a sign of generational change," says Angelo's daughter, Gaia Gaja, who has been taking over from her father, together with brother Giovanni and sister Rossana. "When the Consorzio defined the regulations, Angelo wanted them to allow 5% of another indigenous variety; this was based on the history. But the Nebbiolo is different today; it's more juicy, it has sweeter and softer tannins; Barbera used to cut the tannins. So the wines will taste a little different. The wine can be good with a little Barbera but it doesn't express the site so clearly."

Gaja is constantly renewing itself. "We are changing everything in order to make the same wines," says Gaia. Changes in the vineyards are focused to managing in hotter, drier conditions; changes in the cellar reflect the increased ripeness of the tannins. "Our objective is to make long lived wines. We work to ensure the wines will age as long as they used to. That's been with Nebbiolo, but we can also express the personality of the Langhe in whites. No one knows, it is a pity, but there is an opportunity here for making very long aging white wine." This is a reference to the two Chardonnays, Rossj Bass (from vineyards in Barbaresco and Serralunga) and Gaia & Rey (from vineyards in Treiso and Serralunga), named for Angelo's daughters and grandmother, initiated in 1981 (the first Chardonnay planted in Piedmont). Another revolutionary act was to replant a Nebbiolo vineyard with Cabernet Sauvignon for the varietal wine subsequently named Darmagi—meaning "what a pity" in reference to Angelo's father's reaction.

The elegance and purity of the single vineyard wines is the mark of Gaja's style. The wines are never overbearing, even when young, and for my palate they reach a peak at around fifteen years after the vintage (but will go longer). All reds age for 12 months in barriques or tonneaux of French oak, followed 12 months for Barbaresco or 18 months for Barolo in large casks of Austrian or Slavonian oak. (I find oak more noticeable in the Chardonnays). The style is not as savage as a traditionalist, but nor does it have the full-force overt character of a modernist. It is simply its own.

Bruno Giacosa   ★★★★

Via Xx Settembre 52, 12052 Neive (CN)

@ brunogiacosa@brunogiacosa.it

🌐 www.brunogiacosa.it

20 ha; 300,000 btl

📞 +39 0173 67027

👤 Bruna Giacosa

Barbaresco [map p. 39]

🍷 Barbaresco, Asili

🍷 Barolo, Falletto

A splendid new winery just across the street from the old winery makes a striking contrast with Bruno Giacosa's reputation as the arch-traditionalist of Barbaresco. Built in 2016, it has the lines of a post-modern building. But the wines will stay the same. "We have never changed our philosophy. We prefer elegance to power, we want pure Nebbiolo, we have only big casks, 110 hl and 55 hl. You really smell the terroir in our wines," says Bruna Giacosa, who managed the domain with her father for several years, and then took over after he died in 2018. He was famously shy, but made wonderful wine.

Bruno started to work in the vineyards when he was only thirteen. Before 1961, Giacosa made wine but sold it off in bulk in large containers. When Bruno started estate bottling, all the wines came from purchased grapes. Bruno was legendary for his ability to assess a vineyard by tasting the grapes—"Bruno was a great buyer, he was famous for finding the best grapes of the area," said Francesco Vierzo, winemaker until 2018, when Giuseppe Tartaglino took over. Bruno produced the first single vineyard wine in 1967 from Falletto in Serralunga (Gaja also produced one in

Barbaresco). Slowly he was able to purchase vineyards from which he had previously purchased grapes, starting with Falletto in 1982, followed by Asili and Rabajá in Barbaresco in 1996. In 2006, the subzone of the plot in Rabajà was changed to Asili, but Bruna explains that, "In 2013 I had a chance to buy 1 ha of Rabajà. The cost was unbelievable, but I couldn't leave it—so from 2015 we will again produce Rabajà."

Production was separated in 1996 into wines produced from estate grapes (labeled as Azienda Agricola Falletto) and wines from purchased grapes (labeled as Casa Vinicola Bruno Giacosa). Production from estate grapes is about a third. The estate wines include single vineyard bottlings from the two best Crus in Barbaresco, Asili and Rabajà, and three Barolos, Falletto, Le Rocche del Falletto, and Vigna Croera. There're also Barbera and Dolcetto d'Alba. Under the Casa Vinicola the top wine has been the Barbaresco Santo Stefano di Neive (made since 1964), but production stopped after 2011 as they decided to bottle top wines only from estate grapes. "For Barolo and Barbaresco I prefer to have only estate grapes because I can control everything," Bruna explains. Standard are exacting here, with top wines traditionally not made in vintages Bruno feels aren't good enough. Besides Barolo and Barbaresco, other wines include Dolcetto and Nebbiolo d'Alba, Arneis from Roero (important both historically because Bruno helped to rescue the variety from the edge of distinction, and practically because it is more than a third of all production), and a Spumante which comes from Pinot Noir grapes sourced in Oltrepo Pavese in Lombardy.

Although Giacosa is located in Barbaresco, there are more estate vineyards in Barolo, which is a larger part of production. The wines vary from powerful to elegant. Coming from Serralunga, Falletto has that characteristic sense of underlying power, and is my favorite among the Barolos, which usually spend a year longer in cask than the Barbarescos. In Barbaresco, "Rabajà and Santo Stefano have more power and less finesse," says Francesco. "Asili is near the Tanaro river and has completely different soil from the rest of Barbaresco, because there is some sand in the soil. This makes the most elegant wine." Asili is matured for 12 months in large casks. Riservas are made only in top years, and are identified by red labels. An Asili Riserva has been made about three times each decade; it's matured for 24 months in large casks and then for 24 months in bottle. Asili is my favorite wine from Giacosa, because it has a fantastic combination of delicacy and earthiness, with a distinctly savory edge, but Falletto is probably the most typical. Depending on the Cru, they can be relatively approachable when young, they are never over-stated, but for my palate they really come into their own after fifteen years. The 1997 Asili was brilliant in 2016.

Elio Grasso ★★

Loc. Ginestra 40, 12065 Monforte d'Alba (CN)	📞 *+39 0173 78491*
@ *info@eliograsso.it*	👤 *Francesca Grasso*
🌐 *www.eliograsso.it*	🍷 *Barolo [map p. 38]*

18 ha; 90,000 btl

🔺 *Barbera d'Alba, Vigna Martina*

🔺 *Barolo, Gavarini Chiniera*

The GPS made an error when I was driving to Elio Grasso, so I went a long way round and came around the back through Localita Ginestra along an unpaved one-track road hanging over a cliff edge. This gave me some appreciation of the elevated and isolated character of the vineyards. The estate is a gracious property with a view from its terrace over the surrounding hills. The modern winery was excavated in 2004-2007, and consists of a huge circular tunnel under the hillside. The estate of 42 ha includes 16 ha of vineyards on fairly steep slopes; another 2 ha on the other side of the village were acquired in 2014. The terroir is quite calcareous.

The family has a history of winemaking, and Elio decided in the seventies there was potential in Barolo, gave up his day job in a bank, and renovated an old house and the vineyards. The first official vintage with his label was 1978. His son Gianluca joined him in 1995 and started making the wines.

The wines include Dolcetto and Barbera from Alba, Langhe Nebbiolo, and three Barolos. There is also a Chardonnay. All except the Lage Nebbiolo and the Chardonnay are single vineyard wines. Everything is vinified in stainless steel, and then transferred to wood, except for the Dolcetto and Langhe Nebbiolo. The Barbera is matured in 50% new wood and some first year wood. It's a quintessential representation of the variety, poised between its historic rustic character and the smoothed out modern character. The Chardonnay is matured half in stainless steel and half in barriques with no malolactic fermentation.

"We place ourselves more on the traditional side, even though we have barriques, especially with the work in the vineyards, where Elio is using some of the techniques of his parents and grandparents," says Roberto Bordignon. Neither overtly traditional nor modern, the style of the Barolos tends to elegance. The two single vineyard Barolos, Gavarini Chiniera (a monopole) and Ginestra Casa Matè, are both vinified in botti of Slavonian oak. Gavarini comes from sandier soil and is usually lighter; Ginestra has more clay and limestone and usually displays more sense of stuffing. Barriques are used for the Runcot Riserva, coming from the vineyard immediately below the winery, which has been made only in top vintages since 2004 (previously it was released as a Barolo). "All the oak is new, so the quality of the fruit has to be up to aging in new oak," says Roberto. In other vintages it is declassified into the Langhe Nebbiolo, which comes from Monforte, usually from younger vines. This is not a typical Langhe Nebbiolo because the wine sees no oak. "Our objective is to see the purity of the fruits," says Roberto.

Silvio Grasso ★★

Fraz. Annunziata 112, 12064 La Morra (CN)

 +39 3516 703545

@ *info@silviograsso.com*

👤 *Marilena Grasso & Paolo Grasso*

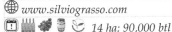 *www.silviograsso.com*

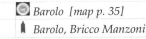 *Barolo [map p. 35]*

14 ha; 90,000 btl

Barolo, Bricco Manzoni

Silvio Grasso is emphatically a small family winery, where cellar work is handled by only four people, Federico Grasso and his wife Marilena, and their sons Paulo and Silvio. The family has been making wine since 1927, but estate bottling dates from the eighties, when Federico took over. There's a very modern tasting room at the front; behind is an expansive and workmanlike winery. There are plans to expand the winery underground, but no plans to expand the vineyards. "14 ha is the maximum for the land," says Paolo. (6 ha are owned by the estate, and 8 ha are leased.) The 15 cuvées include Dolcetto, Barbera, Langhe Nebbiolo, and Langhe Rosso (which comes from within Barolo, but includes Merlot and Syrah as well as Nebbiolo).

Barolo is about half of production. "We have one traditional Barolo," Paolo says, "matured in a larger vat, and five [modern] Barolos matured in barriques." New oak depends on the year, but can be up to 80%. The traditional cuvée is Turnè (which means "return"); it shows a savory, almost savage, edge, with firm tannins on the finish. It has 40 days skin maceration and is matured in large casks. Usually the vineyards are different from the other Barolos. The Barolo *tout court* is a blend from several vineyards, is given 15 days maceration on the skins, and matured in old barriques for 24 months; it shows smoother tannins than Turnè. This is a halfway house to the single vineyard wines, which are vinified in a mix of old and new barriques. The differences between them are striking. Luciani is more powerful, with a rich palate, evident fruits, and the perfume of Nebbiolo coming in at the end. Manzoni is more fragrant, the height of elegance on the palate, with savory fruits making a delicate impression in cooler vintages, but richer in hot vintages. "This is our most modern Barolo," says Paolo. Manzoni, which has the most new oak, comes from a slightly warmer vineyard and the vines are older (planted in 1968 compared to 1982 for Luciani).

I see more of a continuum along the range than a break between tradition and modernism. At Silvio Grasso, "modernism" means increasing refinement, and greater smoothness, rather than power and extraction.

Bruna Grimaldi

Via Parea 7, 12060 Grinzane Cavour (CN)

📞 +39 0173 262094

@ vini@grimaldibruna.it

🔺 Martina Fiorino

🌐 www.grimaldibruna.it

Barolo [map p. 34]

14 ha; 75,000 btl

Located on the northeastern border of the Barolo appellation at Grinzane Cavour, the winery is spread out at ground level because the water table is too high here to excavate underground. "It started as the only farmhouse in the village in 1903," says

Martina Fiorino. "My grandfather started to focus on winemaking and bottling production from about 1957. My mother was one of three daughters and the one who went into winemaking. She studied in Alba, and my parents (Bruna and Franco Fiorino) met at the oenology school. They started to acquire plots and decided to work only with their own grapes." The modern era started when Bruna and Franco began bottling in 1999. Martina and her brother Simone joined the domain in 2015.

Vineyards are dispersed in a semicircle running around the eastern border of the DOC. They extend from the original holding in Grinzane Cavour to a 2 ha plot in the Badarina cru 450m up at the southeastern border of Serralunga, which Bruna inherited from her mother's side. The classic Barolo is a blend from all the plots, and there are single-vineyard releases from vineyards at the extremes of the holdings, Badarina (since 1999) and Bricco Ambrogio (at the north in Roddi, since 2007).

The Nebbiolo d'Alba is not sourced from within Barolo, but comes from east of Grinzane Cavour. "The Nebbiolo d'Alba should be completely different from Barolo, as a direct expression of the variety," Martina says. It ages for 6 months in botti. and has a style in line with the freshness of the Dolcetto and Barbera. Vinified in stainless steel, the Dolcetto d'Alba is named for the San Martino climat where the grapes are grown, just east of Grinzane Cavour at 300m elevation. Barbera d'Alba is a blend of three plots from the north, the center-east, and the southeast, and ages for 10 months in a mix of tonneaux and botti.

The classic Barolo, Camilla, is a blend from 6 plots in 5 villages. The most approachable of the Barolos, it can be started more or less or less on release. Facing southeast with quite a bit of clay, Bricco Ambrogio is a little rounder and deeper with greater expression of fruits. Badarina is the best of the crus, one of the highest plots in Serralunga, with white soils, sandstone, and little clay, facing full south, and shows more of a sheen to the palate, with a finer structure. It's always bottled separately, and in the best vintages a Riserva is produced from the Vigna Regnola plot. Vinification is the same for all the Barolos. Maceration lasts 28 days with a submerged cap, followed by MLF in concrete. Wines age for 30 months in botti in classical manner plus a few tonneaux. The house style is fresh, with a sense of sapidity, even salinity or minerality, running through all the wines. The sense of structure, roundness, depth, and dark fruits increases along range; the crus need a bit of time for fruits to emerge.

Manzone Giovanni

Via Castelletto 9, 12065 Monforte d'Alba (CN)	☎ +39 0173 78114
@ info@manzonegiovanni.com	👤 Giovanni Manzone
🌐 www.manzonegiovanni.com	🔴 Barolo [map p. 38]
🗓 💹 🍇 ✋	🍾 Barolo, Castelletto
8 ha; 45,000 btl	Langhe Bianco, Rossese

"We have been here 98 years. We have more or less the same land we purchased in the 1960s-1980s. All the vineyards are near here, in general north of the town of

68

Monforte. My great grandfather, Giovanni, created the estate in 1925. My grandfather started to bottle the vineyards Castelletto and Gramolere," says Mauro Manzone, who works together with his sister and his father (also called Giovanni)..

Occupying a triangular plot at 450m altitude at the junction of two roads going up to Monforte, the winery is larger than you might expect from the size of the vineyards. The historical building, dating from 1871, is being renovated; the most recent addition to the modern winery was in 2006. The large barrel room can hold 100,000 bottles from each of two vintages. "We want long aging and not that much new oak." There is a 360 degree panoramic view from the tasting room.

All the Barolos have 40 days maceration and then age half in 25-35 hl botti and half in 500-700 liter tonneaux. The lots are blended after three years and then the wine spends a few months in concrete. The Langhe Nebbiolo comes from young vines declassified from Barolo. Spending 6 months in cask and 1 year in stainless steel, it is light but a little tight in style. "The goal is to have 100% Nebbiolo to express the fruits, not so complex in maceration as Barolo, with a fresher, more youthful expression."

Castelletto is the vineyard right under the winery. It was planted in 1999, and has been made as a separate cru since 2004. It is a big step up from Langhe Nebbiolo, smooth and velvety, and the most 'airy' of the crus. From limestone and sandstone, Gramolere is rounder and deeper, firmer and more structured. Bricat is a climat in Gramolere adjacent to the plot for the Gramolere cru. It has more red clay and the plantings are about 10% of the rosé cultivar. It's tighter and more precise, more elegant, and needs more time. Gramolere becomes approachable after about 4 years, but Bricat needs longer. The Riserva from Gramolere comes from 55-year-old vines at the top of the slope. Aged only in tonneaux, it is a step up in generosity with more of a viscous sheen. The style of all the wines shows a dryness to the finish.

Other cuvées include Dolcetto d'Alba and Barbera d'Alba, Le Ciliegie (vinified in stainless steel), both bright and juicy in style, and the Barbera d'Alba Superiore La Marchesa (vinified in tonneaux followed by stainless steel), smoother and nuttier in style. The one white cuvée comes from Rossese, an almost extinct variety that Giovanni planted in 1982. It's acid with a citrus impression when young, moving towards minerality as it ages.

Marchesi Di Barolo   *

Via Roma 1, 12060 Barolo (CN)	📞 +39 0173 564419
@ reception@marchesibarolo.com	👤 Famiglia Abbona
🌐 www.marchesibarolo.com	Barolo [map p. 36]
😊 🏯 ❌ 🍷 🍽 🚜 200 ha; 1,500,000 btl	Barolo, Commune di Barolo

Only a small sign indicates the premises just off the main street in Barolo, and it's a surprise when you enter to find a huge covered courtyard with buildings on all four

sides. Built into the side of the hill, the winery is all around, with vast cellars underneath, and the covered courtyard is not so much a trendy atrium, but is the center for receiving grapes without being exposed to the weather. A large tasting room sells all sorts of products including a wide range of the Marchesi's wines. The cellars have now taken over all available space, including areas that used to be part of the original farm, such as the stables. Everything except bottling is done here.

Marchesi di Barolo has an interesting history. The original owners, the Marchesi di Falletto, were powerful land and property owners in the area (Castiglione Falletto refers to their castle); they died out in 1864, and the property went to a charity. However, a change in the law, intended to restrict the power of the Church, precluded charities from owning commercial enterprises, so the winery and vineyards were sold to the Abbona family, who were already winemakers in the area; now it is run by the fourth and fifth generations.

One of the larger producers in the area, Marchesi makes a vast range of wines, with roughly 40% coming from 70 ha of estate vineyards, and the rest provided by 100 ha of growers; vineyards. Winemaker Flavio Fennocchio, who has been here since 1988, says that, "Barolo and Barbaresco are almost all from our own vineyards. The percent coming from the estate is increasing, mostly because growers sell the vineyards when they want to retire." Flavio refuses to be pegged as to whether he is a modernist or traditionalist. "I usually say I'm not on the side of innovation, I'm not on the side of tradition, I'm on the side of the wines."

Fermentation starts in large stainless steel tanks outside, and then the wine is transferred to cement tanks for the malolactic fermentation. The scale of the cellars is indicated by the fact that it is transferred by gravity feed through a pipeline that is 830 m long, down 60 m, into the aging cellars. The cellars contain both botti, ranging in size from 18,500 l to 3,000 l, and barriques. Maturation depends on the wine.

The style of the Barolo is relatively light, but the Commune di Barolo (which comes only from vineyards around the village of Barolo) is weightier, then with the single vineyard wines, Coste di Rose (from sandy soil) is fairly tight, Cannubi (sand and some clay) moves to a characteristically sleeker style, and Samasso shows the most weight. There is also a Barbaresco, which is quite fine, with a touch of earthiness. In addition, there are both Barolo and Barbaresco cuvées marked Tradizione. Other wines include Nebbiolo, Barbera, and Dolcetto d'Alba, Roero, other wines from the Langhe, and wines from Asti including a Spumante, altogether making around 40 wines.

Marchesi Di Grésy   *

Strada della Stazione n. 21, 12050 Barbaresco (CN)	📞 *+39 0173 635222*
@ *hello@marchesidigresy.com*	👤 *Jeffrey Chilcott*
🌐 *www.marchesidigresy.com*	🔵 *Barbaresco [map p. 39]*
📅 🏭 🍷 *45 ha; 200,000 btl*	🍾 *Barbaresco, Martinenga*

The Grésy family has owned the land here since 1797. The winery is in a valley surrounded by the vineyards, at the end of a steep, narrow track. It was extended in 2000 by excavating into the hill. "Before production started, all the top names used to come here and buy grapes," cellarmaster Jeffrey Chilcott says. The family also own estates, including one in Monferrato. Nebbiolo is about a quarter of production.

The winery is located in the 12 ha Martinenga monopole in Barbaresco. Three cuvées of Barbaresco come from Martinenga: the general blend, and two plots from opposite ends of the vineyards, Guiun, and Camp Gros. You might call the domain a modified modernist, as for the past twenty years, aging has started with 12 months in barriques, including 25% new oak, but then continues for another year (Barbaresco) or 18 months (single-vineyard wines) in botti of old oak.

"For Barbaresco we don't have a regular bottling, it's all Crus, and then there are crus within Crus," Jeffrey says. Releases are staggered. "Every year we bring out three wines, but from different vintages." Guiun ages one year longer in the bottle than Martinenga, and Camp Gros ages two years longer.

The style is quite fine. The Langhe Nebbiolo comes from dedicated plots, consisting of the first 3-4 rows of vines running round the bottom of the amphitheater surrounding the winery. Aged only in stainless steel, it's quite light, with lifted aromatics, and intended for immediate consumption. Martinenga is elegant, and immediately approachable in lighter vintages, needing a little more time in others. Guiun is firmer and more structured. Camp Gros is a Riserva, more powerful and more complex, holding back more than the others, but still quite elegant. The wines age slowly: Martinenga typically begins to show the first signs of development about ten years after the vintage. Camp Gros has the greatest aging potential.

Bartolo Mascarello   *

Via Roma 15, 12060 Barolo (CN)	📞 +39 0173 56125
📠 +39 0173 56125	👤 Maria Teresa Mascarello
	◎ Barolo [map p. 36]
📅 🏭 🚜 5 ha; 30,000 btl	🍷 Barolo

This small domain is famous for continuing its staunch defense of tradition through the generations. Bartolo, who took over from his father in the 1960s, was proud of maintaining the same style; indeed, he famously said, "I don't make wines with fantasy names. I don't make crus, I don't make wine in barriques, my wines don't have perfume of vanilla and Limousin oak. I'm the last of the Mohicans." His daughter, Maria Teresa started making wine in 1993, and has been in sole charge since Bartolo died in 2005. She says the wine is made in exactly the same way as it used to be. "One cannot change the style of the wine according to the whim of the market, I do not want to banalize or vulgarize the wine to please the crowd."

In true traditional style, there is only a single blended Barolo (which comes from the famous vineyards of Cannubi, San Lorenzo, and Rué, in the commune of Barolo, and Rocche from Castiglione). Maria Teresa does not want to follow the French model of Crus. "We should follow tradition, we should make a unique wine that does not resemble the production of other regions. "Fermentation is in cement; maturation is in large old botti of Slavonian oak. The 5 ha of vineyards were assembled by Maria Teresa's grandfather (Bartolo's father, who started the cellar) and great grandfather (who was maitre de chai at a cooperative), and are still the same, producing about 10,000 bottles of Barbera, 6,000 of Dolcetto, 10,000 of Freisa, and 10,000 of Barolo. Vineyards are worked traditionally, but Maria Teresa does not like labels such as organic or biodynamic; she is looking for a middle way that maintains equilibrium, she says.

The style of the wine here is unmistakable, one of the very few that remains truly traditional, with a savage impression when young, melding into fruits with a distinctly savory edge as the wine ages.

Giuseppe Mascarello e Figlio   **

Via Borgonuovo 108, 12060 Monchiero (CN)   📞 +39 0173 792126

@ mauromascarello@mascarello1881.com   👤 Mauro Mascarello

🌐 www.mascarello1881.com   ◎ Barolo [map p. 34]

🔍🖊🍇🚜 13 ha; 60,000 btl   🍷 Barolo, Villero

One of the most famous producers of Barolo, Giuseppe Mascarello's winery is in Monchieri to the south of the Barolo DOCG. Somewhat dilapidated in appearance, just by the railway station, the building dates from the nineteenth century, and the Mascarellos have been making wine here since the 1920s. "We are 3 km out of the Barolo DOC, but we are a historical cellar, so we are authorized to make the wine here," says Elena Mascarello, who together with her brother represents the fifth generation. Her father Mauro, who made Mascarello famous by introducing the single vineyard bottling of Monprivato, and whose name is evident on an old sign in front of the building, is still actively involved, however.

Monprivato, and Mascarello's other vineyards in Barolo, are in Castiglione Falletto. With 6.4 ha planted, Monprivato amounts to about half of the holdings; it accounts for a third of production. The vineyard has a white and gray soil and is rich in limestone. Mascarello owned 3 ha of the vineyard as early as 1904, but over the past century acquired the rest to make it a monopole. Two generations ago, Elena's grandfather mixed the grapes with purchased grapes to produce a Barolo. Monprivato started as a single vineyard wine in 1970. However, it's made only in top

72

vintages: in other years it is bottled as Barolo or even as Langhe Nebbiolo, depending on the year. There are much smaller amounts of Barolos from other plots, of which Villero is the best known. In addition, there are several Barberas and Dolcettos. Strong views are held here about the use of wood. "We are among traditional winemakers, all you see are old botti, up to 60 years," says Elena. "My father tried all sorts of vinification in the seventies and eighties, but it has been settled for the past 15 years," she adds. "With a wine like ours which follows tradition, you see the vintage more clearly. Barriques muddy the expression of vintage." Fermentation is in concrete tanks; then the wine goes into botti, resting for 54 months in the case of Monprivato, followed by two years in bottle before release. Mascarello is traditional, but not necessarily old-fashioned: "We've always done a green harvest," Elena says, "and yields have gone down over the past ten years."

The most striking feature of a tasting here is the strong identity of all the wines: whether it's Dolcetto, Barbera, or Nebbiolo, all offer great purity of fruits. Monprivato is immensely refined, with a silky character; its tannic structure is so fine you may hardly notice it.

Massolino - Vigna Rionda **

Piazza Cappellano 8, 12050 Serralunga d'Alba (CN)	📞 +39 0173 613138
@ *info@massolino.it*	👤 *Franco & Roberto Massolino*
🌐 *www.massolino.it*	🔴 *Barolo [map p. 37]*
📅 🍷 🚜 *42 ha; 307,000 btl*	🍷 *Barolo, Parafada*

Located in the heart of Serralunga, with a clear view across the valley to Castiglione Falletto, the Massolinos have been making wine here for four generations. The estate was founded in 1896 by Giuseppe Massolino. His son built the cellar, and the next generation expanded the estate by buying the Crus in Serralunga that are at its heart today. Today seven family members are involved in the estate. There's a spacious tasting room at the entrance, with the winery below. It's just been expanded underground, right along the edge of the cliff face, in a four year project. A tunnel leads from the older cellars to the latest addition.

Vinification is traditional, with fermentation mostly in cement. "Our new cement vats give extremely pure and clean results. We like this type of vat. We also have stainless steel, of course, but we intend to use more cement," says Franco. He is very fussy about oak. The cellar is full of large botti. The oak comes from Slovenia and the botti are made by Stockinger in Austria. "All our Barolo is aged in traditional large barrels, in very neutral oak, so it's delicate and pure. There's no toast, and the casks are as large as possible."

Wines include the classic varieties, with Dolcetto, both Barbera d'Asti and d'Alba, a Moscato d'Asti (sweet), and a Langhe Chardonnay. "This comes from my passion for the variety," says Franco, "I persuaded my father to buy two plots." The Langhe Nebbiolo and Barolo blend both come mostly from Serralunga, showing a precise, elegant, style. Then in increasing strength, there are the single vineyard wines: Margheria, Parafada, Parussi, and finally the Vigna Rionda Riserva (made only in six vintages since the first in 1996).

With vineyards largely in Serralunga, it's only to be expected that the wines will tend to the more powerful side of Nebbiolo, but they are never out of balance. Due to more sand in the soil, Margheria is the most elegant; coming from the oldest vines on calcareous terroir—"the soil is completely white," says Franco—Parafada is full bodied and deep, a typical Serralunga; and Parussi (the only one outside of Serralunga, from the latest vineyard purchase, in Castiglione in 2006) showing lots of tannins. "It's very masculine with high potential for aging, and not at all easy when young," says Franco. They are more or less ready to drink after successive intervals, Margheria at perhaps 3 or 4 years, Parafada a couple of years after that, and Parussi after another couple of years. Vigna Rionda Riserva should not really be touched for a decade.

That said, the emphasis is on bringing out the character of Nebbiolo. "We did experiments with clones when we needed to replant," says Franco. "We use selection massale (propagating vines from within the vineyard) because the clones give more color or concentration but do not give the necessary elegance. We would prefer to have as little bit less concentration and keep to character (and beautiful color) of Nebbiolo."

Moccagatta   *

Strada Rabajà 46, 12050 Barbaresco (CN)	📞 +39 0173 635228
@ info@moccagatta.eu	👤 Martina Minuto
⊕ www.moccagatta.eu	🖥 Barbaresco [map p. 39]
📅 ⚒ 🍷 12 ha; 65,000 btl	📍 Barbaresco

"When my grandfather and his brother divided the family estate in 1952, Mario Minuto took the name of Moccagatta (after the name of the local area) for his estate to have something on the label that wasn't the family name," says Martina Minuto. Today the estate is run today by Mario's sons Francesco and Sergio and their families. "We have not increased the size of the estate much since then," Martina says, "but grandfather sold a lot of grapes, and my uncle moved into producing wine and built the winery." The building is a modern facility on the main road past Barbaresco, overlooking the main vineyard, Bric Balin (within the Moccagatta cru), which runs down the hill from the winery. The other vineyards in Barbaresco are Bric Basarin (enlarged a little from the original holding) and Cole (the most recent acquisition).

The style is modern. "We tried barriques at the start of the eighties, and by the end of the decade everything was in them," Martina says. Winemaking is the same for all

74

the Barbarescos, with the communal blend staying in wood for one year, and the single vineyards for 18 months, with 50% new barriques and 50% used. The Barbaresco blend comes from the lower part of Basarin and from Bric Balin. Coming from sandy soil, Basarin is the lightest of the cuvées, and the most elegant, although it needs time to resolve the strong oak influence. The range continues to the deeper Bric Balin, with more obvious sense of fruit, and the powerful Cole, where tannins are more powerful than Bric Balin, but slower to show on the palate because of greater fruit density. In terms of approachability, Bric Balin and Cole need about four more years than Basarin. You might say that the range runs from feminine to masculine, but there is no mistaking the modernist approach in any of the wines.

Paolo Monti **

Loc. San Sebastiano, 39, 12065 Monforte d'Alba (CN)   +39 0173 78391
@ wine@paolomonti.com   Paolo Monti
⊕ www.paolomonti.com   Barolo [map p. 38]
18 ha; 50,000 btl   Barolo, Bricco San Pietro

"My family has been involved in construction since 1923, but I am a wine lover," Paolo Monti says. "I was consulted on building a winery in Serralunga, and I decided I wanted to make wine, found this place in 1995, the first sale was of the Barbera 1995 in 1997."The estate is south of Monforte d'Alba, more or less at the southern border of the Barolo DOC. Paolo describes the operation as "A contemporary winery immersed in 200 years of Langhe history." The winery itself is a modern building, fitted to be self-sufficient in energy. Vineyards are all in Monforte d'Alba, half for producing Barolo, the other half planted with different varieties.

Winemaking followed on from the modernist phase; in fact, you might call Paolo an arch-modernist. "I wanted to make wine in a different style, clean, in small barriques," he says. "We are working parcellaire as they say in France. Wine starts out in oak. always in barriques because it's easier to handle small quantities. When it's ready to blend, we move into 16 hl untoasted casks of French oak."

The first wine was just 10 barriques of Barbera d'Alba. Today the Barbera starts in a rotary fermenter, and then ages for 15 months in new French barriques. A Barbera d'Alba Superiore ages in new French barriques for 24 months. This is a top selection of the harvest in special vintages, usually come from a plot on white soil that harvests early. Production is less than 3,000 bottles. Very flavorful, with lots of texture, it might convert people to the variety. "We are famous more for Barbera than Barolo," Paolo says.

Nebbiolo d'Alba comes from vineyards at 400-420m in Monforte and ages for 12 months in 2-year barriques. It's smooth and very flavorful for Nebbiolo d'Alba, in fact I would say it's closer to most producers' entry-level Barolo than to the common fresh and fruity style of Nebbiolo d'Alba. Barolo from the commune of Monforte is a blend of Bussia with Bricco San Pietro, aged in large casks for 28-30 months; it's a classic demonstration of the opulence and power of Monforte. Bricco San Pietro is the estate's major holding, 7 ha in one block, has been made as Cru since 2015. It ages for 3 months in barriques followed by 30-36 months in large casks. The rich, deep, powerful style makes this perhaps the most overtly modernist of the cuvées. Bussia Riserva is made only with the two historic parts of the vineyard, from vines planted in 1971, and is a real vin de garde with a weighty tannic structure. It spends 18 months in 50/50 new/1-year barriques followed by 30 months in big casks.

A range of wines described as 'Creations,' includes a Langhe Merlot (aged for 48 months in new French barriques), the Langhe Dossi Rossi (40% each of Cabernet Sauvignon and Merlot with 20% Nebbiolo, aged for 24-30 months in 2-year barriques), and the white Langhe, L'Aura, an unusual blend of 70% Chardonnay (aged in new barriques) with 30% Riesling (aged in stainless steel).

Nada Fiorenzo *

Via Ausario 12c, 12050 Treiso (CN)	📞 *+39 0173 638254*
@ *nadafiorenzo@nada.it*	👤 *Bruno Danilo Nada*
🌐 *www.nada.it*	💬 *Barbaresco [map p. 39]*
📅 ⚒ 🍇 *10 ha; 50,000 btl*	🏺 *Barbaresco, Manzola*

"My great grandfather bought a 35 ha property in 1921. There were few wineries then, but everyone made wine. He divided the property between his 4 sons (giving none to his 3 daughters). One of the sons was my grandfather, who decided in 1942 to start a winery," says Danilo Fiorenzo, who has been at the estate since 2010. "My father started in 1982 and the focus changed. When he started to do green harvest, my grandfather collected the grapes so the neighbors would not be offended." The 10 ha today are 85% Nebbiolo, 20% Barbera, and 5% Dolcetto. 65% of the estate is in Rombone (in the commune of Treiso). There are 8 wines, all exclusively from estate grapes.

The Dolcetto comes from vines spread all around the estate, with an age over 50 years. All are facing full south. (When they need to be replanted, they will be replaced with Nebbiolo.) The Barbera d'Alba comes from Rombone, and ages for one year in old barriques. Sixtine is a blend between Nebbiolo and Barbera from the oldest vines (planted in 1946) Rombone. It has just a little too much (80%) Nebbiolo to call it a Barbera from Langhe. The blend is made after MLF. It ages for 18 months. The style is definitely Barbera-driven, but it's more elegant than you usually see in Barbera.

Langhe Nebbiolo spends a year in botti; Barbaresco spends 2 years. "Our Langhe Nebbiolo is more like a Barbaresco, that's the terroir. The style of the wines here develops structure and density, it's not possible to make a Nebbuline in stainless steel. The difference between the Langhe Nebbiolo and the Barbaresco is the quality of the grapes. The cru has to taste like the vineyard. We do 15-17 different microvinifications. The best part from each cru goes to make the single vineyard wine. 10-11 microvinifications make the Barbaresco or Langhe Nebbiolo depending on whether they are fruity (Langhe Nebbiolo) or complex (Barbaresco).

The Barbaresco is quite firm. Manzola, from a southwest-facing hill with clay and limestone and some sand, adjacent to Rombone, is a big step up: smooth, silky, very fine, in fact its finesse makes it more approachable than the Barbaresco. "It is never the most powerful wine from the estate." Montaribaldi in Barbaresco commune was planted in 1956 on a plot with no clay or sand, just limestone. The style is more masculine, with the wine more firmly structured. Rombone has clay and limestone, with no sand, and the wine always has freshness. "This is always the hardest cru to get the balance right." Maceration is a bit shorter than the others at 2-3 weeks so as not to over-extract. It is the most elegant and finest, the most aromatic, of the crus. There is a similarity in style between Manzola and Rombone, with Rombone a touch firmer nd more structured, but in the same elegant style. Montaribaldi is definitely more obviously structured, more like a more concentrated version of the classic Barbaresco.

Oddero Poderi e Cantine   *

Loc. Santa Maria, via Tetti 28, 12064 La Morra (CN)	📞 +39 0173 50618
@ info@oddero.it	👤 Mariacristina Oddero
🌐 www.oddero.it	🔴 Barolo [map p. 34]
📅 🏭 🍇 🍷 35 ha; 160,000 btl	🍷 Barolo

"We are one of the oldest families for producing Barolo. We were one of the first to bottle Barolo with the family name, in 1878. We have not changed our style to please the international style of the market, we still use the same principles," says Isabella Oddero, who runs the estate together with her aunt Cristina. "There were six generations of men before my aunt took over," Isabella says.

The Oddero family has been in La Morra since the eighteenth century and began producing wine some time around the end of the century. The family house was built in the 18th century and the winery has grown around it, the last extension being a new storage facility in 2015. The winery owes much of its present form to the efforts of Giacoma Oddero in the fifties, who ran the estate together with his brother Luigi, but the brothers divided the estate in 2006, and Luigi left to found his own winery in 2006 with his half (called Luigi Oddero: see profile). Giacoma's daughter Cristina has been making the wine since 1996.

The approach is traditional. "We were one of the last producers to start producing single vineyard wines. Until 1982 we made only one Barolo. Even today we use grapes from important vineyards for the Barolo Classico, it is important to understand that these are not second line grapes," Isabella points out.

"We are unusual in having very diversified and fragmented vineyards in several communes," Isabella says. "Until 1950 the only vineyards were around the house, but my grandfather bought a variety of vineyards because he wanted to have vineyards in different terroirs." They include a roll call of famous names: Vigna Rionda (Barolo commune), Brunate (La Morra), Mondoca (Monforte), Roche di Castiglione and Villero (in Castiglione Falletto). The Barolo blend comes from vineyards around the winery in La Morra and from Castiglione Falletto. There are also Barbera and Dolcetto d'Alba. There is one Barbaresco, from the Gallina Cru.

The particularity of vinification is that grapes are destemmed, but the grapes go intact into the fermentation vat. The wines ago in botti, mostly Slavonian oak, but some French. There is never any new oak in the Barolos: "When casks are replaced, they are used for the first one or two years for Barbera." "Our wines need more time because of our traditional style," says Isabella. Of course, they can be drunk younger then used to be the case, but they can still be a little stern when young.

The Nebbiolo Langhe comes from a blend that's similar to the Barolo. It's restrained, and you think the tannins have been completely tamed until the characteristic dryness comes out on the finish. The Barolo covers up the tannins more with a glycerinic sheen on the palate. In single vineyard wines, Villero reflects the clay terroir in its muscularity, Brunate reflects sand and limestone in an expression of elegance and purity, Bussia Vigna Mondaco Riserva (it used to be called Bussia Soprano) is the most complete in itself, with great finesse, and Vigna Rionda Riserva (released only after ten years) has a restrained sense of power. The house style shows in some austerity in Barbaresco Gallina. That sense of underlying structure is the mark of the house.

Sori Paitin   *

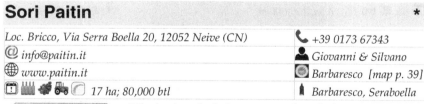

Loc. Bricco, Via Serra Boella 20, 12052 Neive (CN)	+39 0173 67343
@ info@paitin.it	Giovanni & Silvano
www.paitin.it	Barbaresco [map p. 39]
17 ha; 80,000 btl	Barbaresco, Serabaella

"The land we look down on was bought in 1796, and was a farm until the 1860s. My grandfather's grandfather was a professor agronomic science and he used the land to experiment., and transformed this into a business. The first use of Barbaresco on the label was in 1883. We were one of the families who essentially created Barbaresco," says Luca Pasquero-Elia.

The family has Jewish origins, so there were difficulties from 1938. "There was not much commercial production until my grandfather (Second Pasquero-Elia) took over when he was 20 and started production. It took from 1948 to 1974 to get back to full production," Luca says. Second's sons Giovanni and Silvano took over, and today Luca represents the new generation. During the difficult period, holdings fell to 4 ha in Seraboella around the winery, but now are back to 14 ha in Barbaresco altogether, with the rest around Alba.

"We have always been in the traditional approach with long fermentation and aging in big barrels. My father experimented with smaller barrels for Barbera, and in 2001 we tried some tonneaux but we didn't like the results for Barbaresco so we sold the," Luca says. Aging is in 25 hl and 50 hl botti of Slavonian oak, with a couple of Austrian oak, similar for all Barbaresco cuvées at 26 months.

The Langhe Nebbiolo, Starda, originally came from a plot at the bottom of the hill below the winery, but now includes about a third of grapes from Alba. It ages for 9 months, and is a halfway house between the common fresh style of Nebbiolo and the style of Barbaresco. There is no Barbaresco blend; all cuvées come from individual crus. The latest cuvée is Faset, added in 2019 from an 0.5 ha plot rented from a friend of Luca's. "We thought it was in Asili, but it turns out to be one row outside Asili," Luc says. The style is smooth and approachable. Basarin is lighter and more elegant than Faset, and if anything more approachable. As he opens the Seraboella, Luca says, "We have been making Seraboella for 126 years, so we have some experience." It's firmer and riper than Faset or Basarin, and at first fruit density hides the tannins, but even though the tannins are supple, this needs a year or so after release. The Seraboella Riserva is deeper and more intense, more structured, needs more time (say four years), but you see the same character.

Armando Parusso   *

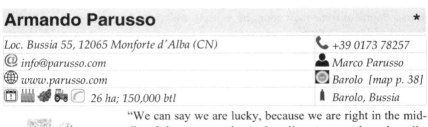

Loc. Bussia 55, 12065 Monforte d'Alba (CN)	📞 *+39 0173 78257*
@ *info@parusso.com*	👤 *Marco Parusso*
🌐 *www.parusso.com*	🔴 *Barolo [map p. 38]*
📅 🏭 🎗 🔖 ◯ *26 ha; 150,000 btl*	▲ *Barolo, Bussia*

"We can say we are lucky, because we are right in the middle of the area, we have clay, limestone, and sandy soils. Our Barolo is quite balanced, with something of the power of Serralunga, but also the more floral properties of the sandy areas." The estate started when Gaspare Parusso bought a plot of land in 1901. Two decades later, the family bought a farmhouse above the Rocche vineyard, at the northeast corner of the Bussia Cru, which is still the location of the cellars, more or less where the communes of Monforte and Castiglione Falletto come together. Originally there was polyculture, with a specialty in peaches. Armando started to bottle wine from the estate in 1971, and the family became committed to viticulture. Marco Parusso, who runs the estate today together with his sister Tiziana, joined after qualifying in oenology in 1986. The next generation, in the form of Tiziano's daughter, Julia, is now involved.

Marco is a modernist, you might even say an arch-modernist. After fermentation in rotary fermenters, all the red wines except the Dolcetto age in barriques with a high proportion of new oak. Grapes are held for several days in the cold before fermentation starts, and then whole bunches are used. During aging there is frequent battonage (twice per day for the first 8 weeks). "It's important for us that the wine gets oxygen, the lees obscure that, so we do battonage." The objective is to extract more from the lees; "we want the wine to be creamy, elegant, and delicate. We want to give up the idea of needing to age the wine for a long time, we prefer a style that is ready to drink."

The Langhe Nebbiolo is declassified from Barolo. The Barolo white label is a blend from all areas. The style is elegant, with savory impressions. The Barolo blue label is made in "unlucky" vintages, such as 2014, when individual crus are not made, and everything goes into one cuvée. Bussia is a blend from two vineyards, and is smoother and more elegant, with a lacy, delicate impression, showing its new wood with a slightly nutty finish. As the wine ages, it from the perfume of roses to truffles. When you get to the Bussia Riserva (only 1,000 bottles), you might describe the style as "truffles and roses." The other crus are Mariondino (in Castiglione Falletto) and Mosconi (in Monforte d'Alba). There is a curious effect in aging, which Marco describes as "the younger appears the older," because fruits hide the tannins better when the wine is younger, and tannins become more obvious as the wine ages. The wines are best enjoyed for the first three or four years, and then after a delay of a few years to let tannins soften. Going from the Barolo white label to Bussia to Riserva there is increasing delicacy, reaching its peak in the Riserva after about ten years.

Other wines include Dolcetto d'Alba and Barbera (Ornati ages for a year in new barriques), two Sauvignon Blancs (Langhe Bianco aged in stainless steel, and Rovella in barriques), a sparkling wine made from early-harvest Nebbiolo, a sweet wine (Parüss) made from late-harvest Nebbiolo, and the Testone orange wine from Sauvignon Blanc.

Pio Cesare **

Via Cesare Balbo 6, 12051 Alba (CN)	📞 *+39 0173 440386*
@ *direzione@piocesare.it*	👤 *Pio Boffa*
🌐 *www.piocesare.it*	⬤ *Barolo [map p. 34]*
📅 🗡 🍇 ⌘ *75 ha; 400,000 btl*	🍷 *Langhe Nebbiolo*

Now in its fifth generation, Pio Cesare was founded by Cesare Pio in 1881. Today, the estate is managed by Pio Boffa, great grandson of the founder. The cellars are located just outside the Barolo production area, in the town of Alba. "We are the only producers in town of Alba," says Cesare Benvenuto (Pio Boffa's nephew), "and the best," he adds wryly. The old cellars, dating from the origins, have been extended by excavating an extra storey underneath; they are one of the historic sights of Alba. It's a mark of tradition that the label has not changed since the 1870s.

Vineyards are all within the Barbaresco and Barolo DOCGs. In Barolo they include the communes of Barolo, La Morra, Serralunga, and Grinzane Cavour. The flagship vineyard is Ornato, in Serralunga. The Barbaresco vineyards are in Treiso and at the edge of Alba, the most important being Il Bricco in Treiso.

The range of wines extends well beyond Barolo and Barbaresco. There are two Barberas: the classic Barbera d'Alba, aged for one year in a mix of 90% botti and 10% used barriques; and Fides, aged equally in botti and second year barriques. Fides used to come from a vineyard in Serralunga that has been replanted to Nebbiolo, and since 2017 has come from the Vigna Mosconi vineyard in Monforte. The same sleek style runs from the Barberas though the Nebbiolos: smooth and silky with a sense of underlying chocolaty texture.

There are two Nebbiolos: Il Nebbio is made in a forward style with no oak exposure, but Langhe Nebbiolo ages like Barolo and Barbaresco, 90% in botti and 10% in (used) barriques. The difference is that Lage Nebbiolo has only two years and the others all have three years. "It's a very serious Nebbiolo," says Cesare Benvenuto, "we don't make it as a declassification." A blend from ten vineyards, it really expresses the house style. The Barbaresco blend comes 70% from Il Bricco, and shows purity and precision, while Barolo comes half from Serralunga and has a greater sense of opulence, with more evident structure. "The Barolo is a selection of different vineyards because we want it to be a complete Barolo," Cesare says. The Il Bricco cuvée is a selection from the best lots, usually from the top of the plot, and adds a touch of opulence to the purity of Barbaresco. Barolo Ornato comes from the central and ripest part of the Cru, and adds a sense of more layers to the Barolo. The Barolos are more powerful but also have more of an opulent sheen. Tannins are fine and can seem deceptively light. Comparing the wines here gives a textbook impression of the difference between Barbaresco and Barolo, seen through the prism of the purity of the house style.

In white wines there's not only Langhe Arneis but also Gavi, Piedmont Chardonnay (Piodilei), and Moscato d'Asti.

E. Pira & Figli ★★

Via Vittorio Veneto 1, 12060 Barolo (CN) 	 +39 0173 56247
@ info@pira-chiaraboschis.com 	 Chiara & Giorgio Boschis
🌐 www.pira-chiaraboschis.com 	 Barolo [map p. 36]
11 ha; 50,000 btl 	 Barolo, Cannubi

On a street corner in the center of Barolo, the building looks like a residence, too small to house a winery, but inside there's a long garden running back, with cellars underneath, extended to two levels. From the garden you can see out over the hills around Barolo.

Chiara Boschis was one of the "Barolo Boys" who revolutionized winemaking in Barolo in the eighties. "My generation had to face the problem of whether to sell the vineyards and abandon winemaking or to take it back.

I was lucky that I was in a group of people who decided to make wine here, I was the youngest, and I was lucky to be included in the group. I was regarded as their mascot because I was the only woman," Chiara recollects.

Chiara comes from a winemaking family who owned Borgogno (see profile), but she did not inherit a share. After working there with her brothers, she purchased the tiny estate of E. Pira, following the death of Luigi Pira in 1980. With under 5 ha, production was not much over a thousand cases. In 2010 her brother Giorgio left Borgogno (after the Boschis family had sold it) and joined her, and that gave them the resources to buy more vineyards, and to expand the cellar by excavating a new barrel room and storage area..

She's definitely a modern winemaker. "Fermentation is in stainless steel, I took out all the concrete." She started fighting with her father, doing green harvest at night to pass unnoticed, but anyway her father heard from other winemakers—"do you know what your daughter is up to?" She remains dedicated to organic viticulture, to the point of persuading all her neighbors in Cannubi to make the whole Cru organic (no mean feat in Piedmont!). Fermentation is in rotary fermenters, but maceration time has been extended, and is now about two weeks. Chiara has moved away from exclusive dependence on barriques, and the cellar also contains botti. "You can get too much taste of oak, this is why I have reduced new oak." The wines now typically age in a mix of botti and barriques.

Dolcetto and Barbera are workmanlike examples of the varieties. The Barbera ages in barriques because there isn't enough production to fill botti. The Langhe Nebbiolo is the only wine not certified as organic, because includes all the grapes from the borders of organic vineyards adjacent to nonorganic vineyards, plus 3 dedicated vineyards in Monforte. The smooth supple style is a preview of the Barolo with less intensity. It can be started on release and lasts for a few years.

Cannubi, aged in botti, is a typical representation of this top Cru, smooth and so silky the tannins are subsumed by the fruits, requiring a minimal amount of time after release. It's my favorite of Chiara's Barolos. Mosconi comes from the purchase in 2010 of a 4 ha vineyard of 40-year old vines in Monforte; this gives a warmer, richer wine, firmer and more powerful than Cannubi, becoming chocolaty as it ages "Mosconi is always bigger, it would be too aggressive in botti, so it ages in smaller casks." Via Nuova used to come from a single plot, but now is a blend from 7 crus. "After we bought more vineyards, it was possible to go back to the tradition of assemblage from different vineyards." Smooth and supple on the palate, it's the roundest and perhaps the easiest to start. Depending on the plot, lots may age in barriques or larger casks. It has more breadth but less precision than Cannubi.

Luigi Pira   *

Via Xx Settembre 9, 12050 Serralunga d'Alba (CN)	📞 *+39 0173 613106*
@ *pira@piraluigi.it*	👤 *Gianpaolo Pira*
🌐 *www.piraluigi.it*	🔴 *Barolo [map p. 37]*
☺ 🏭 🍇 🛢 *12 ha; 60,000 btl*	🍷 *Barolo, Serralunga*

Luigi Pira started in the 1950s by growing grapes in Serralunga; at first grapes, and later wine, were sold to other wineries. The estate took off as an independent producer when Luigi's son, Gianpaolo, joined in the nineties; the first estate bottling was 1993. Today Gianpaolo makes the wine and his brother Romolo manages the vineyards. "We are a classic style of estate," Gianpaolo says, meaning that responsibilities are divided among members of the family, and adding that they stick to the three traditional black grapes.

The winery was originally regarded as modernist, as their first wines were made in rotary fermenters and aged in barriques with significant amounts of new oak. Gianpaolo pays a lot of attention to the balance between oak and fruit, and the style backed off from new oak after 2000. Today Gianpaolo mostly uses 2,500 liter casks, except for smaller barrels for the two top wines. "We don't like the term modernist or traditionalist, it's important for us to express the soil," Gianpaolo says. "Our goal is to put the different personality of each vineyard in the glass."

Except for a plot of Barbera, all the estate vineyards are in the valley below the winery. Each of the 7 cuvées comes from specific terroirs. Langhe Nebbiolo comes from a plot in Serralunga, and its perfumed nose leads into an elegant palate, with chocolate notes on a nuanced finish. Barolo Serralunga is a blend from several vineyards within the commune; adding herbs and spices to the perfume, it's deeper on the palate. Tannins are so fine that it can be started on release. This is the flagship wine. Crus Margheria, from the oldest (60-year) vineyard, is deeper and more intense, broader on the palate; "the soil makes this more salty and mineral," Gianpaolo says. Marenca is the most muscular wine of the domain. The vineyard is adjacent to Gaja's Sperss. "It's usually strong and masculine, so we use French tonneaux for the first year." With sweet tannins gripping the finish, it's still quite fragrant and approachable. Vigna Rionda spends its first year in barriques, and gives the firmest and broadest impression of the range, with some savory notes as it develops. The style is modern in that tannins have been tamed and the wines are immediately approachable, even though they mostly age in large casks with no new oak.

Produttori Del Barbaresco *

Via Turin 52, 12050 Barbaresco (CN)	*+39 0173 635139*
produttori@produttoridelbarbaresco.com	*Aldo Vacca*
www.produttoridelbarbaresco.com	*Barbaresco [map p. 39]*
110 ha; 620,000 btl	*Barbaresco, Montefico*

Occupying one side of the square around the Church at the end of the main street in Barbaresco, the Produttori has a modern tasting room at the front of its original winery. Fermentation still takes place in the cellars underneath, but in 1978 the Produttori bought some land just outside the town, and aging takes place there. The

BARBARESCO

RISERVA

MONTESTEFANO

PRODUTTORI del BARBARESCO

ALC. 14.5% BY VOL. · CONTAINS SULFITES · 750 ML
REO WINE · ESTATE BOTTLED · PRODUCT OF ITALY
SELECTED & IMPORTED BY
V.I.A.S. IMPORTS L.T.D. · NEW YORK, N.Y.

coop represents 110 ha in Barbaresco, which makes it the largest producer in the appellation. Indeed, through the seventies it was one of the only three important producers (together with Gaja and Giacosa).

This is one of the most distinguished cooperatives in Italy. Its origins date from 1894, when a group of nine growers combined their production, but it closed in the 1920s. It reopened as a formal cooperative in 1958 with 19 families; today 54 farmers contribute their grapes. Manager Aldo Vacco explains that it started with three crucial decisions that still stand. The first was only to make wine from Nebbiolo in Barbaresco, even though through the early period Dolcetto or Barbera were more successful. The second decision was 100% delivery. "Our farmers cannot keep back some of their Nebbiolo grapes or sell some to other producers." (This applies only to Nebbiolo, some of the farmers have Dolcetto or Barbera, which they can handle separately.) "The third rule was when we decided to reward quality. Payment depends on tonnage and quality of grapes. It's common sense now, but back in the fifties and sixties it was very unusual." This is a true cooperative in which the 54 farmers share the profits. They are paid for the grapes on delivery, but then later they get a share of the profits.

The Produttori divide production into three categories. The Langhe Nebbiolo is based strictly on selection, but usually comes from lower quality grapes, young vines, or plots lower down the hill. It's about 20% of production. "It's the largest growing category of wine in the region," says Aldo, "but it's very expensive to declassify; every bottle I produce is a bottle of Barbaresco I give up." About half of production is the Barbaresco, a blend from all the villages. The other 30% is a Riserva line that comes from the nine most historic villages in Barbaresco. "We started to make them in 1967 with four, from 1978 there were all nine. It's all or none, depending on vintage."

"All Riservas are made in exactly the same way, some have more perfume, some have more tannin, but we don't do anything to tame them, we just want to showcase the wine," Aldo explains. Riservas were made in 2000, 2001, 2004, and 2005. "Since then we could have made them every year but we gave up 2006 because we thought it was too aggressive and by giving up the single vineyards we made a better Barbaresco. In the old days when we gave up single vineyards we sold off more wine in bulk, now we make more Barbaresco and Nebbiolo Langhe." Then Riservas were made in all vintages except 2010, 2012, and 2018. Production is traditional: the wine stays in Barbaresco in stainless steel until the Spring, and then is transferred to large casks at the new facility.

The wines are good representations of their appellations. The Langhe Nebbiolo shows as a classic second wine, in the style of the Barbaresco, but lighter. It has only six months in cask. "If I wait one more year I have the right to put Barbaresco on it." Because members have vineyards all over the area, the communal Barbaresco is always a good representation of the vintage. 2018 reflects the vintage (there were no crus this year) with a touch of asperity, 2017 had 30% less production than normal but all the cuvées were made, and its round, full, and approachable, 2016 is taut and the most classical, 2015 is already showing elegance, and 2014 is the lightest. Vintage variation in the Barbaresco is evened out a little in poor years by the inclusion of the top lots that would have otherwise have made the Riserva. So 2012 shows quite well relative to the 2013. The Riservas express their terroirs, from the lighter Rio Sordo (where there is sand in the soil), to the fruity Moccagatta, which tends to a classic earthiness, and the most structured Montefico, which shows real elegance once the tannins resolve. In an area where most producers have only a couple of Crus, the Produttori offers an unusual opportunity to compare many terroirs.

Alfredo Prunotto   *

Localita' Bussia Soprana 90, 12065 Monforte d'Alba (CN)	📞 *+39 0173 78334*
@ *bussia@prunotto.it*	👤 *Emmanuele Baldi*
🌐 *www.prunotto.it*	🔘 *Barolo [map p. 34]*
📅 🏭 🍷 🥂 🍇 *65 ha; 850,000 btl*	🍶 *Barolo, Bussia*

Prunotto encapsulates the history of wine production in Barolo. Alfredo Prunotto helped to found the winery in 1905 as a cooperative. When it ran into economic problems in 1922, Alfredo took it over, renamed it, and ran it successfully until he retired in 1956, when it was sold to brothers Beppe and Tino Colla. Marchesi Antinori managed distribution from 1989, and then purchased the estate when the Colla brothers retired in 1994.

Grapes had been sourced from growers, but Antinori established estate vineyards, adding plots in Bussia (in the Monforte commune), Bric Turot in Barbaresco, Costamiole (for Barbera d'Asti), and Treiso (for Moscato). Most recently, 3 ha were added in Serralunga's Cerretta. Barolo and Barbaresco account for about a quarter of production, and the Barbera d'Asti is about half. Communal Barolo and Barbaresco come from purchased grapes, while estate grapes are used for the Bussia Cru (first produced as a single vineyard wine in 1961: today Prunotto owns a large plot shaped like an amphitheater) and the Colonello from a 1 ha lieu-dit within Bussia. Bussia and Colonnella are produced at the winery in Bussia (which Prunotto bought in the seventies), but the other cuvées are produced at a winery built in 1999 in Alba (where the coop in fact started).

"Vinification is more or less similar for all the Nebbiolos, because we believe the differences should come from the soil, not from winemaking," says winemaker Gianluca Torrengo. The style moved in the direction of greater extraction from the late eighties, and then reverted to a lighter, more elegant approach from the late 2000s. There are new tronconique fermentation tanks, so pushing down the cap is gentler, and the wines age in botti mostly of French oak. "Slavonian oak gives a little more austerity, Alliers tends to provide sweeter tannin." There's a big difference between the masculine 2005 Bussia and the more feminine 2009. "In the last ten years we have realized that Bussia is powerful enough anyway, we don't need to express that, but to balance it," says Emmanuele Baldi.

The Prunotto wines are all classically light, you might say translucent, in color, but full of flavor. The Langhe Nebbiolo comes from Roero, and is fragrant and light, the Barbaresco (60% from Barbaresco village, 40% from Treiso), is riper on the palate, and Barolo, from the most powerful villages (50% Monforte, 50% Serralunga) is deeper with more obvious fruits. "Tannins in Barolo are always a bit tighter," Gianluca says. In the Crus, Bric Turot is deeper than Barbaresco, while Bussia is deeper than the communal Barolo. The top wine is Colonnella Riserva, taut when released, and amazingly delicate by a decade after the vintage. While Bussia moves in the same direction and is a more complex version of the communal Barolo, Colonnella is on another level for delicacy. The single-vineyard Barbera, Pian Romualdo, comes from Monforte; ripe and round, it's an unusual Barbera that can age.

Ratti   *

Fraz. Annunziata 7, 12064 La Morra (CN)   📞 +39 0173 50185
@ info@ratti.com   👤 Pietro Ratti
🌐 www.ratti.com   🔴 Barolo [map p. 35]
🗓️ ⚒️ 🍇 🛢️ 🚜 45 ha; 450,000 btl   🍶 Barolo, Marcenasco

Halfway up from the valley to the hilltop village of La Morra is the little village of Annunziata, where Renato Ratti built a new winery on a turn in the road. The estate was created in 1965 when Renato Ratti purchased his first vineyard, and started to produce the Marcenasco Cru (quite an innovation at the time). The approach was modern, using short fermentation in rotary fermenters followed by aging in barriques for two years. During the seventies, Renato purchased more vineyards in the commune of La Morra. Renato became an important figure in Barolo, producing a classification of Barolo and Barbaresco that is still regarded as definitive. In 1988, when he was only 19, Pietro Ratti took over, following his father's death. The striking new postmodern winery was constructed in 2002. The old Abbey of the Annunziata, where the first wine was made, has been turned into a museum of the wines of Alba. With the 50th anniversary in 2015, the name changed simply to Ratti.

Vinification is now more traditional; "we still use barriques, but we are moving back to 50 hl casks for Barolo," Pietro says. The Langhe Nebbiolo Ochetti comes from sandy soils in Roero. It's supple, relatively soft, and a little more lifted aromatically than Barolo. Marcenasco has been used for the name of the Barolo blend since 1970, and comes from three vineyards around the winery and a plot higher up in La Morra. More refined than the Langhe Nebbiolo, it is quite approachable. In 2015 there was a switch to using a submerged cap for fermentation, and the wine is now a little tighter. Conca is now the name of the Cru that used to be Marcenasco, and the 0.7 ha vineyard was replanted in 1994. It shows more varied aromatics than Marcenasco and a great sense of finesse. Rocche dell'Annunziata is 500m up the hill from Conca and has more floral aromatics and a more delicate palate, showing layers of flavor as it ages, Going up the range there is increasing refinement rather than extra power. There are no Riservas. "I do not believe in Riserva as a concept," says Pietro, "it is not a quality determinant, in Italy it's just a matter of aging."

Other wines include Barbera d'Asti and Barbera and Dolcetto d'Alba. In addition, Villa Pattono, which comes from an estate the Rattis inherited in Asti, is a blend of Barbera, Cabernet, and Merlot from Monferrato, and I Cedri is a Sauvignon Blanc.

Francesco Rinaldi   *

via Crosia 30, 12060 Barolo (CN)	📞 *+39 0173 440484*
@ *info@rinaldifrancesco.it*	👤 *Paola & Piera Rinaldi*
⊕ *www.rinaldifrancesco.it*	💿 *Barolo [map p. 36]*
🗓 🏭 🍷 🛢 🚜 *11 ha; 70,000 btl*	🍶 *Barolo*

"My grandfather bought the vineyards that we have today, all in Barolo," says Piera Rinaldi. The estate dates from 1870 (the family split in 1922 when Francesco continued the original domain and his brother Giuseppe founded his own estate; see profile). Luciano Rinaldi took over in 1941, and since the 1990s the estate has been run by his nieces, Paola and Piera. The old buildings are on the road between Cannubi and Brunate.

This old-line family estate is firmly in the traditional camp, with the cellars stuffed with botti of Slavonian oak. "We've produced in a traditional way since the beginning, but we are not so intense as some: for us tradition means long maceration and aging in large botti." The Barolo spends 36 months aging; a Riserva from Cannubi has just been introduced and spends 42 months. Although aging is traditional, the estate has been modernized: bottling was moved to Alba in the 1930s for better distribution, and vinification has now been updated with new presses.

The Nebbiolo d'Alba comes from Roddi (in Verduno). It has an approachable style, quite silky, which you might call feminine. A plot at the bottom of Brunate has just been replanted and will be used for a Langhe Nebbiolo. The communal Barolo includes grapes from four crus; the single-vineyard wines are Cannubi and Brunate. A blend from vineyards in Barolo, La Morra, and Castiglione Falletto, the Barolo makes a very fine impression, very much the delicate style of Barolo, moving towards savory as it ages. You might imagine that the delicacy reflects the Rocche dell'Annunziata cru, which provides a third of the grapes. Cannubi adds some firmness, but stays with the house style of elegance and precision. The Barbera d'Alba and Dolcetto d'Alba come from vineyards in Barolo. About 10-15% of grapes come from long-term relationships with local growers.

Giuseppe Rinaldi ★★★

Via Monforte 2, 12060 Barolo (CN)	📞 *+39 0173 56156*
@ *info@rinaldigiuseppe.com*	👤 *Marta & Carlotta Rinaldi*
⊕ *rinaldigiuseppe.com*	🌐 *Barolo [map p. 36]*
📅 🏭 🍇 🍂 *8 ha; 35,000 btl*	🍶 *Langhe Nebbiolo*

"My sister and I are the fifth generation," says Carlotta Rinaldi. "The family was making wine, although not here, before it split into three Rinaldi wineries. My great grandfather got 10 ha of polyculture, including 6.5 ha of vineyards, which are the same vineyards we have today." (Another 1.3 ha were rented in 2019.) The gothic house, where the family live upstairs, and the winery is downstairs, was built in 1916. It lives up to the reputation of the domain as the most traditional estate in Barolo. Estate vineyards are in four plots, all in Barolo commune within a mile or two of the winery. The largest is 3 ha in Ravera, the coolest plot, now about half Nebbiolo, with the rest divided between Dolcetto, Barbera, and Freisa. "It's the only plot we have that's not south-facing," Carlotta explains. "It used to have early-ripening varieties, but with climate warming my Dad grafted some over to Nebbiolo."

Battista Rinaldi took over in 1947 and was known for producing two wines: the Barolo blend from all the parcels; and the single-vineyard Brunate (which included a small amount of Le Coste). His son Giuseppe (known as Beppe) took over in 1992 and stopped producing the Brunate as a single-vineyard wine. Committed to the tradition of blending—every single-vineyard site has shortcomings, he said—he produced two cuvées, each from a blend of two crus: Brunate-Le Coste and Cannubi San Lorenzo-Ravera. Each represents a blend between a vineyard with heavier soils (the calcareous marl of Le Coste or Cannubi) with one based on lighter sandstone (Brunate or Ravera). "Brunate can be austere, Le Coste is always more lifted and fresher," Carlotta says. "The blend used to change each year to get the best balance, usually around 75% of Brunate for Brunate-Le Coste." It hardly needs saying that both age only in large botti of Slavonian oak: Giuseppe's disdain for barriques was unbounded.

The policy of naming the wines for the complementary vineyards ran into trouble when the definition of the Crus was accompanied by a regulation that only one cru could be named on the label. So the blends changed from 2010. Brunate-Le Coste became simply Brunate, by reducing the proportion of Le Coste to the limit of 15% for an alternative source allowed in a named cru. The remaining juice from Le Coste has been added to what used to be Cannubi San Lorenzo-Ravera, which has been renamed Tre Tine, and is now around 50-60% Ravera, 30-40% Cannubi, and 5% Le Coste. "For Brunate we have to follow regulations, but for Tre Tine we don't have fixed quantities." Production increased slightly in 2018 with the rental of a 1 ha vineyard in Bussia.

Brunate-Le Coste and Cannubi San Lorenzo-Ravera were always regarded as two of the top wines of Barolo; the replacement blends appear set to retain the same mystique. Marta Rinaldi was taking over winemaking, and Carlotta was taking over vineyard management, when Giuseppe died in 2018, and his policy of blending has remained unchanged. The style is traditional. "Barolo must be an austere, powerful wine, without fruit," Giuseppe used to say, but that really under-rates the appeal of the wines even in their first years.

The wines are surely among the most intense in Barolo. Even the Barbera d'Alba gives an impression of power with concentrated fruits. The Langhe Nebbiolo, which is effectively declassified from Barolo, is perhaps the most concentrated example of the appellation I have encountered. The most approachable of the Nebbiolos, it still shows hallmark intensity. Tre Tine is dense to the point of seeming monolithic when it is young; it needs time to develop flavor variety. The Brunate displays characteristic purity, shining through the intense black fruits. Sheer fruit intensity is the first thing you notice in all the wines; the sense of tannic backbone shows after.

The wines taste as though the vines are very old and yields are very low, but that is not in fact the case: yields are around 50 hl/ha, and vine age varies, but averages about 30 years. When pressed for the reason for the difference, Carlotta says it's just the combination of superb terroir and respect for the soil. There are no tricks here. "When I walk through the vineyards," she says, "I see cover crops that have been planted elsewhere, but in our vineyards there are just the flowers that grow naturally." There is no green harvest, because Giuseppe believed that the vine should find its own balance. The wines are unique. It's not particularly easy to arrange a visit here, because the phone is rarely answered, and there is no official email, but *il vaut le detour.*

Albino Rocca *

Strada Ronchi 18, 12050 Barbaresco (CN)   📞 +39 0173 635145

@ roccaalbino@roccaalbino.com   👤 Daniela & Monica Rocca

🌐 www.albinorocca.com   ◉ Barbaresco [map p. 39]

📅 🏭 🍇 🌿 18 ha; 100,000 btl   🍷 Barbaresco, Ronchi

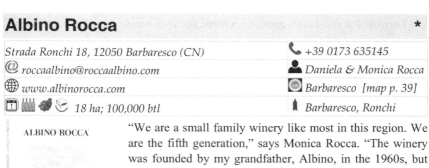

"We are a small family winery like most in this region. We are the fifth generation," says Monica Rocca. "The winery was founded by my grandfather, Albino, in the 1960s, but we've been growing grapes here for generations." The first Barbaresco labeled with the domain name was produced in 1970. Albino's son, Angelo, expanded the vineyards, and began to vinify individual crus separately. Since 2012 the estate has been in the hands of the next generation, Daniela, Monica and Paola, who is the winemaker together with her husband. The original cellars are under the house where Paola lives, and were expanded by building farther into the hillside.

"Today of course we are changing the style of the wine. When my father started to vinify the single vineyards separately, he emphasized their differences with differences in vinification. Vinification now is the same for the Barbaresco and the single vineyard wines. We are not using anything that gives oak influence," Monica says. Angelo began to phase out barriques in 2004, and since 2010 everything has been aged for two years in 20 hl casks of German or Eastern European oak.

The winery is located in the Vigna Ronchi cru, which the family began to plant in 1895; it now provides 70% of production. The other original holdings are in the Ovello cru, and a small vineyard in Cottà (just below the winery); a small plot in the Montersino cru was added in 2012, at the southern boundary of Barbaresco. There are 4 single-vineyard wines. "Total production has remained the same, but we have divided it more," Monica says. In top years one botti is aged longer to become a Riserva from Ronchi. Since 2013 the Angelo cuvée has been produced as a blend of a selection of the best lots from Ronchi, Ovello, and Montersino.

Nebbiolo d'Alba comes from a vineyard owned by Paola's husband's family. The style is fragrant and fresher than Barbaresco. Ronchi is the benchmark for the domain. It's the most approachable of the Barbaresco cuvées, moving in a fragrant direction. Cottà comes from six rows of 60-year old vines just in front of Ronchi, where the soils are clay and limestone. It has a stern structure when young, with a tannic bite, and needs time to reach its mature elegance. Montersino is at 300m elevation with sandier soil, and is finer and tauter. "Ronchi has more of a Barolo style, whereas Ovello and Montersino show more the elegance of Barbaresco," Monica says. Angelo shows its longer maceration and fermentation in wood with the finest structure of all.

Bruno Rocca ★★

Strada Rabajà 60, 12050 Barbaresco (CN)
@ info@brunorocca.it
⊕ www.brunorocca.it
◌ ╱ ❀ ▸ 15 ha; 70,000 btl

📞 +39 0173 635112
👤 Luisa Rocca
▣ Barbaresco [map p. 39]
▯ Barbaresco

The Roccas have owned land in Barbaresco since 1834, but today's winery is a story of the last three generations. The winery is a modest-looking group of buildings off the road about a kilometer from Barbaresco, in the Rabajà Cru. Built around a courtyard and larger than is apparent, there's a splendid terrace behind the buildings with a view right across the vineyards. Standing on the terrace, you feel the microclimate of Rabajà in the wind that is channeled across the vineyard by two hills. Underneath the buildings, the modern cellar is in three storeys, built into the hillside in 2008 to allow wine to be moved by gravity. "The library is now where my father used to park the tractor," says Luisa Rocca.

The land here was bought in the fifties by Francesco Rocca. "The grapes were already known to be good, but 1 km at that time was a long way from the center. Grandfather used to sell the grapes in Alba every year, and the first and easiest grapes to sell were always those from Rabajà," says Luisa. The winery started in 1978 when Francesco's son Bruno started estate bottling. His children, Francesco and Luisa are now involved, Francesco with winemaking and Luisa with marketing. This is very much a family affair—"there is no consultant, the wines are made by Bruno and Francesco," says Luisa. The wines include, Barbera d'Asti, Barbera d'Alba, Chardonnay, Nebbiolo d'Alba, and several Barbarescos. The general Barbaresco blend comes from young vines (although not the youngest, from three vineyards in the Neive area). Coparosa comes from two vineyards (one in Neive and one in Treiso), but 2013 is the last vintage because the lease on one of the vineyards expired. Maria Adelaide is a selection from several vineyards. Rabajà is the leading single vineyard wine. The Currà Riserva will be added with the 2012 vintage. "This is important because it's different from Rabajà, which is powerful and rich, but Currà is elegant and feminine. It's the first Riserva we will make and it's Francesco's project so it symbolizes the passing of the generations," says Luisa.

Winemaking is very particular here, focused on a natural approach to highlight elegance. Fermentation uses yeast which were isolated from the Rabajà vineyard in a four year project. The grapes are broken very gently by using vibration in an interesting looking machine that also selects the berries. "I don't want to crush the bunches, I would rather do more pump-over than crush," says Francesco. Carbon dioxide is used during sorting and crushing to minimize the need for SO2. "We use very gentle fermentation (in a mix of conventional vats and some rotary fermenters), I'm looking for elegance and balance not power."

Barbera is matured entirely in barriques, the Barbarescos also in barriques, Rabajà spends one year in barrique and one year in cask, and the Currà Riserva spends three years in large casks," because the barriques made it too fat, we were looking for elegance." The minimum age for the oak is 14 years—"We prefer wood that doesn't add anything to the wine. You need old wood with not too much toast."

The Roccas do not consider themselves modern. "I consider modernists are people who make wine in the laboratory," says Luisa, "traditionalists are people who make wine in the vineyard." Yet the wines are very approachable. Bruno is not patient, say his children, he has always made wines more on the approachable side. "We don't believe that lots of tannins necessarily mean the wine will age well. When you use more extraction you have a wine that is more powerful and richer, but not elegant." Bruno describes his approach as, "Our philosophy has become much more focused on the terroir. In the past we couldn't do this because of the limitations of the winery. Now that the next generation are interested, we can make more investments, and we plan to move to 100% single vineyards."

The style here is very fine, from the lightest Barbaresco to the weighty Rabajà, there's a sense of extremely finely textured tannins, silky, but always ending in an impression of finesse.

Rocche Dei Manzoni   *

Loc. Manzoni Soprani 3, 12065 Monforte d'Alba (CN)	📞 *+39 0173 78421*
@ *info@rocchedeimanzoni.it*	👤 *Rodolfo Migliorini*
🌐 *www.rocchedeimanzoni.it*	🔵 *Barolo [map p. 38]*
📅 🏛 🦌 🍃 *50 ha; 250,000 btl*	🍷 *Barolo, Big d'Big*

ROCCHE DEI MANZONI®

BAROLO
DENOMINAZIONE DI ORIGINE CONTROLLATA E GARANTITA
ROCCHE

MESSO IN BOTTIGLIA ALL'ORIGINE DAL
PODERE ROCCHE DEI MANZONI
DI VALENTINO
MONFORTE D'ALBA - ITALIA

750 ml ℮   CONTIENE SOLFITI - CONTAINS SULFITES   14,5% vol

This may be the principal remaining arch-modernist in Barolo. Founded by Valentino Migliorini—a Michelin-starred chef in Emilia-Romagna—in 1974, the property started as a farm with a farmhouse and a few vines. The farmhouse has been renovated and is the only original building; a whole set of new winery buildings has constructed on the site, together with a family house and a swimming pool (which is above the storage cellar and serves to insulate it). The building look traditional, but are practical inside. The most striking feature is the rotunda in the barrel cellar—you can see it from miles around—with a ceiling decorated in Florentine style with angels and other biblical scenes, and pillars decorated with mythical figures. They call it the cathedral.

Valentino gave up his restaurant in 1990 and became a full time winemaker. He was called the foreigner locally, not only because of his origins in Emilia Romagna but also because he introduced new types of wines–Bricco Manzoni (80% Nebbiolo and 20% Barbera), which was the first overt blend in Langhe, and a series of sparkling wines. Valentino started with 10 ha. All the vineyards are in Monforte but are more extensive now. After Valentino died in 2007, his son Rodolfo took over.

Vineyards are all in Monforte. The domain expanded in 1998 by purchasing the Pianpolvere Soprano winery, also in Monforte, but they continue to be run separately. The approach has always been modernist, with wines aged in barriques, but since 2008 concrete eggs have been used also. With a generally innovative approach, there's also a focus on art and music; the winery is known for its four cuvées of sparkling wine, made from Pinot Noir and Chardonnay by Méthode Champenois, which are played music while they mature.

In more conventional wines, the communal Barolo comes from Monforte, and other cuvées come from named vineyards. Vinification starts in rotary fermenters. Langhe Nebbiolo ages for 1 year in oak plus 6 months in concrete. Barolo ages for 3 years with racking up to 4 times per year. The entire production ages in new oak (except for Dolcetto). There are both barriques and 500-liter tonneaux of French oak. The Barolo goes into concrete eggs for a few months after the barriques.

The Langhe Nebbiolo is light and fragrant, quite nutty in previewing the Barolo, but the lighter character allows the alcohol to show more obviously. The Bricco Manzoni blend has 14 days maceration and spends two years in new barriques. It is much darker than the Langhe Nebbiolo, more intense, granular, and the new oak is more evident. In fact, oak, in the form of sweet vanillin is the dominant influence on all the wines for several years after release. The Barolo is finer than Bricco Manzoni. but shows the same modernist influence. The Barolo Big d'Big is more of a selection from the same set of sites and is finer than the generic Barolo; in fact, style is more in line with the Langhe Nebbiolo, but rounder and deeper, and again a bit more new oak. It is quite elegant for a modernist. In fact, I would put the wines in pairs, Bricco Manzoni leading to Barolo in a more powerful style, and Langhe Nebbiolo leading Barolo Big 'd Big in more elegant style.

Moving to the Crus, intensity increases in the same modern style. Bricco San Pietro is more refined than Barolo Big 'd Big, but has a lot of tannic structure and is loaded with vanillin from new oak. Perno makes a sleeker and more intense impression in the same general style as Bricco San Pietro. The Riserva comes from Castelletto. Only the Barolo Big 'd Big really has the oak well enough integrated to start soon after release; the others need at least an extra 3 years.

Giovanni Rosso   *

Loc. Baudana 6, 12050 Serralunga d'Alba (CN)	📞 +39 0173 613340
@ info@giovannirosso.com	👤 Davide Rosso
🌐 www.giovannirosso.com	🔘 Barolo [map p. 37]
🗓 ⚒ 🍷 🔩 18 ha; 130,000 btl	❚ Barolo, Commune di Serralunga

This is basically a new estate, started when Davide Rosso returned in 2001 after qualifying in oenology in Alba, and then working in Burgundy, to join his parents Ester and Giovanni. The estate was founded in the 1890s, and was focused on vineyards in Serralunga, with about 11 separate holdings, until Davide expanded. In addition to other areas in the Barolo DOC, in 2016 he bought 6.5 ha of vines on Etna, where he produces both red and white wine. Giovanni Rosso restructured the vineyards in the 1980s, so most of the vines are now around 30-years old. Giovanni mostly sold grapes to the cooperative, although estate bottling started in 1995. Davide took over in 2009 when Giovanni died, and is generally credited with revitalizing the estate.

The approach is traditional with wines aged mostly in botti. The Barbera d'Alba and the Langhe Nebbiolo both come mostly from Roddino with some grapes from Serralunga. The Barbera gets brief exposure to oak, or none at all in warm vintages. The Langhe Nebbiolo has 15 days maceration and ages for up to one year in botti, but with less or no oak in warm vintages. They have very much the same light entry-level style, with red fruit impressions.

Introduced in 2012, the classic Barolo comes 40% from 8 vineyards in Serralunga, 30% from Castiglione Falletto, and 10% from Barolo commune. The lots from Castiglione Falletto and Barolo are provided by collaborations with a winery in each commune. The style is quite different from the Langhe Nebbiolo, light and fruit-driven, but moving in a savory direction. The Barolo Commune di Serralunga cuvée, a blend from 8 vineyards in Serralunga, is a step-up, hiding the power of the commune behind a sleek impression inclined to red fruits, but the tannic backbone is quite powerful and needs 3 years or so after release to resolve, so start to drink about 7 years after the vintage.

All the crus have 25 days maceration, followed by aging up to 36 months in botti, depending on vintage, followed by 6 months in stainless steel. Serra shows minerality on the nose and tension on the palate, and becomes sleek and velvety as it ages. Cerretta has an extremely fine texture and a great sense of precision. Vigna Rionda is the flagship of the domain. In 2010-2011 most (0.8 ha) of the vineyard was replanted. The 0.4 ha of old vines that were not replaced was used to make the Barolo Vigna Rionda cuvee. The new vines were used for the Ester Canale Langhe Nebbiolo, a baby Barolo with shorter aging. This was made until the 2021 vintage. From 2022, the two plots have been blended to make the Vigna Rionda cuvée.

The reputation of the cuvée is so high that the Ester Canale Langhe Nebbiolo priced between the Cerretta or Serra Crus and the Vigna Rionda (now called Ester Canale, previously called Tomasso Canale after an earlier member of the family). It would in fact be marked as an excellent Barolo in most blind tastings. It is sleek with that underlying sense of power marking Serralunga, but more approachable than the Crus, perhaps because of its shorter aging (just 12 months in botti). The last vintages of the Vigna Rionda solely from the old vines show that sleek sense of restrained power that marks Serralunga. The first vintage of the full blend (2022) does not at all diminish that impression. It is one of the most complete expressions of Serralunga from the commune.

Luciano Sandrone ★★

Via Pugnane 4, 12060 Barolo (CN)   📞 *+39 0173 560023*
@ *info@sandroneluciano.com*   👤 *Luciano Sandrone*
🌐 *www.sandroneluciano.com*   ⬤ *Barolo [map p. 36]*
📅 🌿 🚜 *27 ha; 105,000 btl*   🍷 *Barolo, Le Vigne*

"I believe that Luciano straddles the divide between modern and traditional in a way that no one else does. He's constantly experimenting," says Alan Manley, who has been at the Sandrone winery since 2008. Built in 1998, the winery has a group of quite spacious modern buildings around a courtyard, with a workmanlike interior sunk into the hillside. Although there are vines immediately around the winery, "this is not our vineyard, this is a horrible place for Nebbiolo, but many people are planting Nebbiolo in north-facing vineyards where Dolcetto used to be grown."

Luciano Sandrone does not come from a wine family, but went to agrarian school, then started working at traditional producers. In 1977 he put his life savings into buying a piece of land that he heard was for sale at Cannubi Boschis. The first vintage was made in 1978 in his mother's garage, and was only 1473 bottles. Everything developed from the sale of these bottles, when he met a distributor in 1982 who bought them all, and continued to be his export agent for the next twenty years.

Additional vineyards were added every few years, and today Sandrone produces five wines, all from estate grapes (including a small proportion of rented vineyards): Dolcetto and Barbera d'Alba, the Nebbiolo d'Alba Valmaggiore (the vineyard is just north of Alba), Barolo le Vigne, and Barolo Cannubi Boschis. Le Vigne is a blend from four vineyards in Barolo (all the holdings except for Cannubi). "Luciano wanted to make a top blend in the classic tradition." It's been made since 1990, although then it came from only two vineyards, and sources have changed since.

Vinification is very particular here, in stainless steel, although Luciano is experimenting with two wood fermenters. Luciano is fanatical about ensuring not only that indigenous yeast are used, but that every lot is fermented specifically by its own yeast, so every piece of equipment is sterilized between loads of grapes. Fermentation is started by using a pied de cuve (some grapes are selected from the vineyard about a week before harvest and allowed to start fermentation to form a starter colony). Everything goes into 500 liter tonneaux, about 20% new—"we do not use barriques. pump-over, punch-down, or délestage are used according to what Luciano decides is appropriate for the year; that's why he straddles modernism and traditionalism." About 20% of the oak is new for the Barolos. Every tonneau is tasted separately; there is no second wine, as anything not of sufficient quality is sold off in bulk.

I suppose I would call Sandrone a modernist because the wines are so smooth and elegant, with tannins completely mastered. The hallmark of the house is the exceedingly fine structure of the wine. The Nebbiolo d'Alba Valmaggiore is light and fragrant, Le Vigne is slower to develop but makes an elegant, savory impression; this is Sandrone's nod to tradition as it is a blend of several vineyards with complementary characteristics (typically including Serralunga, Castiglione Falletto, Barolo, and Novello). Cannubi Boschis has that silky sheen of the top Barolos with lovely aromatics. The Cannubi Boschis has been labeled as Barolo Aleste since the 2013 vintage (the name is a combination of Luciano's grandchildren).

A new cuvée was introduced with the 2013 vintage (released in 2019). It originated when Luciano noticed a single vine with unusually small berries, deeper color, and less vigorous growth. Essentially it's a new subcultivar of Nebbiolo. During the past thirty years, this has been extended by field grafting, and finally has produced the Vite Talin cuvée. It ages in tonneau with 50% new oak for two years followed by one year in large casks.

Paolo Scavino ★★

Via Alba Barolo 157, 12060 Castiglione Falletto (CN)   📞 *+39 0173 62850*
@ *info@paoloscavino.com*   👤 *Elisa Scavino*

Founded in 1921 by Lorenzo Scavino and his son Paolo, the estate is now run by the third and fourth generations, Enrico Scavino together with his daughters Enrica and Elisa. It was Enrico who really built up its present reputation from the 1950s. Purchased over many years, the vineyards consist of twenty different plots scattered among all the communes. All the vineyards are in Barolo DOC, and about 60% of production goes into Barolo. Much larger than you would expect from the outside, the cellar was extended in 2003, and was renovated again in 2016.

Scavino is a modernist, much concerned about tannin management. They were among the first to introduce rotary fermenters, in 1993. In the 1990s, the Barolos aged in barriques for a year, with one third new oak, one third 1-year, and one third 2-year. Tonneaux were used for the second year, but then there was some backing off from oak exposure, and the second year was spent in large casks, also of French oak. Now Scavino has reverted to more traditional approach; aging is the same for all Barolos, with 22 months in oak, 95% in large casks., followed by 7-8 months in stainless steel. The only difference in aging is for Riserva which spends 30 months in oak and an extra year in

The range of Nebbiolos starts with the Langhe Nebbiolo, which ages for 6 months in used barriques, and then some time in stainless steel. "We don't like to consider the Langhe as a baby Barolo, it is really the expression of Nebbiolo." The style is fresh and light. The Barolo *tout court* is a blend from eight plots in Barolo, Castiglione, and Serralunga; still light in style, it is rounder and deeper. A step up, Caro Bric is a fantasy name, actually an acronym for the constituent vineyards, for a blend that comes from Cannubi, Rocche di Castiglione, and Bric dël Fiasc. However, Scavino's lease on the Cannubi vineyard ended in 2018, so after that both the Cannubi Cru and Caro Bric ceased production. "Carobric wouldn't be the same without Cannubi."

The single vineyards come from all over the DOC. Bricco Ambrogio comes from the northeast border in Roddi. Scavino was the first to bottle this as a single Cru. "For us it is the most feminine expression of Barolo." It's fragrant and perfumed. Moving to Novella in the south, the Ravera Cru is deeper, but still generally elegant in style. At the top of a hill, it has eastern exposure. Global warming was a factor in deciding to buy it in 2015.

First bottled as a single cru in 1978, Bric dël Fiasc, close to the winery in Castiglione Falletto, which the family has owned since the very beginning, is the flagship cuvée. "The secret of this vineyard is that it is really central in Barolo, just between the eastern half of the DOC that's more powerful, and the western side that's more elegant. It gives a balance to the wine that is really unique." It's smooth and silky, with very fine tannic texture, taut in style, and the most elegant of all the cuvées. The top cuvée is Rocche dell'Annunziata, made only as a Riserva only in top vintages,

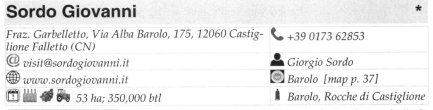

96

never more than 5000 bottles. This has that seamless character of top wines, with lots of flavor variety, but impossible to dissect. The style has lightened over the past ten years, the palate is smoother, tannic structure is less obvious, there is a move towards greater elegance.

Sordo Giovanni *

Fraz. Garbelletto, Via Alba Barolo, 175, 12060 Castiglione Falletto (CN)

@ visit@sordogiovanni.it

🌐 www.sordogiovanni.it

📅 🍴 🚲 53 ha; 350,000 btl

📞 +39 0173 62853

👤 Giorgio Sordo

📷 Barolo [map p. 37]

🍷 Barolo, Rocche di Castiglione

SORDO

BAROLO
DENOMINAZIONE DI ORIGINE CONTROLLATA E GARANTITA
PERNO

This traditional producer has a modern winery, built in 2014, connected to the old cellars by a long tunnel. It is one of the largest producers of Barolo, perhaps the largest owned by a single family. Giuseppe Sordo founded the estate in 1912, handed over to his son Giovanni who expanded by buying some top vineyards, and today it is run by Giovanni's son Giorgio. The new winery has a spacious tasting room and snazzy boutique, with a view across the vineyards and hills looking up to La Morra. It may be unique in owning vineyards in all eight communes of Barolo, and there is a correspondingly wide range of cuvées from different Crus, offering an opportunity to compare different areas and crus. Barolo is 80% of production, although recently Sordo has expanded into Roero and Timorasso. Cuvées include Dolcetto, Arneis, sparkling wine from Nebbiolo and Barolo Chinato and Grappa. Altogether there are 11 red cuvées and five white. The domain is into oenotourism, offering tours to demonstrate all aspects of production, through the winery down to the tasting room.

"We are a traditional producer, you will see only larger casks (mostly 50 hl and 100 hl)) and only Slavonian oak." All grapes are destemmed for both reds and whites, and then fermented in stainless steel. Maceration is 5-20 days for Langhe Nebbiolo, 6-10 weeks for Barolo-"we are keeping the tradition." Vinification is the same for all Barolo-"this is the only way you can taste the difference." Aging is up to 24 months. "We like clean wines, not oaky."

Barbera d'Alba comes from Castiglione Falletto and Serralunga and is vinified in stainless steel. The Barbera d'Alba Superiore comes from Perno, and ages for 12 months in 50 hl Slavonian oak. The first is light and fruity, the second is herbal and forceful: you would never know they come from the same grape variety. The range from Nebbiolo starts with Nebbiolo d'Alba, which is a blend from Roero and Langhe; the Langhe Nebbiolo Valmaggiore comes only from Roero. Both age for 12 months in 50 hl oak casks. The first is light and subdued, the second is riper and sweeter: it may actually have more tannin, but the tannins are less obvious.

The classic Barolo comes mostly from La Morra but includes a large number of plots in different areas. The blend can change each year. "We don't consider the classic Barolo as a lower level, it's a blend of crus." It's quite approachable, but the Rocche di Castiglione cuvée is if anything more immediately accessible, riper and rounder. Monprivato was added to the range in 2013 and is the most elegant cuvée. Monvigliero has greater density, Ravera is a little deeper, and Perno is the strongest—"with the iron in the soil, Perno is the most powerful Cru we have." Until recently, all the Crus were produced also as Riservas, but now only a single cru is selected to be a Riserva each year. House style is classic, elegant rather than powerful, not a trace of oak influence in sight, just the purity of the fruits, but the Riservas are more powerful, and personally I think they really are right to drink after close to twenty years.

Sottimano   *

Loc. Cotta 21, 12052 Neive (CN)	📞 *+39 0173 635186*
@ *info@sottimano.it*	👤 *Andrea & Rino Sottimano*
🌐 *www.sottimano.it*	🅖 *Barbaresco [map p. 39]*
📅 🏭 🍇 🍂 *18 ha; 85,000 btl*	🍷 *Barbaresco, Pajoré*

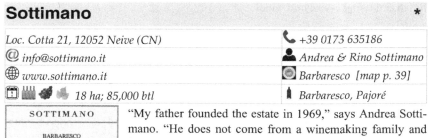

"My father founded the estate in 1969," says Andrea Sottimano. "He does not come from a winemaking family and had to work for another cellar while he began to buy vineyards." This is very much a family estate, with Andrea and his sister Elena now involved.

Reflecting the location at the border of Barbaresco and Neive communes, there are vineyards in all three communes. Rino Sottimano purchased vineyards in five Barbaresco crus; the Barbaresco cuvées from Cottá, Currá, Fausoni, and Pajoré are about a quarter of production, and another quarter comes from young vines (about 15 years old!) in the Basarin cru that are declassified to Langhe Nebbiolo. All wines are treated in the same way to showcase differences in terroir, and are aged in French barriques with about 10% new oak. As well as Nebbiolo, wines include a Piemonte Rosso from the indigenous variety Brachetto, Dolcetto d'Alba, and Barbera d'Alba (all from vineyards in the Barbaresco appellation). "Every wine we produce comes from a single vineyard, it doesn't matter if it's Dolcetto or Nebbiolo," Andrea says.

The style tends to be light and elegant, starting with the immediately approachable Lage Nebbiolo. "This is our equivalent to Barbaresco village—we don't make a Barbaresco blend. It should not be expensive, it should be something that young people can afford and try," says Andrea. "When I was young and working in Burgundy, I was impressed that I could buy village wine, although I had little money."

Barbaresco Pajoré shows a great leap in presence, smooth on the palate, with lively aromatics. Fausoni is more herbal, and deeper and rounder. Both Pajoré and Fausoni are deceptively approachable, because there is certainly tannic structure underneath, more obviously with Fausoni. Coming from the oldest vines, Cottá is richer, with firm tannins moving in a chocolaty direction and a sense of classic phenolics. There's a definite sense of needing more time going up the range. Cottá is a vin de garde that needs time to develop its complexity. Currá is tighter, with a finer structure, but needs even longer. It has the same aging as Cottá, but is kept in bottle a year longer before release. Development starts about eight years after the vintage, showing truffles and an increasing sense of minerality.

A little unusually, the top wine is a blend, the Barbaresco Riserva, selected from the oldest (60-70-year) vines in Cottá and Currá. Andrea has a high standard for Riserva. "My idea of Riserva is Monfortino or Giacosa. It should not be the most expensive wine just because it's kept longer, it should be something different." It spends longer on the skins, with 90 days fermentation, and then ages for 42 months. "It's old school," Andrea says. It is finer and more mineral, rather than more powerful, than the single-vineyard wines.

La Spinetta   *

Via Annunziata 17, 14054 Castagnole Lanze (Asti)	📞 *+39 0141 877396*
@ *info@la-spinetta.com*	👤 *Giorgio Rivetti*
⊕ *www.la-spinetta.com*	◉ *Asti*
🗓 ⛏ 🍇 🍂 *200 ha; 750,000 btl*	🍶 *Barbaresco, Bordini*

La Spinetta is quite an operation. Founded in Castagnole Lanze in Monferrato by Giuseppe and Lidia Rivetti in 1977, it began with Moscato d'Asti. The first red wine was not produced until 1985, a Barbera d'Asti. The first Barbaresco came from the Gallina vineyard in 1995. Other Barbarescos followed. In 2000, the Rivettis purchased a vineyard in Barolo. The Barbarescos are produced at Castognole under a special derogation, but the Barolos are produced at a winery that was constructed near Grinzane Cavour. A large (65 ha) estate was purchased in Tuscany in 2001, and the third winery, La Spinetta Casanova, was built there in 2007. And in 2011, La Spinetta purchased a sparkling wine producer, Contratto, in Piedmont. Today the estate is run by the next generation, Giorgio. Tastings are held at the headquarters in Castagnole, and although it's off the beaten track, there's a constant stream of visitors. There's an unusual policy of selling the most recent four vintages of the top wines at the same price.

The style here is determinedly modern. Barbera d'Alba is unusual in being planted in a south-facing plot in the Gallina cru of Barbaresco (where you would expect to find Nebbiolo, but the vines are 60-years old so are kept). Quite intense, it's similar in style to the Langhe Nebbiolo, which comes from young vines in the Starderi cru of Barbaresco. Both show black fruits with chocolaty overtones, but the Barbera is soft while the Nebbiolo has a tannic bite. There is no communal Barbaresco, but the Bordini cru is the "entry-level" cuvée; intended to be approachable in the short term, it's smoother than the Langhe Nebbiolo. All the reds ferment in rotary fermenters; then Langhe Nebbiolo ages for 12 months in barriques, and the

Barbarescos age for 16 months in one third new, one third 1-year, and one third 2-year barriques. There's been some backing-off from new oak, which used to be 100%.

The modernist approach shows less forcefully with the single-vineyard wines, which are calmer and less obviously fruity. Coming from sandy soils, Gallina is the finest and most elegant, but the most obvious change in style comes with Starderi, which comes from clay and is broader, denser, and more powerful, and Valeriano (in Treiso), which is the most complex and complete, with the greatest aromatic lift. Two Barolos come from the same vineyard in Grinzane Cavour: Garretti, from young vines on the lower part of the hill, is smooth and full, and Campé, a selection from older vines, is more intense, more black, with more lifted aromatics.

Pin, which is the biggest production, started in 1969 as a blend of 80% Barbera and 20% Nebbiolo, but now the proportions have almost reversed, with 65% Nebbiolo. It's been so successful that more vineyards have been bought to increase production.

Giorgio Rivetti would prefer to use only indigenous varieties, but could not find one with which to make a white wine, so the whites come from Chardonnay and Sauvignon Blanc.

G. D. Vajra   *

Piazza della Vite e del Vino,1 12060 Barolo (CN) Italy   +39 0173 56257

@ *welcome@gdvajra.it.*   *Francesca Vaira*

⊕ *www.gdvajra.it*   *Barolo [map p. 36]*

▯ ⚒ 🍇 ⚖   *Barolo, Albe*

60 ha; 400,000 btl   *Langhe Riesling*

"My passion for wine started when I was very young, and my dream was to become a winemaker. My father said I was mad," recollects Aldo Vajra. His father had planted vineyards in 1947, but no one in the family was involved in winemaking. Aldo took over and established the winery in 1972, when he was only 16, and he started estate bottling in 1978. This is now very much a family concern, with Aldo's children, Giuseppe (winemaker), Francesca, and Isidoro, all involved. The winery is located in Verge, the highest village in the appellation. The very large modern building is being expanded.

The estate is known for its dual character: on the one hand, Barolos are made by traditional winemaking, involving long maceration followed by aging in Slavonian botti. (They tried barriques, but Aldo decided that "they're very interesting but not what we are looking for." On the other hand, there is experimentation with varieties other than Nebbiolo. "The important things is to make good wine irrespective of the appellation," Aldo says. Aldo planted the first Riesling in the area, just below the winery. "The soils were not very suitable for Nebbiolo, but they are very good for

Riesling." The wine has a saline minerality that is quite different form the usual amorphous Italian white. "You have to be very precise with whites," he says, "you have more flexibility with reds."

Aldo is sometimes called 'the most modern of the traditionalists and the most traditional of the modernists.' Vajra is known for the lightness of its Barolos, which is partly due to a focus on high altitude vineyards, at 400-500m; in fact, the crus of Fossati, La Volta, Coste di Vergne, and Bricco delle Viole, at the top, were once thought able to produce classic wines only in warmer vintages, but that has changed with global warming. More recently Vajra acquired vineyards in Sinio, just outside the appellation, which go into the Langhe Nebbiolo, together with grapes from within the DOCG.

The house style is smooth, with a glossy sheen to the palate, running from the Dolcetto (where it cuts a faint background bitterness), through Barbera (all sheen and no tannins, but with acidity well tamed), and even the Kyè Langhe made from Freisa (an indigenous black variety where the tannins can bring a monolithic character). Langhe Nebbiolo ages in steel to give a very pure expression of the grape, fragrant, elegant, and glossy. The communal Barolo, called Albe, comes from a blend of three high-altitude plots around the winery, Coste di Vergne, Fossati, and La Volta and shows a firmness reflecting the clay soils. It's the most approachable of the Barolos. A perfect illustration of the difference between clay and sandy soils comes from Bricco delle Viole (from clay soils, which is firmer and deeper than the communal Barolo) and Coste di Rose (exceptionally fine and fragrant reflecting its sandy terroir). Ravera comes from a mix of soils types in the south and has the most lifted aromatics and greatest purity (following on from Coste di Rose), while Baudana (which has some limestone) offers the firmest, most traditional expression (following on from Bricco della Viole).

Giovanni Viberti *

Fraz. Vergne, Via Delle Viole, 30, 12060 Barolo (CN)	📞 *+39 0173 56192*
@ *info@viberti-barolo.com*	👤 *Claudio Viberti*
🌐 *www.viberti-barolo.com*	🔵 *Barolo [map p. 36]*
📅🗡✖🍇🍷🥂🍇 *24 ha; 190,000 btl*	🍷 *Barolo, Buon Padre*

"We concentrate on high altitude vineyards," says Claudio Viberti, whose historic vineyards are around Vergne, the highest point in Barolo DOCG at 400-500m. Antonio Viberti owned a hotel and restaurant in Vergne, and bought two vineyard parcels in 1923 to produce a house wine for the restaurant. He called it Buon Padre, after the restaurant. In 1967 his son Giovanni joined the business, and started the move towards producing wines for general sale. Giovanni's son Claudio took over in 2008. (His brother Gianluca founded a new winery, CasinaBric. His mother Maria remained the chef at the Buon Padre restaurant for forty years.) The small cellars of the original winery are under the restaurant. Another restaurant called Gemella was opened in Barolo in 2019, and the separate facilities for fermentation and aging are being replaced by a new winery with two storeys underground and an adjacent hotel. Visits are presently held at Buon Padre.

The heart of the holdings remains in Vergne, but there are now vineyards in 8 crus, all in Barolo commune, and long term contracts (for grapes from another 4 ha) with two growers in Monforte and Verduno. There are 10 ha of Nebbiolo, 8 ha of Barbera (which has become a major focus), and some Dolcetto and Chardonnay. Winemaking is a mix of modern (using rotary fermenters) and traditional (aging in large vertical casks called tini where the oak is steamed). "The oak is not toasted," Claudio says, "the goal is to use oak but not let it cover the taste of the grapes." Rotary fermenters are used for Barbera and Langhe Nebbiolo; Barolo uses a mix.

Buon Padre continues to be the flagship Barolo cuvée, including grapes from all the holdings. Even though the plots at Vergne are very close, there is substantial variation in exposure and some differences in soils. Specific plots are dedicated to Buon Padre or to single vineyard wines. "Some producers declassify barrels in which they don't see aging potential. In my opinion, that's a mistake. My style is to reflect the grapes of each plot. Bricco delle Viole is minty and balsamic, San Pietro gives the classic tar, La Volte is more powerful." The single-vineyard wines are all Riservas and the only difference in vinification is that they spend one year longer in oak. Some vineyards outside Vergne were added in 2012—Terlo, Albarella, and Ravera. Plots facing more or less south are used for Barolo, while plots facing west are used for the Langhe Nebbiolo.

Light and floral, moving towards balsamic notes, the Langhe Nebbiolo foreshadows the Barolo; Buon Padre is deeper but more delicate and virtually as approachable. Claudio calls his Langhe Nebbiolo the 'baby Barolo.' The single vineyards are all Riservas and spend one year longer in oak. Bricco delle Viole is sterner and firmer, but still leaning towards the perfumed side of Barolo. Balsamic notes are just evident on release, but 'booming' two years later. The sense of concentration and structure increases going to San Pietro and La Volte. The Barbera d'Alba Superiore, Bricco Arioli, is a blend from two vineyards in Bricco delle Viole; more recently Claudio has introduced another Barbera, called Gemella, in lighter style. There's a Chardonnay from vineyards in Vergne.

Vietti   **

Pizza Vittorio Veneto 5, 12060 Castiglione Falletto (CN)	📞 *+39 0173 62825*
@ *info@vietti.com*	👤
⊕ *www.vietti.com*	🏠 *Barolo [map p. 37]*
🗓 🏭 🐛 🍷	🍶 *Barbera d'Alba, Scarrone Vigna Vecchia*
70 ha; 400,000 btl	🍶 *Barolo, Ravera*

An old family estate which has been in Castiglione Falletto for five generations, Vietti is located in the heart—well really one might say at the top of—the hilltop

102

village. Set in two buildings around a charming courtyard, the only place to build the winery was below, so it extends for three storeys underground. The oldest part is right up against the medieval town walls, dating from the fifteenth century. Vietti were engaged in polyculture, and have been bottling Barolo since 1873, but the modern era started when Sabino Vietti returned from the States to take over in the early twentieth century. Known as the "crazy Americano," he had strange ideas such as buying land all over the area. So the family put its energy into buying vineyards not only in Castiglione, but also in the surrounding communes. Sabino's daughter Luciana married Alfredo Currado, who introduced single vineyard bottlings and also made white wine. Their son Luca Currado became the winemaker.

Now they have vineyards in 15 different crus. "We consider ourselves one of the most traditional wineries," says Elena Currado, "for example, in using very long maceration times, but many things that are modern are normal now. It's not just about botti and barriques." She describes Vietti's philosophy. "So long as you do not impose your personality, so long as you respect the soil, it's traditional." Vietti produces one blended Barolo and four single vineyard wines. "It would be very complex to produce 15 different Crus." All the wines are vinified by parcel. "After 24 months we select the lots. We bottle 4 single vineyards. Then we make the Villero Riserva if the year is extraordinary (made in 10 vintages between 1982 and 2007). From the other 10 Crus, we select lots to blend for the Castiglione Barolo, which is the flagship. We want it to be a great wine, of course, with more immediateness, as most of our wines are intended to be put aside." Lots that don't make it into Castiglione are declassified to Perbacco, which is intended to be the most approachable (and is effectively a second wine). Going up the line, the Lage is quite restrained, Castiglione shows more aromatic life and delicacy, and the single vineyard wines are yet more refined. There's also a Barbaresco, which has a more savory, earthy character.

In addition to the five Barolos, Vietti produce five Barberas. "We have always been known as a Barolo producer," says Elena, "but Barbera is very important to us—we try to make extraordinary wines from the ordinary." Some of Vietti's vineyard sites in the Barolo DOC area that could be planted with Nebbiolo are planted with Barbera. La Crena comes from vines planted in the 1930s, and Scarrone Vigna Vecchia comes from vines more than 85 years old. Far from the rustic reputation of Barbera, these offer a creamy sophistication with deep flavors.

Vietti made news in the summer of 2016 when it was announced that the company had been sold to Krause Holdings, the parent company of a chain of convenience stores in the midwest of the U.S.A. Krause added 12 ha of vineyards it purchased to Vietti's holdings, but those grapes are used for the existing Castiglione and Perbacco wines. However, there has been an active program of purchasing vineyards in Barolo and elsewhere. Luca Currado remained as winemaker until 2023 when he and Elena left the estate.

Voerzio Martini *

Strada Loreto 1, 12064, La Morra
@ info@voerziomartini.com
⊕ www.voerziomartini.com
📅 ⚒ 🍇 🥄 12 ha; 60,000 btl

📞 +39 0173 509194
👤 Mirko & Federica Martini
📀 Barolo [map p. 35]
🍷 Barolo, La Serra

The estate represents a transition between two old wine-making families. It was created when the Voerzio property was split between brothers Roberto and Gianni in 1987. Gianni made wine under his own name from his 10 ha, in a more restrained style than those of his brother (see Roberto Voerzio profile). Twins Mirko and Frederica Martini, both oenologists, come from the family that started the Sant'Orsola winery in Piedmont. "Our grandfather and his brothers started a winery in 1947, now it's one of the largest in Italy," Mirko explains. "Our father sold his share in 2010." In 2012, Gianni sold his estate to the Martinis, who added their name to the winery, and Mirko became the winemaker. Gianni stayed on for three years to help the transition.

The estate expanded with the purchase of another hectare in La Morra and 0.5 ha in the Cerequio cru, bringing the holdings in Barolo to 12 h. There are also now 2 ha in Roero (for the white Arneis) and 2 ha in Timorasso (also white). The whites, and the Dolcetto, age in stainless steel. In reds, there is a Barbera d'Alba and four cuvées from Barolo. The Barbera comes from La Morra and ages for a year, 80% in barriques and 20% in tonneaux. It makes a modern expression of the variety, smooth, with blackberry fruits, a little savory.

The Barolo blend comes from three areas in Barolo. It ages for 30 months in tonneaux. "We want it to be easy to drink with smooth tannins," Mirko says. It's quite approachable in the modern style. La Serra shows more flavor variety and a more savory impression; aged half in tonneaux and half in large casks, it starts out wit quite an oaky impression, and needs time to age to a soft, round style. The style changes to a much finer impression with Cerequio, aged for 30 months in one large oak cask, to give very much the elegant, silky style of La Morra, with tannins that seem fine enough to make it approachable soon after release. This is a demonstration of terroir: La Serra and Cerequio are adjacent, but the soils are sandier at Cerequio. There is another change, to a sturdier, former style with Monvigliero (from Verduno), where tannic structure is more evident and at least another couple of years are needed for it to resolve.

Roberto Voerzio **

Loc. Cerreto, 12064 La Morra (CN)
@ info@robertovoerzio.com
⊕ www.robertovoerzio.com
📅 ✂ 🍇 🚜 22 ha; 50,000 btl

📞 +39 0173 509196
👤 David Voerzio
📀 Barolo [map p. 35]
🍷 Barolo, Cerequio

104

BAROLO
Denominazione di Origine Controllata e Garantita

Sarmassa di Barolo

RED WINE PRODUCT OF ITALY
ESTATE BOTTLED BY AZIENDA AGRICOLA
ROBERTO VOERZIO VITICOLTORE - LA MORRA - ITALIA

ALC 14.5% BY VOL   L. 38--04   75 CL

Several buildings labeled Voerzio line up along a street at the edge of La Morra. In their center is a rather old sign saying Roberto Voerzio in front of a rather modern building. Going in through the cellar are ranks of stainless steel fermentation tanks, then around the side you pass into a stylish family house, with children playing with the dog. Much larger than it seems, underneath is a very extensive cellar, with a large barrel room, another room full of wooden vats, and a new extension for storage. As it's underground it's naturally cool, but there is a humidifier running. The modernity of the cellar matches the wine.

Robert Voerzio became an independent producer with a 5 ha landholding in 1986; today his son Davide is making a range of wines, including Dolcetto, Barberas, Nebbiolo, and Merlot from the Langhe, and seven Barolos, all from individual Crus. Originally there was only one Cru, La Serra, but slowly others have been added; the most recent addition (in 2013) was the Reserva from Fossatti (released ten years after the vintage). Half the vineyards are owned by the estate, half are rented. Production levels are small, because yields are among the lowest in Barolo (less than 20 hl/ha). The house is also known for its single vineyard Barbera d'Alba, Pozzo dell'Annunziata, from a small (less than 1 ha) plot of old vines, released only in magnums, with a classic style.

"Our style will stay the same, we like it, we have been making wine in the same style for thirty years," says Davide. "We aim for a pure expression of terroir and vintage. We always look for a natural power that comes from lower yields, but the wine has to have freshness, otherwise it is heavy, not elegant. For me it is important that our wines leave the mouth sweet."

Davide does not think there is much purpose to characterizing the wines as modern or traditional. "We didn't belong to either of the two groups, even if people thought we belonged to the modern group, we have worked in a way that is very traditional; the only modern thing we use is the barrique, but it's a very soft use, it's a very traditional wine, we have never used 100% new oak, we have never been against the big cask. What matters for us is the final result, it can be good with either barriques or large casks." In fact, five of the Barolo Crus are matured in an equal mix of barriques and large casks for around two years (although between 1995 and 2005 only barriques were used); two are matured only in barriques because quantities are too small to use large casks.

With Crus from La Morra (mostly just south of the village), house style varies from the mineral precision of Annunziata or the elegance of La Serra, to the sleekness of Brunate or density of Cerequio, to the greater power of the Fossetti Reserve. The wines certainly reflect their terroirs. They are modern in the sense of avoiding any roughness, but traditional in respecting terroir. Complexity continues to increase for at least twenty years, and the wines become increasingly elegant as they age.

Profiles of Important Estates

Marziano Abbona

Borgata San Luigi 40, 12063 Dogliani (CN)	📞 *+39 0173 721317*
@ *abbona@abbona.com*	👤 *Chiara Abbona*
🌐 *www.abbona.com*	🔘 *Dogliani*
🔲 🏭 📠 🎋 ⬟	*58 ha; 350,000 btl*

The flagship wine here is a Dolcetto, the Dogliano DOC Papà Celso, named for Celso Abbona, who planted the variety in the 1950s. His son, Marziano Abbona, bought vineyards elsewhere in the Langhe in the 1980s, and in 2006 constructed a new winery in Dogliano, just south of the Barolo appellation. Barolo is only a small part of production, but includes top crus from Novello and Monforte d'Alba. There are three holdings in Monforte d'Alba: the communal Barolo and the Langhe Nebbiolo come from Perno, the Pressenda vineyard makes a Barolo Cru, and the Rinaldi vineyard is the source of Nebbiolo d'Alba Bricco Barone and Barbera d'Alba Rinaldi. The plot in Novello makes the Barolo Ravera from a 4 ha vineyard. There is also a Barbaresco. Winemaking is a mix: the Barolo ages in 25 hl botti, but the Crus age in tonneaux followed by 50 hl botti.

Orlando Abrigo

Via Cappelletto 5, Treiso d'Alba, 12050 (CN)	📞 *+39 0173 630232*
@ *info@orlandoabrigo.it*	👤 *Giovanni Abrigo*
🌐 *www.orlandoabrigo.com*	🔘 *Barbaresco [map p. 39]*
🔲 📠 🎋 ⚲	*20 ha; 80,000 btl*

Giovanni Abrigo took over the family winery in 1988, enlarged the domain, and recently built a new underground winery built into the hill. The domain is nominally located in Treiso, but is well to the south. The heart of the domain is Barbaresco, which accounts for about a third of production, with vineyards in Meruzzano and Montersino (both in the Treiso commune. There are separate cuvées from the two crus, and in top years the Rongalio cuvée (a Riserva since 2011) comes from the oldest vines in Meruzzano. Meruzzano ages in 600-liter barrels, Montersino ages in barriques including 20% new oak, and Rongalio ages in a mix of large Slavonian casks and 600-liter barrels. There are also Nebbiolo d'Alba (from Valmaggiore), Barbera d'Alba, Dolcetto d'Alba, Langhe Nebbiolo (a blend of Nebbiolo and Barbera), Langhe Rosso, and Moscato d'Asti. Giovanni is a modernist, but is married to Virna Borgogno (see profile), whose Barolos are firmly on the modernist side.

Cascina Adelaide

Via Aie Sottane 14, 12060 Barolo (CN)	📞 *+39 0173 560503*
@ *wine@cascinaadelaide.com*	👤 *Amabile Drocco*
🌐 *www.cascinaadelaide.com*	🔘 *Barolo [map p. 36]*
🔲 🏭 🎋 🚚	*11 ha; 50,000 btl*

Amabile Drocco bought Cascina Adelaide in 1999. Located in Barolo itself, the winery is a striking modern building. Vineyards are in 12 crus spread across four communes. Barolo Classic and 4 Vigne are blends from Barolo and La Morra communes, Serralunga is a blend from two parcels in Serralunga, the Per Ellen Riserva comes from an 0.5 ha vineyard spanning Preda and Cannubi, and there are five cuvées from individual crus. All age for 24 months in medium size (16 hl) oak, except for the Riserva, which ages for 48 months. The Langhe Nebbiolo is declassified from vineyards in Barolo, and ages for 12-24 months in 27 hl casks. There are three cuvées of Barbara d'Alba, entry-level Le Mie Donne (aged in stainless steel), and the Amabilin blend, and Vigna Preda from the cru, aged partly in 16 hl oak and partly in barriques, using new oak. There's also a Dolcetto and an unusual white, Nascetta di Novello (an almost extinct old variety).

Marco Adriano and Vittorio Adriano

Fraz. San Rocco Seno d'Elvio 13/A, 12051 Alba (CN)   📞 *+39 0173 362294*

@ *info@adrianovini.it*   🧑 *Michela Adriano*

⊕ *www.adrianovini.it*   ◉ *Barbaresco [map p. 39]*

🗓 ⚒ 🍷   *30 ha; 160,000 btl*

The family began as tenant farmers at the start of the twentieth century, and subsequently bought their first vineyards at the southern end of the Barbaresco region, in San Rocco Seno d'Elvio. The first wines were bottled under the estate name in 1994. It's very much a family business, with members from both the paternal and material sides involved. The 50 ha estate includes 10 ha of hazelnuts and 10 ha of forest as well as vineyards. A new cellar was built after a series of trials and tribulations. The Sanadaive Barbaresco comes from the original vineyards in San Rocco; Basarin comes from Neive. The Langhe Nebbiolo comes from San Rocco. They age in small barrels of Slavonian oak. The wide range of wines includes Barbera, Dolcetto, Freisa, Sauvignon Blanc, and Moscato.

Claudio Alario

Via Santa Croce, 23, 12055 Diano d'Alba (CN)   📞 *+39 0173 231808*

@ *info@alarioclaudio.it*   🧑 *Claudio Alario*

⊕ *www.alarioclaudio.it*   ◉ *Barolo [map p. 34]*

🗓 ⚒ 🍷 🍇   *10 ha; 46,000 btl*

Claudio Alario took over the family estate after he graduated in 1988 with a degree in agronomy. He started growing Dolcetto and then added Barbera and Nebbiolo. Estate-bottling began in 1995. His sons Matteo and Francesco now work with him. Vineyards are in Diano d'Alba, Serralunga d'Alba, and Verduno. There are 7 wines: 3 Dolcetto, 2 Barolo, Nebbiolo, and Barbera. All ferment in rotary fermenters. Diano d'Alba Montarillo from 30-year-old vines is the softest and most immediate Dolcetto, and Costa Fiore from 50-year-old vines has more weight. They age for 12 months in stainless steel. The top Dolcetto, Pradurent, ages for 10 months in used barriques. Nebbiolo d'Alba Cascinotto comes from the vineyards in Diano d'Alba and ages in barriques, 50% new, 50% 2-year. The Barolo Riva Rocca comes from Verduno, and Sorano comes from the cru in Serralunga. Both age for 24 months in French barriques followed by 12 months in 30 hl botti. The Barbera comes from 60-year-old vines in Diano d'Alba and ages for 20 months in barriques with 50% new oak, 50% 2-year.

Fantino Alessandro e Gian Natale

Via G. Silvano 18, 12065 Monforte d'Alba (CN)	☎ +39 0173 78253
@ fantinofratelli@hotmail.it	👤 Alesandro & Gian Natale Fantino
🌐 www.vino-fantino.com	🍷 Barolo [map p. 38]
◑ ✒ 🍇 ⚘	6 ha; 45,000 btl

This small family estate is located in the Bussia Cru in the north of Monforte d'Alba. Alessandro managed the vineyards and made the wines at Bartolo Mascarello from 1978 to 1997, when he joined his brother Gian Natale full time at the domain. Their holdings are in the Dardi section of Bussia, with three quarters Nebbiolo and one quarter Barbera. The wines were called as Vigna dei Dardi but now are labeled with the trademark Cascina Dardi, which is used for Barolo (from 25-year old vines), Riserva (from 65-year old vines), and the Vigne Vicchie (old vines) from the oldest (70year) vines. Barolo and Riserva age in large casks, while Vigne Vicchie ages first in large casks and then in barriques. In addition to two cuvées of Barbera (one d'Alba and one d'Alba Superiore, which is aged longer), there is a blend, Rosso dei Dardi, of 90% Nebbiolo with equal amounts of Freisa and Dolcetto. Nepas is an unusual wine, a sweet passito (from Nebbiolo grapes dried on straw mats, along the lines of Recioto).

Crissante Alessandria

Borgata Roggeri 44, Santa Maria, 12064 La Morra (CN)	☎ +39 3333 671499
@ info@crissantewines.it	👤 Alberto Alessandria
🌐 www.crissantewines.it	🍷 Barolo [map p. 35]
📅 🏭 🍇 ⚘	6 ha; 35,000 btl

Located in the hamlet of Santa Maria, in a panoramic position on the road leading up to La Morra, this small domain was founded in 1958 when Crissante Alessandria decided to produce his own wine instead of selling grapes from the family vineyards. Today the domain is run by brothers Michele and Roberto Alessandria together with Michele's son Alberto The domain started making wine traditionally, aging in botti, from vineyards in the immediate vicinity, but with time purchased other vineyards in La Morra, and now ages wine in a mix of barriques, tonneaux, and botti. The range includes Barolos from four Crus, Langhe Nebbiolo, and Barbera and Dolcetto d'Alba.

Fratelli Alessandria

Via Beato Valfrè 59, 12060 Verduno (CN)	☎ +39 0172 470113
@ info@fratellialessandria.it	👤 Vittore Alessandria
🌐 www.fratellialessandria.it	🍷 Barolo [map p. 34]
📅 🏭 🍇 🍾	15 ha; 90,000 btl

This family winery originated in 1870. Gian Battista is in charge of viticulture, and his brother Alessandro and son Vittore make the wines. Vineyards are mostly in Verduno and Monforte d'Alba. Barolo cuvées include the appellation blend and four crus. Wines are aged in tonneaux and 20-30 hl casks of Slavonian or French oak. The brothers are also known for producing wine from the indigenous Pelaverga grape (a specialty of the Verduno commune). In fact, in 2013 the domain abandoned production of varieties such as Chardonnay to focus on indigenous varieties.

108

Gianfranco Alessandria

Loc. Manzoni 13, 12065 Monforte d'Alba (CN)	☎ +39 0173 78576
@ azienda.alessandria@gmail.com	👤 Gianfranco Alessandria
🌐 www.gianfrancoalessandria.com	⬤ Barolo [map p. 38]
📅 🏭 🍇 🚜	8 ha; 55,000 btl

This small family winery has been managed by Gianfranco Alessandria since he took over in 1986 with only 4 ha. Grapes were sold off until estate bottling started when a new winery, attached to the family residence, was completed in 1996. Daughters Marta and Vittoria are now involved. Today the estate has a block of 5.5 ha and another hectare is leased. Vineyards in Monforte d'Alba are planted with all three local varieties. The Nebbiolos comprise the Langhe, Barolo, and the San Giovanni cru. The flagship wines are the San Giovanni and the Barbera d'Alba Vittoria. Gianfranco is a modernist, with the Nebbiolos aged in barriques; The Langhe Nebbiolo ages for 5 months with 10% new oak, and the Barolo ages for 24 months with 20% new oak. There are two cuvees from the 1.5 ha San Giovanni vineyard in Monforte, planted with 65-year-old vines. EnPiasì, produced only in magnums, ages in 3-year barriques for 24 months; San Giovanni ages in barriques with 40% new oak. Barbera and Dolcetto age in stainless steel.

Famiglia Anselma

Loc. Castello della Volta 3, 12060 Barolo (CN)	☎ +39 0173 560511
@ info@anselma.it	👤 Maurizio Anselma
🌐 www.anselma.it	⬤ Barolo [map p. 36]
📅 🏭 🍇 🐌	51 ha; 80,000 btl

This is a new estate but very traditional in its approach. Renato and Giovanna Anselma began buying vineyards in the 1970s, and now have one of the largest privately owned holdings in Barolo, but produced their first Barolo only in 1993. Their son Maurizio made waves as a new young winemaker. He has changed his position since he said, "We will only make Barolo, because this is the history of our land. We will not make any single vineyard wines because this is not our tradition, but we will make two wines." This attitude is reflected in the Communes blend (from three villages) and the Adasi Riserva (a blend from 7 crus)." For a while, grapes from a major part of production were sold off, but the range has now extended to three communal wines (Barolo, Monforte d'Alba, and Serralunga d'Alba), plus several cuvées from individual crus, making a total of 10 wines altogether. There are also Langhe Nebbiolo and Dolcetto.

Barale Fratelli

Via Roma 6, 12060 Barolo (CN)	☎ +39 0173 56127
@ info@baralefratelli.it	👤 Sergio Barale
🌐 www.baralefratelli.it	⬤ Barolo [map p. 36]
🚹 🏭 🍇 🍷	13 ha; 80,000 btl

Founded in 1870 by Francesco Barale, the domain operates from a historic house in the center of Barolo, with underground cellars nearby. Sergio Barale is Francesco's great grandson. Most of the vineyards are in Barolo commune. There are 7 ha of Nebbiolo in Barolo DOCG, with the major holding in Castellero (which has the oldest vines), and plots around a hectare each in other crus. In addition to the Barolo blend, there are cuvées from Seraboella, Castellero, and Cannubi. There's a Riserva from Bussia. A research project has identified yeasts that are indigenous to the cellar, and these are used for fermentation. The wines age in 15-30 hl casks of French oak. There are two Barberas from Alba, and a line of other varietals, including Arneis and Dolcetto, from the Langhe.

Beni Di Batasiolo

Fraz. Annunziata 87, 12064 La Morra (CN)	📞 +39 0173 50130
@ *info@batasiolo.com*	👤 *Fiorenzo Dogliani*
🌐 *www.batasiolo.com*	🍷 *Barolo [map p. 35]*
📅 👪 🍇 🚜	*140 ha; 2,500,000 btl*

This is a huge domain for the Barolo area. The Dogliani family have long owned significant estates in the area, and in 1978 they purchased the Kiola winery in La Morra, which had been founded in the 1950s and comprised seven separate estates. A new winery was built in the Batasiolo vineyard, and the domain was renamed Beni Di Batasiolo. There are holdings in several major crus, 4 in La Morra, 2 in Serralunga, 2 in Barolo commune, and Bussia Bofani in Monforte. The Briccolina cru shows sweeter, riper tannins than Cerequio. Most of the Barolos age in casks of Slavonian oak, and the general impression tends towards traditional. The range extends to all major DOCs of the area.

Bel Colle

Fraz. Castagni 56, 12060 Verduno (CN)	📞 +39 3451 524828
@ *visite@belcolle.it*	👤 *Luca Bosio*
🌐 *www.belcolle.it*	🍷 *Barolo [map p. 34]*
📅 👪 🍇 🍷	*10 ha; 180,000 btl*

Brothers Carlo and Franco Pontiglione and Giuseppe Priola founded Bel Colle in 1976 in Borgo Castagni, in Verduno at the border with La Morra. In 2015 they sold the property to Luca Bosio, a producer from Asti. There are vineyards in La Morra, Treiso, and Barbaresco, as well as Verduno. The domain's top holdings are in the Monvigliero cru of Verduno and in Pajoré in Barbaresco. They are also known as one of the few remaining growers of Pelaverga, a rare black variety confined to Verduno, making a light red wine. The Langhe Nebbiolo is intended for immediate consumption. The Nebbiolo d'Alba, La Reala, comes from sandy terroir in Roero and ages for a year in French barriques. Barolo Simposio is the blend from multiple areas and ages for 36 months in botti. Pajoré and the Barolo Riserva age in 40-45 hl botti; Monvigliero ages in French oak. There are both Barbera d'Alba and Barbera d'Asti. In white wines, Langhe Favorita comes 100% from the local variety, Favorita, and there is also a Langhe Chardonnay, vinified partly in stainless steel and partly in French barriques.

Franco Boasso

Borgata Gabutti 3/a, 12050 Serralunga d'Alba (CN)	📞 +39 0173 613165
@ *boasso@gabuttiboasso.com*	👤 *Ezio Boasso*
🌐 *www.gabuttiboasso.com*	🍷 *Barolo [map p. 37]*
📅 👪 🍇 ✂	*7 ha; 20,000 btl*

110

Also known as the Gabutti Winery after its location, the winery was established in the 1970s when the Boasso family started to produce wine from the family vineyards. Barolo comes from 4.5 ha of vineyards in Serralunga, with the 1.5 ha of Gabutti the largest holding. There's a single vineyard wine from Gabutti and also from Margaria; the Serralunga cuvée is an assemblage from many small plots. There are also 1.5 ha of Dolcetto and 1.5 ha of Barbera (also in Serralunga). Winemaking is between traditional and modern: fermentation is relatively short at 14-16 days, and the Barolo ages for 36 months, in medium-sized casks of new oak.

Cascina Bongiovanni

Via Alba Barolo 4, 12060 Castiglione Falletto (CN)	📞 *+39 0173 262184*
@ *info@cascinabongiovanni.com*	👤 *Davide Mozzone*
🌐 *www.cascinabongiovanni.com*	🔴 *Barolo [map p. 37]*
🏠 ⛏ 🍇 🍷	*7 ha; 50,000 btl*

The estate was founded in 1950 when Giovanni Bongiovanni bought a plot of land and replaced the trees with grapevines. His daughter Olga took over and then passed the estate to her nephew, Davide Mozzone (Giovanni's grandson). Davide moved in a modernist direction with his first vintage in 1993. (Like some other modernists, he took to green harvesting at night to avoid criticism from within the family). He also planted some Cabernet Sauvignon. The Barolo is a blend from Castiglione Falletto, Serralunga d'Alba, and Diano d'Alba. The Riserva comes from Castiglione Falletto. There is also a cuvée from the cru Pernanno in Castiglione Falletto. They ferment in stainless steel and age in barriques with some new oak, usually for 24 months. The Langhe Nebbiolo is declassified from Barolo and follows the same approach but with aging only for 8 months. Faletto is a Langhe Rosso from Cabernet Sauvignon, aged in barriques. The Barbera d'Alba comes from Diano d'Alba and Monforte d'Alba and has the same aging as the Barolo. Both Dolcetto d'Alba and Dolcetto di Diano d'Alba age in stainless steel. The only white is a Langhe Arneis.

Boroli

via Pugnane 4, 12060 Castiglione Falletto (CN)	📞 *+39 0173 62927*
@ *info@boroli.it*	👤 *Achille Boroli*
🌐 *www.boroli.it*	🔴 *Barolo [map p. 37]*
🏠 ⛏ 🏠 🍇 🍷	*8 ha; 45,000 btl*

This old Piedmont family has been involved in a variety of activities; Silvano was in publishing until he changed careers to make wine in the 1990s. His son Achille joined the domain in 2000. There were initially cellars and vineyards in Alba, but those have been sold; a new winery. looking over the Villero cru, designed by Silvano's son Guido, was built in 2006, and is devoted exclusively to Barolo. The home vineyard is La Brunella in Castiglione Falletto, and there are also vineyards in Villero, Cerequio and Serradenari (in La Morra). The Barolo comes from Castiglione Falletto, and there are cuvées from Brunella, Cerequio, and Villero. They go through malolactic fermentation in barriques, and then age in a mix of barriques and larger barrels. Villero sees some new wood. There is also a Chardonnay from Castiglione Falletto.

Agostino Bosco

Via Fontane 24, 12064 La Morra (CN)	📞 *+39 0173 509466*
@ *info@barolobosco.com*	👤 *Andrea Bosco*
⊕ *www.barolobosco.com*	🅾 *Barolo [map p. 35]*
📅 🏭 🐝	*6 ha; 28,000 btl*

Pietro Bosco founded the estate in the late 1940s and started by selling grapes to Prunotto and Pio Cesare. He started bottling wine in 1979. His son Agostino took over in 1983, and was joined by his son Andrea in 2000. They built a new winery in 2006. All the vineyards of this small domain are close to La Morra. La Serra comes from the cru in La Morra. Barolo Neirane comes from the cru in Verduno, just across the border from La Morra. They ferment in stainless steel and age in barriques and tonneau for 6 months before transferring to 20 hl botti of Slavonian oak for 24 months. The Langhe Nebbiolo is declassified from Barolo and ages in 500-liter barrels of French oak. Barbera d'Alba ages in barriques with 30% new oak. Dolcetto d'Alba is vinified in stainless steel.

Gianfranco Bovio

Frazione Annunziata, Borg. Giotto 63, 12064 La Morra (CN)	📞 *+39 0173 50667*
@ *boviogianfranco@boviogianfranco.com*	👤 *Alessandra Bovio*
⊕ *www.boviogianfranco.com*	🅾 *Barolo [map p. 35]*
📅 🏭 ❌ 🐝 🚜	*9 ha; 55,000 btl*

Bovia is probably just as well, if not better, known for its restaurant Belvedere, in a commanding position just outside La Morra, as for its wines. Gianfranco, who took over the business, and renovated the vineyards and started making wine in 1976, died in 2016 and the estate is now run by his daughter Alessandra and her husband Marco. All the Barolos, the Langhe Nebbiolo, and the Barberas, come from La Morra. The two Crus are Gattera and Arborina. Winemaking is traditional, with long maceration on the skins and aging in large casks for the Barolos; the Barbera d'Alba is aged in stainless steel.

Brandini

Fraz. Brandini 16, 12064 La Morra (CN)	📞 *+39 0173 50266*
@ *brandini@agricolabrandini.it*	👤 *Serena & Giovanna Bagnasco*
⊕ *www.agricolabrandini.it*	🅾 *Barolo [map p. 34]*
📅 🏭 ❌ 🐝 🍂	*20 ha; 90,000 btl*

In the context of Barolo, Brandini is relatively new, dating only from the 1990s. Originally only a winery, it was purchased by the owners of the Eataly supermarket group in 2007 (so it shares ownership with Fontanafredda), and now is well into oenotourism, with a guest house and restaurant, located on a hilltop in La Morra. Vineyards are in La Morra, with the recent addition of a small holding in Serralunga. Wines are aged in traditional manner, only in botti. Beppe Caviola is the consulting oenologist. In addition to Barolo, there are Langhe Nebbiolo, Barbera, Dolcetto, and Arneis.

112

Giacomo Brezza e Figli dal 1885

Via Lomondo 4, 12060 Barolo (CN)	☎ +39 0173 560921
@ brezza@brezza.it	👤 Enzo Brezza
🌐 www.brezza.it	⬤ Barolo [map p. 36]
📅 👥 ✖ 🍷 🍶	20 ha; 100,000 btl

The estate has been bottling wine since 1910, and Antonio Brezza handed over to his son Enzo, the third generation in this family winery, a few years ago. Located in the heart of the town of Barolo, there is also a hotel and restaurant. The Barolo and the individual crus all come from the commune of Barolo, the Langhe Nebbiolo is declassified from Barolo, Nebbiolo d'Alba comes from near Alba, and Barbera d'Alba comes from Barolo, while Barbera d'Alba Vigna Santa Rosalia comes from Alba. The Barolo Crus are Castellero (sandy soil), Cannubi (sandy and silty), and Sarmassa (with more clay, so this is the best performer in dry years). In some vintages a Riserva is made from the Vigna Bricco part of Sarmassa. Winemaking is traditional in large casks.

460 Casina Bric

Località Bruni 8, 12050 Serralunga d'Alba (CN)	☎ +39 3352 83468
@ info@casinabric-barolo.it	👤 Gianluca Viberti
🌐 www.casinabric-barolo.it	⬤ Barolo [map p. 37]
📅 👥 🍷 ☙	12 ha; 80,000 btl

The 460 in the name refers to its altitude in meters; close to the 500m limit for Barolo, it is located at one of the highest points in the DOCG. Gianluca Viberti worked for twenty years at the family domain, Giovanni Viberti (see profile) until he left to start this new venture in 2010. (His younger brother Claudio runs the Viberti domain.) Recently he expanded by adding a property in Serralunga d'Alba (where the winery is now located). Casina Bric is local dialect meaning 'perched on a hilltop.' Returning to an old tradition, the wines are bottles in 'Poirinotta,' rather squat bottles that were used in Piedmont in the eighteenth century. In another old tradition, his Langhe Rosso Ansì is a blend of a majority of Nebbiolo with both Barbera and Dolcetto. More conventionally, there are Barolo (a blend from plots in La Morra and Barolo communes) and Barolo Bricco delle Viole (from plots between 420-480m). They age in 25 hl and 50 hl botti for 18-24 months, followed by 6 months in concrete. The white is a Langhe Arneis.

La Briccolina di Grasso Tiziano

Via Roddino, 7, 12050 Serralunga d'Alba (CN)	☎ +39 0173 380231
@ labriccolina@gmail.com	👤 Daniele Grasso
◔ ✑ 🍷 🍶 7 ha; 6,000 btl	⬤ Barolo [map p. 37]

La Briccolina is a south-facing amphitheater in Serralunga that Tiziano Grasso's father purchased in 1923. Tiziano worked at Fontanafredda with Danilo Drocco, and then in 2012, together with his son Daniele (who works at Bataisolo), decided to produce his own wine from La Briccolina. The vines are about 50 years old. Production was 3,000 bottles. Tiziano died just after the vintage was bottled, and now Daniele makes the wine (from about 20% of the crop; the rest continues to be sold off). Fermentation takes place in tines (large casks of untoasted oak), and the wine ages in 20 hl botti of Slavonian oak. It's generally regarded as very refined for Serralunga.

Fratelli Brovia

Via Alba Barolo 145, 12060 Castiglione Falletto (CN)	📞 *+39 0173 62852*
@ *info@brovia.net*	👤 *Alex Sanchez*
🌐 *www.brovia.net*	🍷 *Barolo [map p. 37]*
📅 ⛪ 🍇 🥄	*17 ha; 70,000 btl*

The estate dates from 1863, but economic difficulties led to wine production being abandoned in the 1930s. It resumed in 1953 under Giacinto Brovia; today the estate is run by the next generation, Elena, the winemaker, Cristina, the vineyard manager, and Alexis Sanchez, Elena's husband, who is the marketing manager. This is very much a traditional producer, with wine fermented in cement cuves for 15-20 days (except stainless steel for Dolcetto and Arneis), with Barolos matured in botti of Slavonian oak for three years. Vineyards are in two communes, including Villero, Rocche, and Garblèt Sué in Castiglione Falletto, and Cà Mia in Serralunga. The Barolos account for just over half of production, another quarter is Dolcetto, 10% is Barbera, and the rest comes from other grapes in the area. The Barolos are light and elegant; the Barbera is fruity.

Alberto Burzi

Frazione Santa Maria 9, 12064 La Morra (CN)	📞 *+39 3381 800860*
@ *info@albertoburzi.it*	👤 *Alberto & Caterina Burzi*
🌐 *www.albertoburzi.it*	🍷 *Barolo [map p. 35]*
📅 ⛪ 🍇 🚜	*7 ha; 20,000 btl*

This is in effect a new domain, with its first vintage in 2012. Alberto and his sister Caterina are the first in the family to make wine; their grandfather belonged to a cooperative. Production started with a Barbera, and then extended to Nebbiolo. The Langhe Nebbiolo Runcaja comes from young vines (less than 15 years old) in Santa Maria in La Morra, and the wine ages in 500 liter tonneaux. The Barolo is a blend from around five plots and ages in Slavonian oak. Capelot comes from a single plot of the oldest (80-year) vines, with an extended maceration using a submerged cap, followed by aging in botti of Austrian oak.

Ca'Viola

Borgata San Luigi 11, 12063 Dogliani (CN)	📞 *+39 0173 742535*
@ *info@caviola.com*	👤 *Beppe Caviola*
🌐 *www.caviola.com*	🍷 *Dogliani*
📅 ⛪ ❌ 🍇 🚜	*12 ha; 60,000 btl*

Beppe Caviola is a well-known oenologist, and this is his home estate, which started in 1991 with a rented vineyard in Montelupo Albese (near Serralunga d'Alba) and moved to a new winery in Dogliani in 2002. Most of the vineyards are in Montelupo, on calcareous clay and marl soils, producing two cuvées each of Dolcetto and Barbera, but in 2005 a small plot of about a hectare was added in the Sottocastello cru in the Novello commune

114

in Barolo, where the soil has an unusually high content of chalk. The vineyard produces both the Barolo Sottocastello, which shows a ripe, round, modern style, and a Langhe Nebbiolo. In addition, Barolo Caviòt is a blend from other plots on Novello. The Barolos age in large (50 hl) casks. The Barbera d'Alba Bric du Luv, comes from 1.5 ha of 60-year old vines in Montelupo, and was originally aged in barriques and tonneaux, but since 2011 has been aged in a mix of 80% large casks and 20% tonneaux. It's extremely supple for Barbera and almost delicate.

Cantina Del Glicine

Via Giulio Cesare 1, 12052 Neive (CN)   📞 *+39 0173 67215*

@ *info@cantinadelglicine.com*   👤 *Roberto Bruno*

🌐 *www.cantinadelglicine.it*   🍷 *Barbaresco [map p. 39]*

6 ha; 37,000 btl

The winery dates back to 1582; located at the entrance to Neive, it is popular with tourists for its ancient cellars. Adriana Marzi and Roberto Bruno founded the winery in 1980. Although the family estate is small, there is a wide range of wines, with the Barbaresco Vignesparse constituting a blend from several plots, and Marcorino and Currà coming from individual crus. The Nebbiolo d'Alba comes from Roero. The two Barbera cuvées are in fact blends that include 10-15% of Nebbiolo (the varieties are co-fermented). Production is traditional, with fermentation in stainless steel followed by aging in botti.

Cantina Pertinace

Loc. Pertinace 2, 12050 Treiso (CN)   📞 *+39 0173 442238*

@ *info@pertinace.it*   👤 *Cesare Barbero*

🌐 *www.pertinace.com*   🍷 *Barbaresco [map p. 39]*

100 ha; 750,000 btl

This is a well-regarded cooperative in Treiso, founded in 1973 by Mario Barbero and 13 other growers. Today it has 17 members, and Mario's son, Cesare, is the manager and winemaker. The style is sweet and ripe, but there is a curious reversal going from the communal Barbaresco, where flavor develops early but tannins dry the finish and really need time to resolve, compared with the Crus, Marcarini and Nervo, where greater fruit density absorbs the tannins better, and counter-intuitively may make them ready to drink sooner. Nervo is softer and more approachable than Marcarini, but Marcarini is more complex and may have greater longevity. The Barolo comes from La Morra and occupies a position in the range between Barbaresco and the Crus. The Langhe Nebbiolo comes from vineyards outside Barolo, and is lighter. The wines age in traditional botti. There are also several cuvées of Dolcetto, and other red and white wines from Langhe.

Cappellano

Via Alba 13, 12050 Serralunga d'Alba (CN)   📞 *+39 0173 613103*

@ *info@cappellano1870.it*   👤 *Augusto Cappellano & Orsi Emma*

🌐 *www.cappellano1870.it*   🍷 *Barolo [map p. 37]*

4 ha; 11,000 btl

Founded in 1870 by Filippo Cappellano, who bought 60 ha of vineyards, the domain was well known in the nineteenth century, and the central square in Serralunga is named after the family. His son Giovanni took over the estate; his other son, Giuseppe, was a pharmacist who in 1895 invented Barolo Chinato, the aperitif consisting of Barolo wine infused with herbs and spices. Giovanni died in 1912 when he was searching for phylloxera-resistant vines in Tunisia. Giuseppe then took over the estate, which became known as Dott. Giuseppe Cappellano. After Giuseppe's death in 1955, the estate was run by his nephew Francesco, whose son Theobaldo lived in Eritrea, and returned to take over the estate in 1970. By this time, the estate no longer owned any vineyards. Theobaldo acquired its present holding of a single plot in the Gabutti Cru in 1985 by a deal with a farmer called Fiorin, from whom he had been buying the grapes since 1976. The labels continue to show his name. Theobaldo became a well-known personality in the area, totally committed to traditional production—from 1983, he refused to allow journalists to visit unless they agreed to review the wines without scores—and Cappellano became something of a cult producer, with its wines very difficult to obtain, and formidably high prices. Theobaldo died in 2009 and his son Augusto took over, continuing the traditional approach. The two Barolos both come from the Gabutti vineyard, Rupestris from vines that were planted in the 1940s (consisting of various clones on Rupestris rootstock), and Piè Franco, from a parcel planted with the Michet clone of Nebbiolo on its own roots in 1989 when it became necessary to replant part of the vineyard that collapsed. The Barbera d'Alba also comes from Gabutti. Until 2014, there was a Nebbiolo d'Alba from a vineyard leased in Novello.

Ca'Rome'

Strada Rabajà 86-88, 12050 Barbaresco (CN)	📞 *+39 0173 635126*
@ *info@carome.com*	👤 *Giuseppe Marengo*
⊕ *www.carome.com*	🟢 *Barbaresco [map p. 39]*
📅 🏭 ✖ 🍇 🌿	*5 ha; 30,000 btl*

Romano Marengo founded Ca'Rome' in 1980 and runs it today with his children Giuseppe (now the winemaker) and Paola (manager), producing only Nebbiolo and Barbera from Barbaresco and Serralunga d'Alba (with vineyards inherited from Romano's grandmother). Wines are aged in a mix of 25 hl botti of Slavonian oak and barriques of French oak. There are three Barbarescos from the Rio Sordo area, and two Barolos from Serralunga; Langhe Nebbiolo Calimpia is declassified from young vines in Barbaresco, and Langhe Da Pruvé is a blend of Nebbiolo and Barbera. Two Barberas come from Serralunga. The wines tend to be powerful.

Tenuta Cucco

via Mazzini 10, 12050 Serralunga d'Alba (CN)	📞 *+39 0173 613003*
@ *info@tenutacucco.it*	👤 *Famiglia Rossi Cairo*
⊕ *tenutacucco.it*	🟢 *Barolo [map p. 37]*
📅 🏭 🍇 🍶	*13 ha; 70,000 btl*

The winery dates from the 1960s, but the modern era started when it was acquired by Piero Rossi Cairo. an entrepreneur who already owned the La Raia winery in Gavi and works with his son Giorgio. The winery is located in the cru Ceratti together with most of its vineyard plots. Vineyards were extended by the recent addition of 2.5 ha in Bricco Voghera, just a little farther north along the eastern slope of Serralunga. Cerrati is a monopole, historically with only three owners, planted only with Nebbiolo. In addition to the Barolo Cerrati, which comes from 4 ha of (slightly) richer soils on the lower parts, the cuvée Vigna Cucco Riserva is produced from 1.5 ha of the highest plots ('cucco' means the highest part in Piedmont dialect), where the vines include plantings up to 50 years old. In addition to the cuvées from each Cru, there is a blend from Cerrati and Bricco Voghera, labeled as Commune dei Serralunga d'Alba. The Serralunga, Cerrati, and Bricco Voghera age in 25 hl botti of Slavonion oak; the Riserva ages in barriques. The Langhe Nebbiolo comes from Diano d'Alba, just north of Serralunga, and ages in stainless steel. There are also plots in Roddi, planted with Barbera for the Barbera d'Alba, which ages in the botti, and with Cabernet Sauvignon and Merlot used in the Langhe Rosso, which ages in barriques with a third new oak.

Cascina Luisin

Via Rabajà 34, 12050 Barbaresco (CN)	☎ *+39 0173 635154*
@ *cascinaluisin@gmail.com*	👤 *Luigi Minuto*
🌐 *www.cascinaluisin.it*	🔘 *Barbaresco [map p. 39]*
👤 🏭 🍷 🚜	*8 ha; 30,000 btl*

The estate was founded in Barbaresco by Luigi Minoto in 1913 (Luisin means 'small Luigi' in local dialect). The holdings in Barbaresco include the top crus Rabajà and Asili in Barbaresco commune and Sori Paolin in Neive. Separate cuvées are made from each Cru; the only blend is the Barbaresco Riserva. There is also a holding in Serralunga d'Alba, the source for the Barolo Leon. The vines vary from 40-65 years of age. Plantings are 50% Nebbiolo. Roberto Minuto came into the winery in 1995. They introduced rotofermenters in 1998, but decided to use them only for Dolcetto and Barbera. Nebbiolo is macerated and fermented in the traditional way in large concrete vats, with frequent racking to ensure strong extraction, followed by aging in 30 hl botti of Slavonian oak. The Langhe Nebbiolo comes from San Rocco Seno d'Elvio (just south of Barbaresco), and ages in slightly smaller botti for not quite as long. Barbera d'Alba comes from the same location, with the Maggiur cuvée aged in 40 hl botti, and the Axilium cuvée aged in small barrels.

Cascina Morassino

Strada Bernino 10, 12050 Barbaresco (CN)	☎ *+39 3471 210223*
@ *morassino@gmail.com*	👤 *Roberto Bianco*
📇 🏭 🍷 🍂 *5 ha; 20,000 btl*	🔘 *Barbaresco [map p. 39]*

This small family winery was founded in 1984 by Mauro Bianco, and is run today by his son Roberto. Most of the vineyards (3.5 ha) are in the Ovello cru at the northern border of the Barbaresco commune, with another 1 ha in Cottà in Neive. (Most of the Ovello cru is owned by Gaja or the Barbaresco cooperative.) Plantings are mostly Nebbiolo, with just 0.5 ha of Dolcetto and 0.3 ha of Barbera. Barbaresco is half of production, divided between the Morassino cuvée and the single-vineyard Ovello. They age for 18 and 24 months respectively in 25 hl casks of Slavonian and French oak. The Langhe Nebbiolo and the Barbera d'Alba age in stainless steel.

Castello di Neive

Via Castelborgo,1, 12052 Neive (CN)
@ *info@castellodineive.it*
🌐 *www.castellodineive.it*
📅 ⚒ 🍇 ✎

📞 *+39 3292 125171*
👤 *Claudio Roggero*
🔴 *Barbaresco [map p. 39]*
26 ha; 150,000 btl

Giacomo Stupino acquired vineyards during the 1960s, and purchased the castle over-looking Neive in 1964 together with the surrounding 60 ha estate. His son Italo started estate bottling in the 1970s, and expansion led to construction of a new cellar in 2012. The Barbaresco is a blend from several plots, and the flagship is the Santo Stefano cru, also produced as a Riserva in top vintages. It ages in 35 hl botti of French oak. (Grapes from Santo Stefano have been sold to Bruno Giacosa for his famous cuvée.) There is also a Barbera from Santo Stefano, and a wide range of other wines.

Le Cecche

Via Moglia Gerlotto, 10, 12055 Diano d'Alba (CN)
@ *info@lececche.it*
🌐 *www.lececche.it*
📅 ⚒ 🏠 🍇 ✎

📞 *+39 3316 357664*
👤 *Jan Jules de Bruyne*
🔴 *Barolo [map p. 34]*
8 ha; 40,000 btl

Le Cecche is an unusual property for the area as it is no longer owned by local growers. Slightly off the beaten track in Diano d'Alba, it belonged to the Marengo family until the last generation had no heirs and sold the property in 2001 to Belgian physician Jan de Bruyne and his Italian wife. They restored the buildings, created a modern winery, and planted vineyards with Nebbiolo, Barbera, and Merlot around the house. The first vintage in 2002 was only 3,000 bottles, but subsequently they planted a vineyard for the local white variety Manzoni, at the high elevation of 750m, bought plots in Sorano cru in Serralunga d'Alba, Borzone in Grinzane Cavour, and Bricco San Pietro in Monforte d'Alba, and planted another 2 ha in Diano d'Alba. Barolo cuvées from the three crus all ferment in stainless steel and then age in a mixture of tonneaux and barriques of French oak with 30% new wood. Even the Nebbiolo d'Alba gets 20% new oak, as does the Barbera d'Alba. There's a Diano d'Alba Dolcetto, and Langhe Rosso blended from Dolcetto with Barbera and Nebbiolo. The Langhe Rosso Fiammingo is a blend of 60% Merlot, 20% Nebbiolo, and 20% Barbera aged in 20% new barriques.

Ciabot Berton

Fraz. Santa Maria 1, 12064 La Morra (CN)
@ *info@ciabotberton.it*
🌐 *www.ciabotberton.it*
📅 ⚒ 🍇 ✎

📞 *+39 0173 50217*
👤 *Marco Oberto*
🔴 *Barolo [map p. 35]*
14 ha; 75,000 btl

The name of the domain comes from a ruined building close to the winery, a ciabot (small building) owned by a maker of fireworks called Berton. The estate is owned by the Oberto family, which can trace its presence in La Morra for centuries. They bought the first vineyard four generations ago in 1876. They were growers until Giovenale Oberto started estate-bottling in 1961, and then expanded the vineyard holdings. His grandchildren, oenologist Marco and his sister Paolo. now run the domain. All the vineyards are in La Morra, with five separate crus. The communal La Morra bottling is a blend from young vines, Ciabot Berton 1961 comes the estate three oldest vineyards, from 30-50-year old vines, and there are separate cuvées from crus Roggeri and Rocchettevino. They age in Slavonian botti followed by some time in concrete, Lage Nebbiolo 3 Utin comes from vineyards in La Morra and ages only in stainless steel. There are also Barbera and Dolcetto d'Alba, and Langhe white and rosé.

Fratelli Cigliuti

Via Serraboella 17, 12052 Neive (CN)	📞 *+39 0173 677185*
@ *info@cigliuti.it*	👤 *Claudia Cigliuti*
🌐 *www.cigliuti.it*	🔴 *Barbaresco [map p. 39]*
📅 ⛏ 🍇 🌿	*8 ha; 30,000 btl*

Renato Cigliuti describes himself as a farmer. He started to bottle Barbaresco from the family estate, then only 4 ha, in 1964. This remains a small family estate, comprising Renato and his wife and two daughters. The vineyards are in two crus: Barbaresco, Barbera d'Alba, and Dolcetto come from Serraboella, and Barbaresco Vie Erte and Langhe Nebbiolo come from Bricco di Neive. The Barbarescos are aged in large casks, mostly Slavonian oak, the Langhe Nebbiolo in a mix of steel and Slavonian casks, and the Langhe Rosso Briccoserra, an equal blend of Nebbiolo and Barbera, is aged in barriques.

Col dei Venti

Strada San Lazzaro 14, 12053 Castiglione Tinella [cn]	📞 *+39 0141 793071*
@ *info@coldeiventi.com*	👤 *Ornella Cordara*
🌐 *www.coldeiventi.com*	🔴 *Asti*
📅 ⛏ 🍇 🚜	*10 ha; 35,000 btl*

I suppose you would call Ornella Cordara a modernist, because the phrase most often used to describe her wines is 'fruit-driven.' She grew up in a winemaking family, founded her own winery in 2003, and now works with her children Ivan and Sara. The major cuvée is the Barbaresco Túfoblu, which comes from Neive. Long fermentation and maceration with frequent punch-downs and pump-overs is followed by aging for 24 months in barriques. The Debutto Barolo comes from Serralunga d'Alba and La Morra, and has similar vinification, except that aging lasts for 36 months. The Langhe Nebbiolo comes from Neive and ages in barriques of French oak for 15 months. There are also cuvées from local holdings in Asti.

Poderi Colla

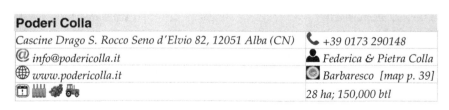

Cascine Drago S. Rocco Seno d'Elvio 82, 12051 Alba (CN)	📞 *+39 0173 290148*
@ *info@podericolla.it*	👤 *Federica & Pietra Colla*
🌐 *www.podericolla.it*	🔴 *Barbaresco [map p. 39]*
📅 ⛏ 🍇 🚜	*28 ha; 150,000 btl*

The Colla family has a long history of winemaking since the eighteenth century, and became involved with Barolo when Beppe Colla took over Prunotto in 1956. Then his younger brother Tino founded Poderi Colla in 1994. There was an expansion with the purchase of Cascine Drago in 2015, followed by the vineyards and winery of Bricco Bompè in 2016, where a new underground winery has been constructed. There's a wide range of wines from the Langhe, including varietals and classic blends. The flagship is the Barolo Bussia Dardi Le Rose, from the Bussia Soprano di Monforte cru, which Beppe first vinified as a separate cuvée in 1961. The Barbaresco comes from Roncaglie. These are traditional wines, vinified in botti of Slavonian oak.

Collina Serragrilli

Loc. Serragrilli, no.30, 12052 Neive (CN)	☎ +39 0173 677010
@ info@serragrilli.it	👤 Bruno Piernicola
🌐 www.serragrilli.it	⬤ Barbaresco [map p. 39]
📅 ⚒ 🍷 🍂	15 ha; 100,000 btl

The name of the winery reflects its location on the Serragrilli hill in Neive, where the Lequio family is now in its fourth generation. It's very much a family affair, currently managed by winemaker Piernicola Bruno and enologist Gianfranco Cordero. The inclination is towards modernist, with most wines aged in barriques and tonneaux and 10 hl casks, but all of French oak from Allier. There is a fair amount of new oak as barriques are used only for 4 years. The Serragrilli Cru is the most modern cuvée, aged in new barriques for 18 months. The Starderi cru has more conventional aging, with 70% in 10-20 hl casks and 30% in new barriques, for two years. The Barolo, La Tur, which comes from the Giacomo cru in La Morra, is the most traditional, aged in 20 hl casks (albeit French oak) for 36 months. The Langhe Nebbiolo, Bailé, is declassified from grapes from Neive; it ages in tonneaux. The range also includes Barbera d'Alba, with one cuvée seeing only partial oak and the Grillaia cuvée aged in barriques, and whites from Langhe and Roero.

Diego Conterno

Via Monta 27, 12065 Monforte d'Alba (CN)	☎ +39 0173 789265
@ info@diegoconterno.it	👤 Diego Conterno
🌐 www.diegoconterno.it	⬤ Barolo [map p. 38]
📅 ⚒ 🍷 🛢 🍂	8 ha; 65,000 btl

Diego Conterno worked with his cousins Claudio and Guido at Conterno Fantino (see profile) for twenty years, before founding his own winery in 2000. His son Stefano joined him in 2010. The winery was extended in 2014. Estate grapes are supplemented by about 10% with purchased grapes. Winemaking is conventional, with static fermenters and larger casks used for the Barolos, and 500 liter tonneaux for the other wines. There are three Barolos, all from Monforte d'Alba: the communal cuvée, Le Coste Cru, and the top Cru, Ginestra. The Nebbiolo d'Alba, Baluma, the Barbera d'Alba, Ferrione, and the Dolcetto d'Alba, also come from Monforte. Monguglielmo is a blend of Nebbiolo and Barbera. There's also a white, from the old variety Nascetta.

Conterno Fantino

Via Ginestra1, 12065 Monforte d'Alba (CN)	☎ +39 0173 78204
@ info@conternofantino.it	🧑 Claudio Conterno& Guido Fantino
🌐 www.conternofantino.it	🍷 Barolo [map p. 38]
📅 🏭 🦌 🦌	27 ha; 150,000 btl

Conterno Fantino is a modernist producer, from the stylish eco-friendly winery built on the top of a hill overlooking Monforte d'Alba to the use of French barriques for aging. It was founded by cousins Claudio Conterno (viticulturalist) and Guido Fantino (winemaker) in 1982, and the next generation is now involved. All the Barolos are single vineyard wines, from various crus with Sorì Ginestra in the lead, aged in barriques with about half new oak; Langhe Nebbiolo Ginestrino is declassified from Barolo and aged in second year barriques, as is the Barbera d'Alba, also from Monforte d'Alba.

Paolo Conterno

Località Ginestra 34, 12065 Monforte d'Alba (CN)	☎ +39 0173 78415
@ ginestra@paoloconterno.com	🧑 Giorgio Conterno
🌐 www.paoloconterno.com	🍷 Barolo [map p. 38]
📅 🏭 ❌ 🦌 🦌	37 ha; 85,000 btl

When Paolo Conterno founded the estate in 1886, it was known as Casa della Ginestra, after its location in the famous Cru of Monforte d'Alba. Today it is in the hands of Giorgio, the fourth generation. The vineyard is in a prime part of the Cru, facing south and southeast, on a steep slope at an altitude of 300-350. There are three Barolos. Riva del Bric comes from younger vines in Ginestra, then there is Ginestra and the Ginestra Riserva. The Langhe Nebbiolo and the Barbera d'Alba also come from Ginestra. Winemaking is classical, with the wines aged in 35 hl botti. Giorgio expanded by renting vineyards between Asti and Monferrato) where he makes a range of wines from other varieties, and in 2015 he bought the 13 ha estate of Tenuta Ortaglia in Tuscany.

Cordero Di Montezemolo

Fraz. Annunziata 67, Cascina Monfalletto, 12064 La Morra (CN)	☎ +39 0173 50344
@ info@corderodimontezemolo.com	🧑 Elena & Alberto Cordero di Montezemolo
🌐 www.corderodimontezemolo.com	🍷 Barolo [map p. 35]
📅 🏭 🦌 🦌	45 ha; 300,000 btl

This very old estate was in the Falletto family from 1340, part of a very extensive land holding among which was Castiglione Falletto. It came into the Cordero di Montezemolo family by the marriage of Luisa Falletto in 1920. Enrico Cordero di Montezemolo moved the domain from its original location in the village of La Morra to its present location on the hill of Cascina Monfalletto (near the famous cedar of Lebanon planted in 1856). It's a beautiful location with panoramic views across to La Morra on one side, and to Serralunga and Castiglione Falletto on the other. Visits are organized to be educational. The home estate of 28 ha extends around the hill; "we have a contiguous estate, which is unusual for Barolo," says Alberto, who now runs the domain. Another important vineyard is

Villero in Castiglione Falletto, bought in 1965. Other holdings extend elsewhere in the Langhe. Enrico moved the domain into a modern style, with short maceration and aging in barriques. "We've always been a producer who uses short maceration to get wines that are approachable," Alberto says. "Historically we have aged a little in oak, but more in bottle. We like to make long bottle aging so the wine is ready on release." The Langhe Nebbiolo comes from young (under 10-year-old) vines, and is declassified from Barolo, and also some dedicated vineyards. "It should express Nebbiolo without any influence such as oak," so it ages in stainless steel. In a tasting it comes before the Barbera d'Alba, which is a little richer. The Monfalletto Barolo is a blend from the holdings in La Morra; "it is known to be very approachable," Alberto says. Gattera is a selection from three plots of older vines; "Gattera plays to richness, while Monfalletto shows freshness." Gorette Riserva comes from the oldest vines, and is produced only as magnums, and is sold only at the estate. The top Enrico VI cuvée comes from Villero, and is more masculine, and the only cuvée really to show any tannins. Barbera d'Alba is a blend from Monfalletto and Roero, while the Barbara d'Alba Superiore Funtanì comes from the oldest vines at Monfalletto. Whites wines includes Arneis and a Chardonnay (from the lower slopes at Monfalletto). The style is modernist to the extreme that virtually all the wines are ready to drink on release.

Renato Corino

Fraz. Annunziata Pozzo 49a, 12064 La Morra (CN)	📞 *+39 0173 500349*
@ *info@renatocorino.it*	👤 *Renato Corino*
⊕ *www.renatocorino.it*	📷 *Barolo [map p. 35]*
📅 🏭 🚜	*8 ha; 50,000 btl*

Renato created this estate in 2005 when he and his brother split the Giovanni Corino estate (see profile) of their father. Renato built a new winery in the Arborina cru (less than a mile away), and now works with his son Stefano and daughter Chiara. The Barolo comes from the commune of La Morra, mostly from the Roncaglie vineyard, and there are cuvées from two crus: Arborina and Rocche Annunziata (the flagship wine). A Riserva comes from 50-year-old vines. Following the style of the original Corino estate, Renato is a modernist, aging wines in French barriques with about 30% new oak.

Giuseppe Cortese

Via Rabajà 80, 12050 Barbaresco (CN)	📞 *+39 0173 635131*
@ *info@giuseppecortese.it*	👤 *Tiziana Cortese & Occhetti Gabriele*
⊕ *www.cortesegiuseppe.it*	📷 *Barbaresco [map p. 39]*
📅 🏭 🛏 🌿	*9 ha; 68,000 btl*

The Cortese family lived on the Rabajà hill, and Giuseppe Cortese started to bottle Barbaresco from the cru in 1971. The estate was expanded by buying more vineyards in Rabajà and neighboring areas. Giuseppe's son, Pier Carlo, became the winemaker. The Rabajà is aged in Slavonian oak casks for 20-22 months; a Riserva is made in top years and aged in slightly smaller casks for 40 months. The Langhe Nebbiolo also comes from Rabajà, and is aged in the casks for 12 months. In addition there are Barbera, Dolcetto, and Chardonnay. There is now also a bed and breakfast.

Rocche Costamagna

Via Vittorio Emanuele 8, 12064 La Morra (CN)	☎ *+39 0173 509225*
@ *barolo@rocchecostamagna.it*	👤 *Alessandro Locatelli*
🌐 *www.rocchecostamagna.it*	🔴 *Barolo [map p. 35]*
🖰 🍴 🏠 🥂 🚜	*14 ha; 95,000 btl*

The estate originated in 1841, and produced wine commercially until the 1930s, when the estate was reduced to the vineyards in La Morra and grapes were mostly sold off. Claudia Ferreresi, a painter, inherited the estate at the end of the 1960s, and resumed production. (Some of Claudia's paintings hang in the accommodation that is available in the farmhouse.) Her son Alessandro Locatelli took over in the 1980s. The heart of the estate are 5 ha in the Rocche del'Annunziata Cru. There are three Barolos: the communal Barolo is a blend from La Morra and Verduno, Roche del'Annunziata comes from the Cru, and Bricco Francesco Riserva comes from the very top (the 'bricco') of the Cru. They age in botti of Slavonian oak. Other wines include Langhe Nebbiolo and Barbera d'Alba.

Damilano

Strada Provinciale Alba-Barolo 122, 12064 La Morra (CN) (winery); Via Roma 31, 12060 Barolo (shop)	☎ *+39 0173 56105*
@ *info@damilanog.com*	👤 *Guido Damilano*
🌐 *www.cantinedamilano.it*	🔴 *Barolo [map p. 35]*
🕴 🍴 ✖ 🥂 🚜	*40 ha; 365,000 btl*

You can hardly miss the Damilano winery, a large modern building on the main road from Alba to Barolo. In spite of its appearance, it's one of the older estates, started by Giuseppe Borgogno in 1890. His son-in-law, Giacomo Damilano, took over in 1935; his grandchildren, Guido, Mario, and Paolo, have been in charge since 1997. In addition to the Lecinquevigne Barolo blend from five vineyards, there are releases from crus Cannubi, Cerequio, Brunate, and Liste, and a Riserva from Cannubi (the most important of the estate vineyards, in the heart of the cru). Other wines include Langhe Nebbiolo, Barbera d'Alba, Barbera d'Asti, and Dolcetto, as well as Langhe Arneis and Chardonnay. There are also sparkling wines, Chinato, and Grappa. The winery is distinguished by including the Michelin-starred restaurant Massimo Camia (with a separate entrance at the side). In addition to the winery, which has a tasting room and boutique, there's also a shop in Barolo village.

Cantina Del Pino

Via Ovello 31, 12050 Barbaresco (CN)	
@ *cantina@cantinadelpino.com*	👤 *Franca Miretti*
🌐 *www.cantinadelpino.com*	🔴 *Barbaresco [map p. 39]*
🔍 🥂 🚜	*10 ha; 54,000 btl*

Renato Vacca was the technical director at the well-regarded Produttori del Barbaresco, but now runs his family estate, which his great grandfather purchased. Vineyards are exclusively in Barbaresco, with many old vines (35-year-old vines are regarded as young). The top holdings are the flagship cru, Ovello, and the Albesani vineyard in Santo Stefano, including a Riserva since 2005. The crus, and the Barbaresco blend, are aged in barriques, but are not overtly modern in style; the Langhe Nebbiolo, which also comes from Barbaresco, is aged in stainless steel. The Maria Grazia Langhe Nebbiolo comes from a small plot in Ovello and ages in large casks.

Giacomo Fenocchio

Loc. Bussia 72, 12065 Monforte d'Alba (CN)	📞 *+39 0173 78675*
@ *info@giacomofenocchio.com*	👤 *Claudio Fenocchio*
🌐 *www.giacomofenocchio.com*	🔴 *Barolo [map p. 38]*
🗓 🏭 🍇 🔖	*17 ha; 100,000 btl*

The estate dates from 1894, but gained its modern form when Giacomo took over in 1964 and expanded the estate with purchases in the top Crus. Claudio and his brothers took over when Giacoma died in 1989, and continued the policy of traditional winemaking, with aging in 25-35 hl botti of Slavonian oak. Vineyards are in three communes, Bussia in Monforte d'Alba, Villero in Castiglione Falletto, and Cannubi in Barolo. The communal Barolo comes from Monforte, and in addition to the cuvées named for their Crus, Castellero comes from Cannubi, and there is a Riserva from Bussia. The Langhe Nebbiolo, Barbera d'Alba, and Dolcetto d'Alba all come from Monforte. The wines are known for their reasonable prices.

Cascina Fontana

Vicolo della Chiesa 2, Loc. Perno, 12065 Monforte d'Alba (CN)	📞 *+39 0173 789005*
@ *visite@cascinafontana.com*	👤 *Mario Fontana*
🌐 *www.cascinafontana.com*	🔴 *Barolo [map p. 37]*
🚶 ✏ 🍇 🔖 🍷	*6 ha; 35,000 btl*

"I learned winemaking from my grandfather Saverio and I still do many things *come una volta* — as in the past, as my grandfather himself would have done," says Mario Fontana, who is the 6th generation at the small family winery. He started left school at 17 to work with his parents and grandfather, and started to make the wine in 1994.The estate grows only the traditional grape varieties, Nebbiolo, Barbera, and Dolcetto. The Barolo is a blend from three vineyards, Vollero and Valleti in Castiglione Falletto, and Gallinotto in La Morra. There is also a Barolo specifically from the commune of Castiglione Falletto. The wines age in 26 hl botti of Slavonian oak. The Langhe Nebbilo is a blend from vineyards at the Castello di Sinio (just to the east of Barolo), which has been in the family for a century, with grapes from Castiglione Falletto. The Barbera d'Alba comes from the Barolo area and ages in a mix of used barriques and concrete.

Fontanabianca

Via Bordini 15, 12052 Neive (CN)	📞 *+39 0173 67195*
@ *tour@fontanabianca.it*	👤 *Matteo Pola*
🌐 *www.fontanabianca.it*	🔴 *Barbaresco [map p. 39]*
🚶 🏭 🍇 🔖	*17 ha; 92,000 btl*

Franco Pola and Ottavio Ferro founded the domain in 1969, and today it is run by their sons, Aldo Pola and Bruno Ferro. In addition to the 15 ha of estate vineyards, another 2 ha are rented. There are three cuvées of Barbaresco: a blend from three plots in Neive; the Serraboella cru; and the Bordini cru, where the winery is located. Style has moved from modernist to more varied aging protocols. Barbaresco ages in a mix of casks and barriques, Serraboella ages in casks; Bordini ages in barriques. Aging is relatively short at 12-15 months. Langhe Nebbiolo comes from Neive, aging in casks for 6 months.

Fortemasso

Loc. Castelletto, 21, Monforte d'Alba (CN)	📞 *+39 0173 328148*
@ *info@fortemasso.com*	👤 *Piero Ballario*
🌐 *www.fortemasso.it*	💿 *Barolo [map p. 38]*
🗓 👓 🍷 🚜	*8 ha; 40,000 btl*

The Beretta firearms company owns several wine producers through its subsidiary Agricole Gussalli Beretta, including Lo Sparviere in Franciacorta, Castello di Radda in Chianti Classico, Orlandi Contucci Ponno in Abruzzo, and Fortemasso in Barolo. They distribute the wines of another twenty producers. Fortemasso is the most recent addition to the portfolio, with a new winery built in a top location, the Castelletto subzone of Monforte, in 2013. The range includes Barbera d'Alba, Langhe Nebbiolo, Barolo Castelletto, and the Castelletto Riserva.

Gianni Gagliardo

Borg. Serra dei Turchi 88, 12064 La Morra (CN)	📞 *+39 0173 50829*
@ *gagliardo@gagliardo.it*	👤 *Gianni Gagliardo*
🌐 *www.gagliardo.it*	💿 *Barolo [map p. 34]*
🗓 👓 🍷 🍶	*30 ha; 350,000 btl*

The Colla family started working vineyards in Roero 1847, and fourth generation Paolo Colla bought a vineyard in La Morra where he established a winery and started bottling Barolo in 1961. In 1973 his daughter Marivanna married Gianni Gagliardo, and the winery was established under the name of Vinicola Paolo Colla. Gianni took over in 1981, and the name changed to Gianni Gagliardo in 1986. Gianni's sons, Stefano (winemaker), Alberto (viticulturalist), and Paolo (marketing), run the estate today. Vineyards were divided between Barolo and Roero until the most recent acquisition in 2017 of Tenuta Garetto, planted with Barbera, in the Nizza DOCG. In Barolo, there is a classic blend from many plots a communal La Morra release, both aged in 35 hl casks. There are six releases from individual crus, aged in medium-size casks or used barriques depending on the total volume. The Nebbiolo d'Alba and Langhe Nebbiolo both come from Roero, and there are also Barbera and Dolcetto. One unusual cuvée is Fallegro, which is Vermentino from Roero.

Garesio

Località Sordo 1, 12050 Serralunga d'Alba (CN)	📞 *+39 3667 076775*
@ *info@garesiovini.it*	👤 *Giovanna Garesio*
🌐 *www.garesiovini.it*	💿 *Barolo [map p. 37]*
🗓 👓 🍷 🍶	*25 ha; 90,000 btl*

Originally from Puglia, the Garesio family have been buying vineyards in Piedmont since 2010, divided between Serralunga d'Alba, Monferrato in Asti, and Perletto in Alta Langa. They converted an old farmhouse in Serralunga into a modern winery, partly underground. They produce Barbera under Asti and Nizza DOCs (at Monferrato) and Nebbiolo from Alta Langa, as well as Barolo. From Barolo there are the communal Serralunga and the crus Cerretta and Gianetto. They age in 25-50 hl botti of Austrian oak for 24 months.

Ettore Germano

Loc. Cerretta 1, 12050 Serralunga d'Alba (CN)   +39 0173 613528

@ info@ettoregermano.com   Sergio Germano & Elena Bonelli

www.germanoettore.com   Barolo [map p. 37]

20 ha; 150,000 btl   Barolo

The family estate at Serralunga d'Alba dates from 1865, but sold grapes until Sergio Germano started to bottle wine in 1985; in 1993 he came to the estate full time (after making wine at Fontanafredda) and started to bottle all the production. His son Elia and daughter Maria have now joined him. The winery is high up in the hills of Serralunga with a spectacular view from its tasting room over the vineyards, including the estate holdings, which are spread around the winery in three different Crus. "We started with 4 ha in Serralunga, mostly in Dolcetto and Barbera, and my grandfather started to grow Barolo in 1958," Maria says. "My father is passionate about Riesling and sparkling wine, and has started to grow other varieties in cooler locations in Alta Langhe." Now there are 12 ha in Alta Langhe as well as 10 ha in Barolo. Nascetta white and the well-regarded Herzù Riesling come from Alta Langhe.

From Serralunga, there are Nebbiolo d'Alba (from a vineyard near the castle with vines of 5-15 years age), the communal Barolo (a blend of young vines from Crus Prapò and Ceretta), Prapò and Ceretta (from near the winery) and Vignarionda (at the other end of Serralunga), and the Lazzarita Riserva (on the other side of the hill from Ceretta and Prapò). Aging depends on the cuvée.

Langhe Nebbiolo is fresh and easy, given short maceration and aged for 6 months in stainless steel, a different style from Barolo, which has a good sense of the power of Serralunga, aged in 20 hl botti for 2 years, with 80% Slavonian and 20% French oak. There is a big jump going to Prapò (from 45-year-old vines right below the cellar) and Ceretta (from 50-year-old vines on the adjacent hill, where Germano has 6 ha, with 4 ha for Barolo and 2 ha for Barbera). Prapò ages for two years in large casks, and Ceretta ages for two years in 700-liter barrels. Prapò seems broad and sturdy, until you get to Ceretta, which is rich and deep. Lazzarita Riserva (from 0.5 ha over another hill, aged for three years in 20 hl botti) moves up a notch in both power and finesse.

Carlo Giacosa

Strada Ovello 9, 12050 Barbaresco (CN)   +39 0173 635116

@ info@carlogiacosa.it   Carlo Giacosa

www.carlogiacosa.it   Barbaresco [map p. 39]

  5 ha; 42,000 btl

126

Donato Giacosa founded the estate in 1968 when he purchased vineyards in Barbaresco. Today the next three generations are involved, his son Carlo, granddaughter Maria Grazia, and great grandson Luca. The vineyards lie in several important crus. There are three cuvées: Narin and Luca Riserva are both blends from Asili, Cole and Ovello, while Montefico comes from a single vineyard. Aging is mostly in large casks of French oak, but Narin uses some barriques.

Fratelli Giacosa

Via Xx Settembre 64, 12052 Neive (CN)	☎ +39 0173 67013
@ *giacosa@giacosa.it*	👤 *Maurizio & Paolo Giacosa*
🌐 *www.giacosa.it*	*Barbaresco [map p. 39]*
🔲🏭🍷🍾🌿	*50 ha; 1,000,000 btl*

Giuseppe Giacosa founded the estate when he bought a vineyard in Neive in 1895. His two sons took over after the second world war and moved in to estate bottling. Their sons Maurizio and Paolo took over and expanded the vineyards. This is now a large domain with vineyards in Barolo as well as Barbaresco, including with holdings in Bussia and San Pietro in Monforte d'Alba (bought in 1991) and in Castiglione Falletto (bought in 1994) and increased holdings in Neive (added in 2003). From Barbaresco there is a DOCG wine and the Basarin cru (aged in botti), and Vigna Gianmatè, from a single plot in Basarin (aged in barriques). From Barolo there is the DOCG wine, the Bussia cru, and Vigna Mandorlo from the Scarrone cru. I find Bussia to be sweeter and rounder than Scarrone. The Nebbiolo d'Alba comes from the other side of the Tanaro river. There are four cuvées of Barbera d'Alba, including a generic wine, a cuvée sourced from Bussia, one from Madonna di Como (in Alba), and the top cuvée Maria Gioana, a selection of the best grapes from several sources, aged in barriques. There are also two Dolcetto d'Alba cuvées from specific sources as well as the generic wine.

Luigi Giordano

Via Secondine 5, 12050 Barbaresco (CN)	☎ +39 0173 635142
@ *luigigiordano@luigigiordano.it*	👤 *Luigi Giordano*
🌐 *www.luigigiordano.it*	*Barbaresco [map p. 39]*
🍷🚜	*7 ha; 80,000 btl*

Giovanni Giordano founded the domain in the 1930s and sold grapes. His son Luigi moved into estate-bottling in 1960, and expanded the estate, which is now run by his daughters, Silvia and Laura. There are holdings in Barbaresco in the crus of Montestefano, Asili, and Cavanna, and there is a cuvée from each cru; all age for 18-24 months in 30-50 hl botti of Slavonian oak. The Barbaresco is a quarter of all production. The Langhe Nebbiolo is a 100% varietal from vineyards in Barbaresco. Langhe Rosso is a blended wine from vineyards in Barbaresco. There are also Barbera and Dolcetto d'Alba. The only white is Arneis from Roero.

Giacomo Grimaldi

Via L. Einaudi 8, 12060 Barolo (CN)	☎ +39 0173 560536
@ *info@giacomogrimaldi.com*	👤 *Ferruccio Grimaldi*

⊕ *www.giacomogrimaldi.com*

🗓 🏭 🚜

◉ *Barolo [map p. 36]*

16 ha; 70,000 btl

The estate was founded in 1930 by Ernesto Grimaldi. His son Giacomo took over in 1983 and continued the policy of selling most of the grapes from the 2 ha estate. Ferruccio took over in 1996, expanded the estate by purchasing vineyards to bring the total in Barolo to 6 ha, and switched to estate bottling. The communal Barolo is a blend from the Terlo and Ravera crus, and two crus come from Le Coste (the original family vineyard) and Sotto Castello di Novello. The Nebbiolo d'Alba comes from the Valmaggiore vineyard in Roero. The style is traditional, producing wines that can be austere when young.

Icardi

Via San Lazzaro 24, 12053 Castiglione Tinella (CN)

@ *info@icardivini.com*

⊕ *www.icardivini.com*

🗓 🏭 🚜 📄

📞 *+39 0141 855159*

👤 *Mariagrazia or Claudio Icardi*

◉ *Asti*

44 ha; 310,000 btl

The winery was founded in 1914, and established a commercial basis in the 1960s when Pierino Icardi began to produce Moscato d'Asti, subsequently expanding to the west to produce Barolo and Barbaresco. His children Mariagrazia (manager) and Claudio (winemaker) now run the domain, focusing on Barolo. Barolo Parej is a traditional blend, coming from three areas ('this is the interpretation of how Barolo should be'). However, vinification is modern, with fermentation in stainless steel followed by 36 months aging in new barriques. The cuvée from the cru, Fossati, ages similarly. Barbaresco is about 10% of production, and comes from the Montubert and Starderi Crus. Other wines in the range are Barbera from Alba and Asti, Langhe Rosso and Nebbiolo, and, of course, Moscato d'Asti.

Lodali

Viale Rimembranza 5, 12050 Treiso d'Alba (CN)

@ *lodali@lodali.it*

⊕ *www.lodali.it*

🗓 🏭 🚜

📞 *+39 0173 638109*

👤 *Walter Lodali*

◉ *Barbaresco [map p. 39]*

16 ha; 100,000 btl

Giovanni Lodali was the son of a peasant farmer who started a trattoria in Treiso and began to produce wine for his customers in the 1930s. His son, Lorenzo, qualified in oenology and started to produce wine commercially in 1958. Lorenzo died young in 1982, and his wife Rita took over the business. Their son Walter graduated in oenology in 1998 and took over the estate. There is quite a large range of wines for a small estate. For most sources there are two cuvées: a regular cuvée, and the Lorens cuvée at a higher level, added in 2005. Barbaresco Rocche dei 7 Fratelli is the original cuvée; Barbaresco Lorens is the top Barbaresco. Both come exclusively from the commune of Treiso. Similarly there is a regular cuvée from Barolo Bricco Ambrogio and a Lorens cuvée. The Nebbiolo d'Alba comes from just to the west of Alba. Barolo and Barbaresco age in 25 hl botti. Also from Treiso, Barbera d'Alba ages in stainless steel, while Barbera d'Alba Lorens ages in barriques. Similarly, Langhe Chardonnay ages in stainless steel, and Chardonnay Lorens in barriques.

Paolo Manzone

Loc Meriame 1, 12050 Serralunga d'Alba (CN)	📞 +39 0173 613113
@ paolomanzone@barolomeriame.com	👤 Paolo Manzone & Luisella Corino
⊕ www.barolomeriame.com	◉ Barolo [map p. 37]
🖪 👑 🗃 🍷 ☡	14 ha; 85,000 btl

The estate is located in the tiny Meriame Cru and has been in Luisella Manzone's family for many generations, but the grapes were sold off. Paolo was a consulting oenologist until he started to produce wine from the family estate in 1999. The Barolo *tout court* comes from Meriame but is labeled 'Commune di Serralunga d'Alba.' The Meriame Cru comes from a plot of 65-year old vines; there is also a Riserva. They are aged in a mix of Slavonian botti and French barriques or tonneaux. The Nebbiolo d'Alba and the Barbera d'Alba come from Sinio, just to east outside the Barolo DOCG. There are also a Barbaresco, two Langhe reds from blends of indigenous varieties, and an Arneis.

Poderi Marcarini

Via Umberto I 34, La Morra (shop)	📞 +39 0173 50222
Piazza Martiri 2, 12064 La Morra (cn)	
@ marcarini@marcarini.it	👤 Manuel Marchetti
⊕ www.marcarini.it	◉ Barolo [map p. 35]
🏃 👑 🍷 🚜	20 ha; 125,000 btl

The estate originated in the mid nineteenth century, and is now in its sixth generation of family ownership under Manuel Marchetti and his children. (Luisa Marchetti inherited the estate in 1990, and her husband Manuel continued after her death). Barolo comes from estate vineyards in La Morra, including Brunate (more masculine) and La Serra (more feminine). The style is traditional, with four weeks maceration followed by aging in Slavonian botti, and the wines usually regard time to come around. The domain has expanded into Neviglie and Roero. The Langhe Nebbiolo is a blend from the younger vineyards in Barolo and from Neviglie. The Barbera d'Alba also is a blend from La Morra and Neviglie. The Dolcetto d'Alba Fontanazza comes from La Morra, and the Boschi di Berri cuvée comes from pre-phylloxera ungrafted vines (probably the oldest Dolcetto in Italy). A Moscato d'Asti comes from the vineyards at Neviglie. The white Arneis comes from 2 ha in Roero.

Mario Marengo

loc. Serra Denari 2a, 34, 12064 La Morra CN	📞 +39 0173 50115
@ marengo@cantinamarengo.it	👤 Marco Marengo
🖪 👑 🍷 ☡ 8 ha; 38,000 btl	◉ Barolo [map p. 35]

This small estate was established in 1899. Marco began in the winery in 1993,and took over from his father in 2001; today he works with his son, oenologist Stefano. A new cellar was built for the 2011 vintage. The top vineyards are about a hectare each, one in Brunate (in La Morra commune) and one in Bricco della Viole (in Barolo commune). Both holdings date almost from the beginning of the domain. There is a Riserva as well as the regular cuvée from Brunate. The general Barolo cuvée is a blend from four plots in La Morra, and there are also Nebbiolo d'Alba (from plots in Roero) and Barbera d'Alba (from a vineyard in Castiglione Falletto). Marco is a modernist, using short maceration followed by aging in French barriques including 15% new oak.

Casa E. di Mirafiore

Via Alba 15, 12050 Serralunga D'Alba (CN)	📞 *+39 0173 626117*
@ *info@mirafiore.it*	👤 *Andrea Farinetti*
🌐 *www.mirafiore.it*	🔴 *Barolo [map p. 37]*
📅 🏭 🍇 🍷 ○	*25 ha; 200,000 btl*

The estate originated together with Fontanafredda (see profile), when Vittorio Emmanuele II (who became the first King of Italy) bought the adjacent estates for his mistress. Their son, Emmanuele Alberto, Count of Mirafiore, started to produce wine at the estates in 1878. Purchased together in 2008 by Oscar Farinetta, who founded the Eataly chain, they remain under the same ownership, but the wines are produced independently. In fact, the Mirafiore label was not used for seventy years until it was resurrected after the change of ownership. Casa Mirafiore is also used as the name of the hotel at Fontanafredda. Vineyards are basically at the estate in Serralunga (actually somewhat north of the village of Serralunga and in reality closer to Grinzane Cavour), although there is a holding also in the commune of Barolo.

Mauro Molino

Fraz. Annunziata Gancia 111a, 12064 La Morra (CN)	📞 *+39 0173 50814*
@ *info@mauromolino.com*	👤 *Matteo Molino*
🌐 *www.mauromolino.com*	🔴 *Barolo [map p. 35]*
📅 🏭 🍇 🌱	*20 ha; 160,000 btl*

Mauro Molino started as a winemaker in Emilia Romagna in 1973, returned to the Langhe in 1979, and founded his own domain in 1982. His children Martina and Matteo have now taken over. The original vineyards are in La Morra, more recently some were added in Monforte d'Alba, and there are three crus as well as the Gallinotto single vineyard wine and a communal Barolo. Molino is a modernist, using short maceration followed by aging in French barriques; the wines are on the lighter side for Barolo. The top wine is the Barolo Conca. Half the production is Barolo; the rest is an extensive range from other areas in the Langhe.

Fratelli Monchiero

Via Alba-Monforte 49, 12060 Castiglione Falletto (CN)	📞 *+39 0173 62820*
@ *monchierovini@monchierovini.it*	👤 *Vittorio Monchiero*
🌐 *www.monchierovini.it*	🔴 *Barolo [map p. 37]*
📅 🏭 🏠 🍇 🚜	*12 ha; 40,000 btl*

The family owns vineyards in La Morra and Castiglione Falletto and in Alba. Brothers Reno and Maggiorino took over in the 1950s, and started bottling wine in the 1970s. They were based in La Morra until they purchased the winery in Castiglione Falletto in 1982. Maggiorino's son, Vittorio, who qualified at the oenology institute in Alba, now runs the domain, with his son Luca, who joined in 2017. Their approach is traditional, with wines aged in botti of Slavonian oak. The Barolo comes from Castiglione Falletto, and there is also a cuvée specifically labeled Commune di Castiglione Falletto. From within the commune there are Rocche di Castiglione and Montanello (the area around the winery). Roere de Santa Maria comes from La Morra. They all age in 50 hl botti for 30 months, except for Montanello which ages in 500 liter tonneaux. There are Riservas from Rocche di Castiglione and Montanello. The Nebbiolo d'Alba comes from vineyards in Alba. The Barbera d'Alba comes from a variety of sources and the Dolcetto d'Alba from old vines in Treiso.

Ada Nada

Via Ausario 12b, 12050 Treiso (CN)	📞 *+39 0173 638127*
@ *info@adanada.it*	👤 *Elvio & Annalisa Nada*
🌐 *www.adanada.it*	🔘 *Barbaresco [map p. 39]*
📅 🏭 🏠 🌱 🍷	*9 ha; 50,000 btl*

This is one of the Nada domains in Treiso started when Carlo Nada bought 3 ha of vines in what is now the Rombone cru. The Ada Nada domain descends from Carlo's son Giovanni, who worked with his son Giancarlo, who daughter Annalisa and her husband Elvio took over in 2001. Wines ferment in stainless steel and age in the traditional botti. The Langhe Nebbiolo, Serena, comes from younger vines in Rombone. Valeirano comes from vines planted in the cru in 1971. Elisa is the cuvée from vines planted in Rombone cru in 1947. The Riserva Cichin comes from a half hectare plot in Rombone planted in 1958. Other wines includes Barbera and Dolcetto d'Alba.

Giuseppe Nada

Via Giacosa, 12a, 12050 Treiso d'Alba (CN)	📞 *+39 0173 638110*
@ *enrico.nada@live.it*	👤 *Enrico Nada*
🌐 *www.nadagiuseppe.com*	🔘 *Barbaresco [map p. 39]*
📅 🏭 🌱 🍷	*6 ha; 50,000 btl*

This Nada estate started in 1900 with a purchase of a vineyard in the Casot cru from the Gaja family. The domain started estate-bottling in 1964, then in 1968 moved from Casot to a new winery higher up in Marcarini. Giuseppe's son Enrico has been the winemaker since 2008. The Langhe Nebbiolo is a blend from the Casot and Marcarini Crus, and the wine ages in a mix of tonneaux and botti. From Barbaresco, the Casot cru ages for a year in 10 hl botti followed by a year in 30 hl botti. Marcarini makes a Riserva, which ages in 10-30 hl botti for four years.

Negretti

Fraz. Santa Maria, 53, 12064 La Morra (CN)	📞 *+39 0173 509850*
@ *info@negrettivini.com*	👤 *Ezio & Massimo Negretti*
🌐 *www.negrettivini.com*	🔘 *Barolo [map p. 35]*
📅 🏭 🌱 🌿	*13 ha; 45,000 btl*

The Negretti brothers started their domain in 2002. Vineyards are in La Morra and Rodi, mostly dating from the 1980s. They are modernists, with wines fermented in stainless steel then aged in barriques of French oak or small botti of Swiss or Austrian oak. The Barolo is a blend from La Morra and Rodi. Mirau comes from plots in La Morra, aged in 25 hl Swiss botti for 24 months, Rive comes from the cru in La Morra, aged in a mix of French and Austrian 25 hl botti, and Bricco Ambrogio comes from the cru in Rodi, aged in French barriques for 24 months. The Nebbiolo d'Alba comes from Monforte d'Alba, aged in French barriques for 12 months, and the Barbera d'Alba comes from La Morra, aged in a mix of French barriques are German botti. The Langhe Chardonnay ages in a mix of barriques and stainless steel.

Andréa Oberto

Borgata Simane 11, 12051 La Morra (CN)	☎ +39 0173 50104
@ info@andreaoberto.it	👤 Fabio Oberto
🌐 www.andreaoberto.it	🔴 Barolo [map p. 35]
📅 🏭 🍷 🚜	16 ha; 100,000 btl

The domain started two generations ago when Andréa's father bought a small farm in La Morra in 1959, practicing polyculture. Andréa left but came back to take over in 1978 when his father died, focusing on viticulture, at first sending some grapes to the cooperative and making some wine for bulk sales. Slowly the estate turned to growing grapes exclusively and bottling its own wine. A new winery was built in 2003. Andréa's son Fabio is now making the wine. The Barolos include three Crus, Brunate, Rocche and Albarella, accounting for about a quarter of the estate; another half is Langhe Nebbiolo, and the rest is Barbera and Dolcetto.

Figli Luigi Oddero

Tenuta Parà 95, Fraz. Santa Maria, 12065 La Morra (CN)	☎ +39 0173 500386
@ info@figliluigioddero.it	👤 Alberto Zaccarelli
🌐 www.figliluigioddero.it	🔴 Barolo [map p. 35]
📅 🏭 🍷 🚜	32 ha; 90,000 btl

Brothers Giacomo and Luigi inherited Oddero (see profile), but Giacomo's daughter Cristina and her uncle had a disagreement that led Luigi to leave with his half the estate to form his own domain in 2006. After Luigi died in 2009, his widow Lena continued to run the estate. The wines are made traditionally, with long maceration, and aged in botti, with advice from Dante Scaglione, formerly of Bruno Giacosa. The range naturally is similar to Oddero, with top cuvées from Santa Maria in La Morra, Rocche dei Rivera (Castiglione Falletto) and Broglio (Serralunga d'Alba).

Azienda Vinicola Palladino

Piazza Cappellano 9, 12050 Serralunga d'Alba (CN)	☎ +39 0173 613108
@ info@palladinovini.com	👤 Veronica Santero
🌐 www.palladinovini.com	🔴 Barolo [map p. 37]
📅 🏭 🍷 🍾 🚜	11 ha; 180,000 btl

The property that houses the winery dates from 1870, but the current domain dates from 1974, when the Palladino family bought the estate. It's now in the third generation. Wine

132

production started with the 1978 vintage after some renovations. The core of the estate is in Serralunga, and the Barolo is labeled Commune di Serralunga d'Alba. Holdings include three Crus in Serralunga: Ornato, Parafada, and San Bernardo which comes as a Riserva. Winemaking is not committed to a single style, but varies with the cuvée, using both large casks and barriques. The range is supplemented by purchased grapes, and includes Nebbiolo d'Alba, Barbera d'Alba, Dolcetto d'Alba, Roero Arneis, Gavi, and even Moscato.

Pelissero

Via Ferrere 10, 12050 Treiso (CN)	📞 *+39 0173 638430*
@ *pelissero@pelissero.com*	👤 *Giorgio Pelissero*
🌐 *www.pelissero.com*	🔴 *Barbaresco [map p. 39]*
🗓️ 🏭 🍴 🍷	*42 ha; 250,000 btl*

Luigi Pelissero founded the domain in 1960, and it has expanded steadily under current owner Giorgio Pelissero. The Langhe Nebbiolo comes from Treiso, and is ripe, soft, and immediately approachable. The Barbaresco Nubiola comes from six small plots in all three villages of the appellation, and has a similar style, but a bit more weight to the palate. It is made in a traditional style, with fermentation in stainless steel followed by aging in 50 hl botti. Vanatu comes from a single vineyard, and is a little tauter; the Riserva is a selection of the best lots. The Barbera d'Alba comes from Treiso, and there is also a Riserva. I find the wines overall to be a bit ho-hum.

Pasquale Pelissero

Via Crosa, 2, 12052 Neive (CN)	📞 *+39 0173 67376*
@ *info@pasqualepelissero.com*	👤 *Ornella Pelissero*
🌐 *www.pasqualepelissero.com*	🔴 *Barbaresco [map p. 39]*
🗓️ 🏭 🍴 🍷	*8 ha; 35,000 btl*

The family bought the farm, Cascina Crosa, in 1921. Pasquale Pelissero was one of the first producers in Neive to bottle his own wine, starting with a Barbaresco in 1971. The vineyards of this small estate surround the winery, at 400m elevation at the top of the Bricco San Giuliano hill. Pasquale's daughter Ornella took over the estate when he died in 2007. She has renovated the cellars and expanded the range of wines. The range of Nebbiolo starts with the Langhe, sourced from Neive, aged in 3-year barriques for 12 months. Bricco San Giuliano is the cru, from 25-year-old vines, and ages 90% in 25-30 hl botti of French oak and 10% in new French barriques. Casina Crosa comes from older vines in the cru, aged entirely in 25-30 hl botti of French oak. Riserva Ciabot comes from 25-year-old vines, and ages for 36 months entirely in new French barriques. The Barbera d'Alba comes from Neive and ages for a year in 3-year French barriques. There are also Dolcetto d'Alba, a Langhe Freisa (light red), and Langhe Favorita (100% of the white variety).

Guido Porro

Via Alba 1, 12050 Serralunga d'Alba (CN)	📞 *+39 0173 61306*
@ *guidoporro@guidoporro.com*	👤 *Guido Porro*

www.guidoporro.com

🗓 👪 🏭 🚜

Barolo [map p. 37]

8 ha; 35,000 btl

This family estate is now in its fourth generation under Guido, together with his son Fabio. The transition from selling grapes to the cooperative to producing estate wine occurred in the 1980s. Close to the castle in Serralunga, the winery was renovated in 2010, and is more or less surrounded by the estate vineyards. The two historic estate vineyards are both within Cru Lazzarito, just to the west of the village: Lazzairasco has the oldest (50-year) vines and is the warmest site and more masculine, while Santa Catarina is adjacent, but more exposed to the wind and more feminine. Two vineyards on the other side of Serralunga are more recent: Cru Gianetto was added in 2011, and Guido inherited a half hectare of Vignarionda in 2011, which has its first release with the 2014 vintage. The wines are classically aged in 25 hl Slavonian botti.

Prinsi

Via Gaia 5, 12052 Neive (CN)

@ *info@prinsi.it*

www.prinsi.it

🗓 👪 🏭 🌿

📞 *+39 0173 67192*

👤 *Daniele Lequio*

Barbaresco [map p. 39]

15 ha; 60,000 btl

Ottavio Prinsi started estate bottling in thee 1940s, and his grandson Daniele Lequio, who started in 1999, is now the winemaker, although his father Franco is still involved. The three Barbarescos each come from single vineyards: Gaia Principe is around the winery, Gallina comes from one of Barbaresco's top Crus, and Fausoni comes as a Riserva. Daniele has something of a reputation as a modernist who wants to make his wines more approachable, but in fact is flexible, with Gaia Principe aged in barriques, Gallini in tonneaux followed by large casks, and Faustino Riserva in botti. Langhe Nebbiolo and Barbera d'Alba also age in wood, but everything else ages in stainless steel.

Raineri

loc. Panerole 24, 12060 Novello (CN)

@ *info@rainerivini.com*

www.rainerivini.com

🗓 👪 🏭 🌿

📞 *+39 3396 009289*

👤 *Gianmaetto Raineri*

Barolo

6 ha; 40,000 btl

Raineri started in 2005 as a collaboration between three friends, Gianmatteo Raineri (known as Jimmy), Fabrizio Giraudo, and Luciano Racca. Their first production was Dogliani, rather a lesser appellation, but now they are known for their Barolo. The Barolo comes from Perno in Monforte d'Alba, the Monserra cuvée is a blend from Perno and Serralunga d'Alba, and the Perno cuvée comes from the single vineyard of Santo Stefano di Perno. They age in large casks of French oak, including some new oak. The cuvée from the Castelletto cru of Monforte ages in barriques with 25% new oak. The Langhe Nebbiolo, Snart, comes from Monforte, and ages in stainless steel. There is also a Barbera d'Alba Superiore from Monforte, aged in old French oak. The Langhe Bianco is a blend of Chardonnay with Cortese (the grape of Gavi), aged in stainless steel.

Réva

Località S. Sebastiano, 68, 12065 Monforte d'Alba (CN)	☎ *+39 0173 789269*
@ *francesco.spadaro@revawinery.com*	🚹 *Miroslav Lekes*
⊕ *www.revawinery.com*	◉ *Barolo [map p. 38]*
🗓 ⛏ 🏠 🦐 ♨	*23 ha; 70,000 btl*

This is effectively a new domain, created in 2013 by Miroslav Lekes, a Czech entrepreneur, when he bought 6 ha of vineyards in the southern part of the DOCG, divided more or less equally between Monforte and Novello. He has also created a small boutique hotel with a Michelin-starred restaurant at the domain. Gianluca Colombo came as winemaker. Vineyards have now been expanded all over the DOCG, from the original 3 ha each in Monforte and Ravera (in Novello), to include 1 ha in Lazzarito (Serralunga), 0.3 ha in Cannubi (Barolo), 0.3 ha in Grinzane, and 15 ha in Roddino. The Barolo is a blend from all the communes and ferments in stainless steel before aging for 14 months in barriques. The crus ferment in conical vats and then age for 24 months in botti. The Nebbiolo d'Alba actually comes from Monforte; there are also Barbera and Dolcetto d'Alba. A white cuvée, Grey, comes from Sauvignon Blanc (actually 70% Sauvignon Gris and 30% Sauvignon Blanc), aged for a year in botti.

Revello Fratelli

Fraz. Annunziata 103, 12064 La Morra (CN)	☎ *+39 0173 50276*
@ *revello@revellofratelli.com*	🚹 *Elena or Simone Revello*
⊕ *www.revellofratelli.com*	◉ *Barolo [map p. 35]*
🗓 ⛏ 🏠 🦐 ☕	*12 ha; 60,000 btl*

The Revello family moved to La Morra in 1945 and bought a vineyard in 1954, selling off the grapes until they started estate bottling in 1967. They moved to a new location in the Gattera Cru in 1971. Brothers Lorenzo and Carlo took over the family domain in 1990, following the advice of family friend Elio Altare. The winery was renovated and expanded in 2003, and a tasting room was built. Lorenzo was the winemaker and Carlo managed the vineyards until they split into two estates in 2016, dividing the vineyards each cru. Lorenzo kept the name and original winery, and his children Elena and Simone are now taking over. Carlo Revello (see profile) makes wine separately under his own name. The brothers' first Barolo in 1993 was a blend from all the plots, and over the next few years they introduced separate cuvées from the Crus, Giachini, Rocche dell'Annunziata, Conca, Gattera, and Cerretta. The style is in the modernist camp, with fermentation in rotary fermenters followed by aging in French barriques including 20% new oak for the Barolo, and 40-50% for the Crus, except Gattara which ages in Slavonian oak. Two Barberas come from the local vineyards, one aged in stainless steel, and Ciabot du Re aged in barriques with 80% new oak. L'Insieme is a modernist Langhe Rosso, blended from Nebbiolo, Barbera, and Cabernet Sauvignon.

Carlo Revello & Figli

Frazione Santa Maria, Serra dei Turchi 96/a, 12064 La Morra Cn	☎ *+39 0173 509524*
@ *info@carlorevello.com*	🚹 *Carlo and Erik Revello*

 *carlorevello.com*

📅 ⚒ 🍇 🌿

🔴 *Barolo [map p. 34]*

7 ha; 30,000 btl

Brothers Lorenzo and Carlo Revello took over the family estate of Fratelli Revello (see profile) in 2010, and then in 2016 divided into two separate estates. Enzo kept the name and original winery; Carlo works with his son Erik, making wine at a new winery in La Morra. Vineyards include 5 ha of Nebbiolo, 1.5 ha of Barbera, and 1 ha of Dolcetto. The first releases were assemblages from different crus, including R.G. which comes from Conca, Rocche dell'Annunziata, and Giachini; releases of the individual crus, Giachini and Rocche, started with 2016. Winemaking is more traditional than at Revello Fratelli, with aging in large casks.

Michele Reverdito

Borgata Garassini 74, Frazione Rivalta, 12064 La Morra (CN)   📞 *+39 0173 50336*

@ *reverdito-m@libero.it*   👤 *Michele Reverdito*

🌐 *www.reverdito.it*   🔴 *Barolo [map p. 34]*

📅 ⚒ 🍇 🌿   *26 ha; 100,000 btl*

Silvano Reverdito started buying vineyards in the late 1960s and sold the grapes, then helped his son Michele to found the domain in 2000. The focus is exclusively on indigenous varieties. The Barolo is a blend across communes, and then there are seven Crus across three communes: Bricco Cogni, La Serra, Castagni, and Ascheri in La Morra; Bricco San Pietro in Monforte d'Alba; Badarina in Serralunga d'Alba; and Riva Rocca in Verduno. The Langhe Nebbiolo comes from La Morra. Winemaking varies: the Barolos are aged mostly in large casks, but some tonneaux are used. The three Barberas see wood and can show a touch of oak. Wines from two old varieties, the Langhe Nascetta and the Verduno Pelaverga, age in amphora.

Fratelli Seghesio

Fraz. Castelletto 19, 12065 Monforte d'Alba (CN)   📞 *+39 0173 78108*

@ *info@fratelliseghesio.com*   👤 *Riccardo Seghesio*

🌐 *www.fratelliseghesio.com*   🔴 *Barolo [map p. 38]*

📅 ⚒ 🍇 🌿   *10 ha; 60,000 btl*

Aldo and Riccardo Seghesio began bottling their own wine at this family estate in 198. Today Riccardo runs the winery with his niece Michaela and nephews Sandro and Marco. Located in the top Castelletto subzone of Monforte, their approach varies with the cuvée, although all winemaking starts with rotary fermenters. The Langhe Nebbiolo and both Barolos come from the Castelletto cru, distinguished by the age of the vines. Langhe Nebbiolo comes from the youngest (20-year old) vines (aged in a mix of stainless steel and barriques), the Barolo DOCG from 20-30-year old vines (aged in 50 hl botti of Slavonian oak), and La Villa from the oldest (40-60-year old) vines (aged for 12 months in French barriques and for 18 months in the Slavonian botti). Dolcetto d'Alba and Barbera d'Alba age in stainless steel, and Barbera d'Alba La Chiesa ages in French barriques. Langhe Rosso Bouquet is an 'international' wine, a blend of Merlot, Cabernet Sauvignon, and Nebbiolo, ages in French barriques.

136

Massimo Rivetti

Via Rivetti 22, 12052 Neive (CN)	📞 *+39 0141 89568*
@ *massimo@rivettimassimo.it*	👤 *Massimo Rivetti*
🌐 *www.rivettimassimo.it*	🔵 *Barbaresco [map p. 39]*
🧍 🍶 🍇 🍂	*25 ha; 100,000 btl*

The estate was founded in 1947; Massimo is the founder's grandson. The home estate is the 12 ha Froi vineyard around the winery, part of the Serraboella Cru; planted with indigenous varieties, some vines date from the establishment of the domain. Farther off, vineyards in Alba are also planted with Nebbiolo, Barbera and Dolcetto, while at Mango (east of Barbaresco), the Garassino vineyard has international varieties. The generic Barbaresco ages in botti; the Froi cuvée, from the home estate, also ages in botti; Serraboella comes from 60-year old vines and ages in barriques (including new oak) as well as botti. The style of the Barbarescos points towards modernism, with aromatic complexity increasing from Froi to Seraboella. There are two cuvées of Barbera d'Alba Superiore: Serraboella comes from the oldest (75-year) vines and ages in barriques, while Froi ages in cement. There's a range of international varieties under the Langhe label: Garassin is a blend of Cabernet Sauvignon and Merlot, and there are also Chardonnay and Pinot Noir, as well as whites, rosés, and Moscato.

Azienda Agricola Rivetto DAL 1902

via Roddino 17, 12050 Serralunga d'Alba	📞 *+39 0173 613380*
@ *info@rivetto.it*	👤 *Enrico Rivetto*
🌐 *rivetto.it*	🔵 *Barolo [map p. 37]*
📅 🍶 🍇 ⚙ 🔘	*15 ha; 100,000 btl*

Originally founded in 1920, Rivetto has been in its present location southeast of Serralunga since 1938. Enrico is the fourth generation and took over in 1999. The property extends over 35 ha, including 6 ha of nut trees and 1 ha of other crops, with the vineyards surrounded by woods. Vineyards were reduced slightly in size when Enrico converted to biodynamic viticulture, taking out some vines to make room for donkeys, which provide manure. The winery is located at the top of the Lirano hills at an elevation of 400m. There principal cuvée is the Barolo labeled as Commune di Serralunga; the Leon Riserva is selected from the best barrels. The top cuvées comes from an 0.5 ha plot in Cru Briccolina. The Lage Nebbiolo is a blend of 95% Nebbiolo and 5% Barbera. The Barbaresco comes from grapes purchased from Treiso commune. Barbera d'Alba Loirano Soprano comes from plots at the top of the hill; Zio Nando comes from a third of the plot, from vines planted in 1944.

Rizzi

Via Rizzi 15, 12050 Treiso (CN)	📞 *+39 0173 638161*
@ *cantinarizzi@cantinarizzi.it*	👤 *Enrico & Jole Dellapiana*
🌐 *www.cantinarizzi.it*	🔵 *Barbaresco [map p. 39]*
📅 🍶 🍇 🌿	*40 ha; 100,000 btl*

Ernesto Dellapiana left his career as an entrepreneur in Turin almost fifty years ago to make wine from land that belonged to the family. The domain takes its name from the Cru where it is located; there is also a vineyard in the adjacent Nervo Cru to the east. Other vineyards have been added over the years. Enrico (production) and Jole (management) joined in 2004. All four Barbaresco cuvées come from Crus: Rizzi, Nervo, and Pajoré. The Vigna Boito Riserva comes from the Boito vineyard within Rizzi (which is a large Cru). All ferment in stainless steel and age in 50 hl botti of Slavonian oak. The Langhe Nebbiolo and Barbera d'Alba come from Treiso; Moscato d'Asti comes from a vineyard in the nearby commune of Neviglie.

Roagna

Loc. Paglieri 9, 12050 Barbaresco (CN) or Str. della Pira 3, 12060 Castiglione Falletto (CN)	☎ +39 0173 635109
@ info@roagna.com	👤 Luca Roagna
⊕ www.roagna.com	Barbaresco [map p. 39]
◯ ✐ 🦋 ☀	15 ha; 60,000 btl

Vincenzo Roagna created the estate at the start of the twentieth century with a key holding of 2 ha in the famous Cru of Pajè. It has passed from father to son to Luca, the fifth generation, who took over in 2001. Roagna expanded into Barolo with the purchase of the 7 ha Pira Cru in Castiglione Falletto in 1989 (it's a monopole and now Roagna's largest single holding). A small cellar has recently been built there so the wines can be vinified on site. Other vineyards have been added in Barbaresco: Asili and Faset (in 2013), and Albesani and Gallina (rented in 2014), so the holdings are a roll-call of top names. The three historic cuvées are Pajè, Pajè Vecchie Vigne (from 60-year old vines), and Crichet Pajè (from the oldest vines in the top few rows). Other notable cuvées are the Vecchie Vigne from Asili and Montefico, but production is very small, because the plots are only a quarter hectare each. The Langhe Rosso is a blend using the top 10-20 liters of each vat. Roagna is a traditionalist: sixty days maceration before aging in botti of Slavonian oak from three to five years (up to ten years for Crichet Pajè). The range also includes Dolcetto and Langhe Bianco.

Josetta Saffirio

Via Castelletto 32, 12065 Monforte d'Alba (CN)	☎ +39 0173 78660
@ josettasaffirio@hotmail.com	👤 Sara Vezza
⊕ www.josettasaffirio.com	Barolo [map p. 38]
📅 ⚒ 🦋 🍂	5 ha; 30,000 btl

The family has been in Monforte d'Alba since 1890, and Josetta took over the vineyards in 1975 when she was only 23. Grapes continued to be sold off until she started to produce wine in 1982. Her daughter Sara took over in 1999 and built a new winery in 2006, based on ecological principles. All the vineyards are in the Castelletto subzone Monforte; the oldest date from plantings in 1948 by Josetta's father. Nebbiolo plantings for Barolo are all exclusively the Michet clone. The range starts with Langhe Nebbiolo, aged in 30 hl botti for 12 months. The Barolo and the Persiera cuvées come age in a mix of new and used barriques. The Riserva Millenovecento48 has been made since 2007 as a separate cuvée from the oldest vines, giving only about 1,000 bottles; it ages for 24 months in a

138

mix of new and used barriques followed by a further 24 months in concrete. Other wines include Barbera d'Alba (aged in large casks), Langhe white (from the variety Rossese), a Moscato d'Asti, and Langhe rosé and sparkling wine from Nebbiolo.

Elio Sandri

Località Perno 14, 12065 Monforte d'Alba (CN)   📞 *+39 0173 787337*

@ *info@cascinadisa.com*   👤 *Elio Sandri*

🌐 *www.cascinadisa.com*   🅾 *Barolo [map p. 38]*

📅 🍷 🍂   *7 ha; 35,000 btl*

At this tiny domain in Perno, with a view across the hills to Serralunga, Elio Sandri is known for his uncompromising artisanal approach. There's only minimal pruning in the vineyard, where the oldest vines (for the Barolo) date from 1937. The cellar (and family home) is just below the vineyards, so grapes come straight down into the concrete fermentation tanks outside. The Langhe Nebbiolo originally came only from east-facing plots, but some southwest-facing plots were added in 2014, the Barolo is a Riserva (released only seven years aging in botti, well, actually one botte, making about 300 cases), and there are Dolcetto and Barbera. Elio's father purchased the property in 1965, and he's been making the wine here in his own manner since 2000.

Scarzello Giorgio e Figli di Federico Scarzello

Via Alba 29, 12060 Barolo (CN)   📞 *+39 0173 56170*

@ *info@scarzellobarolo.com*   👤 *Federico Scarzello*

🌐 *www.scarzellobarolo.com*   🅾 *Barolo [map p. 36]*

📅 🏭 🍇 🛢 🍂   *7 ha; 45,000 btl*

Giorgio Scarzello established his reputation for making ageworthy Barolos at this tiny estate. His son Federico took over in 2001 and continued the tradition. Giorgio largely replanted the vineyards in the 1990s at high density. Half the holding is in the Sarmassa Cru, and the top wine is the Vigna Merenda from the parcel in Sarmassa. There are also a Barolo blend, a Langhe Nebbiolo (declassified from Barolo), and a Barbera d'Alba (the grapes come from Sarmassa and Pajagallo). Vigna Merenda is only made in the best years, and production is only around 400 cases. It ages for 30 months in large oak casks of Slavonian and German oak before spending another three years in bottle before release. Fermentation has used wild yeast since the 2006 vintage, and can be slow, sometimes up to a couple of months. The Barbera is treated as seriously as the Barolo: fermentation may last a month, followed by two years aging in Slavonian oak.

Schiavenza

Via Mazzini 4, 12050 Serralunga d'Alba (CN)   📞 *+39 0173 613115*

@ *schiavenza@schiavenza.com*   👤 *Luciano Pira*

🌐 *www.schiavenza.com*   🅾 *Barolo [map p. 37]*

📅 🏭 ❌ 🍷 ✂   *11 ha; 47,000 btl*

Founded in 1956 by brothers Vittorio and Ugo Alessandria, the estate is run today by the second generation, Maura Alessandria and her husband Luciano Pira. The estate was originally part of the Opera Pia Barolo, the local castle which functioned as a charitable foundation, and whose vineyards were worked by sharecroppers. The name of the domain is the local dialect for sharecropper. The style is traditional, with wines aged only in botti of Slavonian oak. Vineyards are mostly in Serralunga, with a further 1.5 ha in Monforte D'Alba. The communal Barolo is labeled Serralunga d'Alba, and there are cuvées from three Crus: Prapò, Cerretta, and Broglio. The Langhe Nebbiolo comes from Serralunga, and the Barbera d'Alba comes from the holding at Perno in Monforte d'Alba. The cellars are just by the castle of Serralunga, and include a restaurant, where the Schiavenza wines are available.

Mauro Sebaste

Via Garibaldi, 222 bis, Frazione Gallo, 12051 Alba (CN)	📞 *+39 0173 262148*
@ *info@maurosebaste.it*	👤 *Sylla Sebaste*
🌐 *www.maurosebaste.it*	🔴 *Barolo [map p. 34]*
🏠 🏭 🍷 🛢 🚜	*30 ha; 150,000 btl*

Mauro Sebaste is the son of Sylla Sebaste (see profile), and founded his own winery in 1991. Vineyards were built up over several years and now extend widely in the region. Trèsurì is the Barolo blend, from three vineyards (in the villages of La Morra, Verduno and Serralunga) as indicated by its name. The Crus are all in Serralunga d'Alba, and include Prapò and Cerretta, and the Ghé Riserva. The style is modernist, with the Barolos aged in a mix of 1,600-liter casks and 400-liter barrels. The Nebbiolo d'Alba, Parigi, and the Barbera d'Alba, Contessa Rosalia, come from immediate area of Alba. "Dolcetto is an important part of our story, so we keep it and we produce two Dolcetto wines," Mauro says. Dolcetto d'Alba Contessa Rosalia is fresher and easier, and Diano d'Alba is more structured. There are also Barbera d'Asti, where Valdevani is aged in stainless steel, and Centobricchi comes from the best parcel and ages in new 400-liter barrels. Costemonghisio is a Barbera from Nizza DOC, aged in barriques to give a powerful expression of the variety. In whites, Roero Arneis is focused on freshness, while Langhe Viognier comes from calcareous terroir (fermented and aged in oak). An Alta Langa sparkling wine from Pinot and Chardonnay makes its first appearance in 2021.

Sylla Sebaste

San Pietro delle Viole 4, 12060 Barolo (CN)	📞 *+39 0173 56266*
@ *syllasebaste@syllasebaste.com*	👤 *Fabrizio Merlo*
🌐 *www.syllasebaste.com*	🔴 *Barolo [map p. 36]*
🏠 🏭 ✖ 🍷 🛢 🚜	*7 ha; 70,000 btl*

The domain was founded in 1985 by Sylla Sebaste (whose son Mauro has his own winery: see profile). Since Sylla's premature death, for the last twenty years it has been owned by Fabrizio Merlo and his brother. The winery is on the San Pietro hill between Novello and La Morra with a view over the vineyards, which are in the Bussia and Bricco Viole areas of Barolo commune. The approach is modernist, with cold maceration before fermentation in stainless steel, and Barolos aged in oak casks of various sizes, including 30% new oak. The Barolo comes from the village of Bricco, and the two top wines are the Crus, Bricco delle Viole and Bussia. The range is extended by the Nebbiolo d'Alba, the Langhe Rosso (a traditional blend of Nebbiolo and Barbera), Barbera d'Alba and d'Asti, and a Gavi, some of which come from purchased grapes.

Giulia Negri Serradenari

Via Bricco del Dente 19, 35, 12064 La Morra (CN)	📞 +39 0173 50119
@ *info@giulianegri.com*	👤 Giulia Negri
⊕ *www.giulianegri.com*	🔵 Barolo [map p. 35]
🗓 🏭 🍷 🧴	*7 ha; 45,000 btl*

Serradenari is the name of the highest hill in Barolo, and the vineyards here rise above 500m. Giulia Negri took over her family estate in 2014 when aged only 24, after gaining experience in Burgundy. When she took over, the wines were mostly aged in barriques, but she has replaced them with the traditional botti. Her father planted some Chardonnay and Pinot Noir on cooler north-facing slopes, and the Pinot Noir ages in barriques, and the Chardonnay in 350-liter barrels, both with 30% new oak. In Nebbiolo, the Langhe Pian delle Mole comes from slopes at 500m facing north in Serradenari, and ages in a mix of stainless steel and tonneau. The Barolo La Tartufaia is a blend from Serraddenari (80%) and grapes purchased from Brunate (20%). Serradenari comes from slopes facing southwest at 520m, and Marassio comes from a subparcel facing west. The Barolos all age for 24-30 months in 25hl botti of Slavonian oak. The Barbera comes from purchased grapes.

Aurelio Settimo

Fraz. Annunziata 30, 12064 La Morra (CN)	📞 +39 0173 50803
@ *aureliosettimo@aureliosettimo.com*	👤 Tiziana Settimo
⊕ *aureliosettimo.com*	🔵 Barolo [map p. 35]
🗓 🏭 🍷 🌱	*7 ha; 40,000 btl*

Domenico Settimo settled in Annunziata in 1943 and grew grapes, bottling a little in the 1950s under the label of Settimo Domenico. His son Aurelio took over in 1962 and since 1974 all production has been bottled under the Aurelio Settimo label. Since Aurelia's death in 2007, his daughter Tiziana has run the estate. Cuvées include the appellation Barolo (aged for 12 months in concrete, followed by 18 months in botti of French oak, and then 6 months in botti of new Austrian oak), the cru Rocche dell'Annunziata (slightly longer aging with a similar regime), and a Riserva from the cru (aged only in botti of French oak). The Langhe Nebbiolo is declassified from the vineyards in La Morra, and ages for 36 months only in concrete. Other wines are a Dolcetto and a rosé.

Francesco Sobrero

Via Brunella 5, 12060 Castiglione Falletto (CN)	📞 +39 0173 62864
@ *info@sobrerofrancesco.it*	👤 Flavio Sobrero
⊕ *www.sobrerofrancesco.it*	🔵 Barolo
🗓 🏭 🍷 🚜	*16 ha; 90,000 btl*

Francesco Sobrero established his estate in 1940, selling grapes until his children started to produce wine in the 1960s. Third generation Flavio Sobrero has been in charge since

2000. Most (13 ha) of the vineyards are in Castiglione Falletto, divided among 6 crus: Villero, Pernanno, Ornato, Piantà, Valentino and Parussi. The other 3 ha are planted with Moscato in the area of Canelli. The Barolo Ciabot Tanasio is the cuvée from the commune of Castiglione Falletto, and there are cuvées from the individual crus of Parussi, Villero (Riserva) and Pernanno (Riserva). The Barolos age in botti. There's a Langhe Nebbiolo and also Barbera d'Alba, Selectio, and Barbera d'Alba Superiore, :a Pichetera.

Socré

Strada Terzolo 7, 12050 Barbaresco (CN)	☎ *+39 3487 121685*
@ *info@socre.it*	👤 *Marco Piacentino*
⊕ *www.socre.it*	◉ *Barbaresco [map p. 39]*
🗓 ⛏ 🍷 🌿	*9 ha; 50,000 btl*

The domain was founded in 1869 but sold off the grapes. It took its modern form in 1990 when architect Marco Piacenteno left his career in Turin to take over the family vineyards. A new cellar was built in 2010. The core holding is the 3 ha vineyard in Barbaresco just below the winery; since the early 200s, only Nebbiolo has been grown here. There are also 1 ha in Alba, producing Langhe Nebbiolo, Barbera d'Alba, and Dolcetto d'Alba, and 2 ha in Cisterna d'Asti (between Monferrato and Roero), where Cabernet Sauvignon and Merlot are grown as well as indigenous varieties. The Barbaresco shows a modernist approach, aged in French barriques. The top wine is the Barbaresco Roncaglie, aged first in barriques including a third new oak, and then in 20 hl casks. In international varieties, the Langhe Chardonnay, 'Paint it Black' offers a Piedmont take on the variety, quite smoky and mineral.

Terre Del Barolo

Via Alba Barolo 8, 12060 Castiglione Falletto (CN)	☎ *+39 0173 262053*
@ *info@terredelbarolo.com*	👤 *Paolo Boffa*
⊕ *www.terredelbarolo.com*	◉ *Barolo [map p. 37]*
🚶 ⛏ 🍷	*650 ha; 3,000,000 btl*

The only cooperative in Barolo, Terre del Barolo (it has dropped Cantine from its name) was founded in 1958 with 22 growers, and today has more than three hundred members from all the villages in the Barolo appellation. Its reputation has been somewhat mixed. The wide range of wines includes Barolo and Barolo Riserva, but they are outnumbered by wines from other appellations in the Langhe. However, there are ongoing efforts to lift up the level, including a range of organic wines from Barolo, Nebbiolo d'Alba, and Barbera d'Alba, and the new Arnoldo Rivera range, launched with the 2013 vintage, and named after the coop's founder. The name of the Arnoldo Rivera Undici indicates that it's a blend from Crus in each of the 11 villages in the appellation; other wines in the range come from single vineyards, across 15 ha of the coop's holdings.

Trediberri

Borgata Torriglione, 4, 12064 La Morra (CN)	☎ *+39 0173 509302*
@ *info@trediberri.com*	👤 *Nicola Oberto*

142

This small family estate was founded in 2007, when Nicolo Oberta, his father Federico (who retired from Ratti in 2005), and his associate Vladimiro Rambaldi, bought 5 ha of Nebbiolo in Berri, a hamlet in La Morra, at the far west of the DOCG. The first wine went on the market in 2012. There are now also smaller holdings in Torriglione, where they built a winery, Rocche d'Annunziata (the oldest vineyard with 40-year-old wines), and a rented plot in Capalot. The Langhe Nebbiolo comes from Berri, the Barolo is a blend, and there is a special cuvée from Rocche d'Annunziata. In addition there are Barbera d'Alba, a Langhe rosé from Barbera, and a Sauvignon Blanc from the home vineyard at Torriglione.

Mauro Veglio

Fraz. Annunziata, Cascina Nuova 50, 12064 La Morra (CN)

📞 *+39 0173 509212*

@ *mauroveglio@mauroveglio.com*

👤 *Mauro & Alessandro Veglio*

🌐 *www.mauroveglio.com*

⚪ *Barolo [map p. 35]*

⬛🏭🐌🦪

22 ha; 130,000 btl

Angelo Veglio bought a vineyard in Gattera in the 1960s and moved into making wine. The house where the winery is now located in La Morra followed in 1979 together with the Arborina and Rocche dell'Annunziata vineyards. Mauro, the only one of his children to be interested in winemaking, took over in 1986. Vineyards in Monforte d'Alba were added ten years later. Today there is a Barolo blend (coming from the youngest vines), and cuvées from four crus. The wines are aged in barriques, with 20% new for the Barolo *tout court*, and 40% new for the crus.

Castello Di Verduno

Via Umberto I 9, 12060 Verduno (CN)

📞 *+39 0172 470284*

@ *info@cantinecastellodibverduno.it*

👤 *Marcella Bianco*

🌐 *www.cantinecastellodiverduno.it*

⚪ *Barolo [map p. 34]*

🧍🏭❌🦪🌿

12 ha; 68,000 btl

This is not in fact a castle, but a rather gracious mansion at the top of the village, partly converted into a hotel and restaurant, with its cellars used for the winery. The Burlotto family purchased it in 1909. It was subsequently inherited by one of the sons of Giovanni Bastista Burlotto; another son inherited G. B. Burlotto (see profile), and the third son inherited Casina Massara. The current owners are Franco Bianco and his wife Gabriella (Burlotto). Estate grapes provide 95% of the supply. Mario Andrion has been the winemaker since 2000. There is also cellar in Barbaresco. Barolo vineyards are mostly in the commune of Verduno, and there are three crus of Barolo. From Barbaresco there is a blend and cuvées from the Faset and Rabajà crus; the Langhe Nebbiolo is declassified from Barbaresco. Winemaking is completely traditional, with fermentation in open-topped vats, and aging in botti. The top wines are the Barolo Monvigliero Riserva and the Barbaresco Rabaja.

Virna Borgogno

Via Alba 24/73, Barolo (CN)

@ info@virnabarolo.it

🌐 www.virnabarolo.com

📅 🏭 🍇 🛢 🥂

📞 +39 0173 56120

👤 Virna Borgogno

🖼 Barolo [map p. 36]

12 ha; 60,000 btl

The family has owned vineyards in Barolo since 1720, and the domain was called Enrico & Lodovico Borgogno, until Lodovico's daughter Virna joined her father in 2001. Today she runs the estate together with her sister Ivana under the name of Virna Borgogno. The Barolo Noi blend is an assemblage from Novello, Monforte, and La Morra, and ages in botti. There's also cuvée from the commune of Barolo, also aged in botti. The crus Cannubi and Sarmassa age in a mix of botti and tonneaux. There are two Barbera d'Alba cuvées, with San Giovanni sourced from La Morra. Other wines include Dolcetto and Arneis. Estate grapes are 20% of production, the rest are purchased. The style here is traditional, but Virna is married to Giovanni Abrigo, who is a modernist making Barbaresco under the Orlando Abrigo label (see profile).

Alberto Voerzio

Borgata Brandini, 1a, 12062 La Morra (CN)

@ info@albertovoerzio.com

🌐 www.voerzioalberto.com

📅 🏭 🍇 🚜

📞 +39 3333 927654

👤 Alberto Voerzio

🖼 Barolo [map p. 35]

6 ha; 18,000 btl

Alberto Voerzio is not related to the other Voerzio domains but comes from a family that was not in the wine business. He qualified in oenology in Alba in 2003 and then bought his first vineyard in the La Serra cru in La Morra, planted half with Nebbiolo and half with Barbera. He made his first wine on a very small scale, just one barrel, with the 2006 vintage. Slowly he added other vineyards and now produces Barolo (from La Morra), Barolo La Serra (from the cru), Langhe Nebbiolo, Barbera d'Alba, and Dolcetto d'Alba. Alberto is a modernist: the Barolos aged for 24 months in barriques with 30% new oak, and another 8 months in stainless steel; the Langhe Nebbiolo, which comes from La Morra, ages in used barriques for 12 months and in stainless steel for 8 months.

144

Index of Estates by Rating

Index of Organic and Biodynamic Estates

Marziano Abbona
Fratelli Alessandria
Azelia Di Luigi Scavino
Barale Fratelli
Bel Colle
Enzo Boglietti
Giacomo Borgogno & Figli
Brandini
Giacomo Brezza e Figli dal 1885
Fratelli Brovia
Piero Busso
Cappellano
Tenuta Cucco
Cascina Delle Rose
Cavallotto
Ceretto
Aldo Conterno
Diego Conterno
Conterno Fantino
Cordero Di Montezemolo
Giuseppe Cortese
Fontanafredda
Gianni Gagliardo
Garesio
Ettore Germano
Fratelli Giacosa
Bruna Grimaldi
Icardi
Casa E. di Mirafiore
Ada Nada
Nada Fiorenzo
Giuseppe Nada
Oddero Poderi e Cantine
Sori Paitin
Armando Parusso
E. Pira & Figli
Réva
Giuseppe Rinaldi
Massimo Rivetti
Azienda Agricola Rivetto DAL 1902
Bruno Rocca
Rocche Dei Manzoni
Josetta Saffirio
Elio Sandri
Scarzello Giorgio e Figli di Federico
Scarzello

Giulia Negri Serradenari
Sottimano
La Spinetta
Trediberri
G. D. Vajra
Mauro Veglio
Vietti
Voerzio Martini

Producers Making Natural Wines or Wines With No Sulfur

Crissante Alessandria
Beni Di Batasiolo
Enzo Boglietti
Cascina Morassino
Col dei Venti
Collina Serragrilli
Cascina Fontana
Fontanafredda
Bruna Grimaldi
Poderi Marcarini
Casa E. di Mirafiore
E. Pira & Figli
Azienda Agricola Rivetto DAL 1902
Mauro Sebaste
Trediberri
Giovanni Viberti

Index of Estates by Appellation

Giacomo Fenocchio
Cascina Fontana
Fontanafredda
Fortemasso
Gianni Gagliardo
Garesio
Ettore Germano
Elio Grasso
Silvio Grasso
Bruna Grimaldi
Giacomo Grimaldi
Manzone Giovanni
Paolo Manzone
Poderi Marcarini
Marchesi Di Barolo
Mario Marengo
Bartolo Mascarello
Giuseppe Mascarello e Figlio
Massolino - Vigna Rionda
Casa E. di Mirafiore
Mauro Molino
Fratelli Monchiero
Paolo Monti
Negretti
Andréa Oberto
Oddero Poderi e Cantine
Figli Luigi Oddero
Azienda Vinicola Palladino
Armando Parusso
Pio Cesare
E. Pira & Figli
Luigi Pira
Guido Porro
Alfredo Prunotto
Raineri
Ratti
Réva
Revello Fratelli

Carlo Revello & Figli
Michele Reverdito
Fratelli Seghesio
Francesco Rinaldi
Giuseppe Rinaldi
Azienda Agricola Rivetto DAL 1902
Rocche Dei Manzoni
Giovanni Rosso
Josetta Saffirio
Elio Sandri
Luciano Sandrone
Scarzello Giorgio e Figli di Federico
Scarzello
Paolo Scavino
Schiavenza
Mauro Sebaste
Sylla Sebaste
Giulia Negri Serradenari
Aurelio Settimo
Francesco Sobrero
Sordo Giovanni
Terre Del Barolo
Trediberri
G. D. Vajra
Mauro Veglio
Castello Di Verduno
Giovanni Viberti
Vietti
Virna Borgogno
Alberto Voerzio
Voerzio Martini
Roberto Voerzio
Dogliani
Marziano Abbona
Ca'Viola
Podere Luigi Einaudi

148

Index of Estates by Name

Made in the USA
Middletown, DE
29 August 2024

59955407R00086